AF579991

BOIOTIA
IN THE
FOURTH CENTURY B.C.

BOIOTIA
IN THE
FOURTH CENTURY B.C.

EDITED BY
SAMUEL D. GARTLAND

PENN

UNIVERSITY OF PENNSYLVANIA PRESS

PHILADELPHIA

Published by
University of Pennsylvania Press
Philadelphia, Pennsylvania 19104-4112
www.upenn.edu/pennpress

Printed in the United States of America on acid-free paper
10 9 8 7 6 5 4 3 2 1

A Cataloging-in-Publication record is available from the Library of Congress
ISBN 978-0-8122-4880-7

CONTENTS

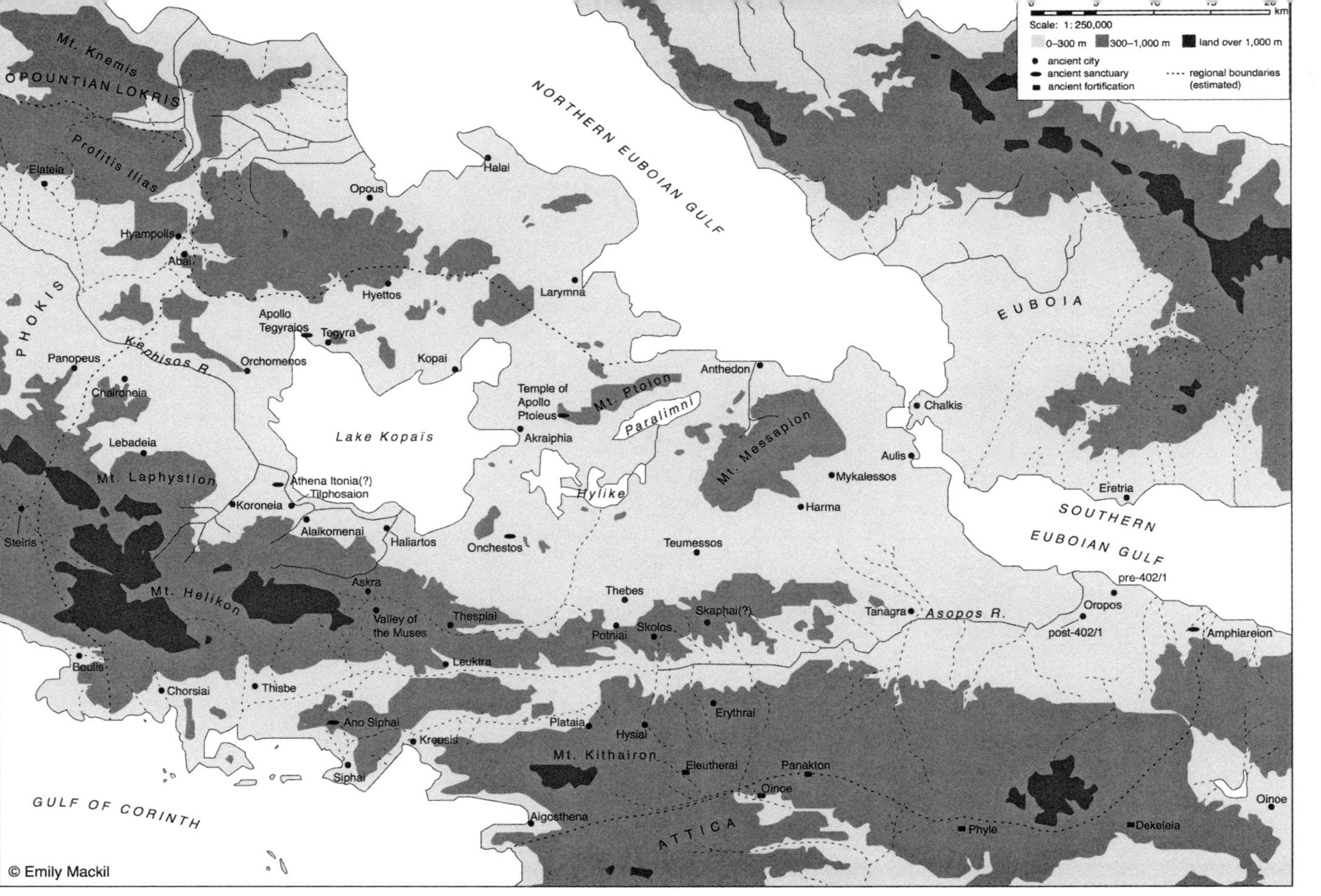

Boiotia in the Classical and Hellenistic periods. Permission of Emily Mackil.

Introduction

SAMUEL D. GARTLAND

The study of the history of the fourth century B.C. in Boiotia has been dominated by interest in Thebes. The century witnessed the apparently sudden rise and dramatic fall of the city, and its legendary leaders have always been alluring to historians and undoubtedly provide rare glamour in Boiotian studies. This collection seeks to place this traditional focus on hegemony and great men in a wider context. This approach is based on the belief that the orthodox presentation of that ephemeral primacy, apparently made possible only by a single great generation of leaders, often obscures more interesting and important trends and developments in the region.

In tandem with the lack of glamour attached to anything in Boiotia other than Epameinondas and Pelopidas, the fourth century is often considered the less attractive half of the so-called Classical era. However much successive generations of scholarship have moved away from viewing the fifth century as the apogee of Greek civilization, that period still has a strong hold on modern approaches to Greek history, particularly with regard to the mainland. To the undergraduate, too, used to the simplified oppositions of the fifth century (Greeks/barbarians, Athens/Sparta, land/sea, democracy/oligarchy), the fourth century can be something of an unpredictable, polyvalent anticlimax, with Boiotia acting mischievously to complicate these binaries. The reassuring authority of Herodotus and Thucydides is replaced by a series of overlapping literary sources whose inadequacies are more obvious, if no greater, than those of their fifth-century predecessors. These writers were themselves well aware of the difficulties in imposing a framework on the events of the century; even Xenophon, a man of great intellectual range and well versed in the vicissitudes of Greek power, gave up writing fourth-century history in frustration after the inconclusive battle of Mantineia in 362 B.C., which he claimed only created more *akrisia* and *tarache*, confusion and disorder, than before.

But Xenophon, together with Herodotus and Thucydides, had little affection for, or knowledge of, Boiotia. For them, Boiotia always represented an other, a region in opposition, with the capacity to surprise and unsettle but not the capability to dominate. But even if this problematic supposition were true, Boiotia would still be central to the history of the fourth century: the inherent problems of Sparta's imperialism and later its spectacular collapse were played out in the region from the end of the Peloponnesian War. The development of effective northern powers in Phokis, Thessaly, and Macedon are all most clearly intelligible through their interactions with Boiotia in the middle decades of the century. And nascent Hellenistic paradigms can be seen in the recalibration of the Boiotian landscape after 338 B.C., which witnessed the creation of a new vocabulary with which poleis and big men interacted, an invention necessitated by the power of Macedonian kings to create and destroy communities and reshape landscapes. Only through a better understanding of the diverse experiences of Boiotia will these other histories become more intelligible.

Apart from the narrative of the rise and fall of the big powers, Boiotia also provides a model for understanding the relationship between the small community and the larger group, which acts as a bridge between the fifth century B.C. and the cofluorescence of poleis and koina in the third century B.C. The interaction between the ethnos and the polis was an important feature of Boiotian history in every period, and although the periodic re-formation of a Boiotian federal political body highlights that cohesion was often deemed beneficial, the political character of each incarnation was dependent on the context of its creation.

Boiotian federalism is a subject that has received much attention over the past century and a half, and interest has recently reached a new zenith. The publication of Mackil's *Creating a Common Polity*, an excellent study of ancient federalism that uses Boiotia as a keystone, and Beck and Ganter's contribution "Boiotia and the Boiotian Leagues" in *Federalism in Greek Antiquity* are just two of the longer contributions made in the past few years that emphasize the importance of this phenomenon within Boiotia, and of Boiotia to this phenomenon. With many parts of the European Union and North America engaged in energetic debates over devolution, relations between smaller and larger members of federal groups, and the purpose and limits of sovereignty, this aspect of Boiotian history has in some ways never been more relevant. Drawing any modern parallels with Boiotia would be unhelpful, but that is not to say that the fourth-century picture lacks subtlety or sophistication. On the contrary, within the region there was a matrix of power relations that resulted in every community being in some way dependent on another.[1] Even Thebes, often predominant in population and territory, was effectively locked into the center of the southern part of the region by its neighbors and needed either to cooperate with or to dominate other communities to be able to exercise power outside its immediate surroundings. However, despite its undeniable importance for both Boiotian and wider Greek history, an explicit treatment of federalism is eschewed in this volume because of the recent treatments of the subject and a desire to explore new avenues. Instead, it is sufficient here to provide a short overview of the political developments of the fourth century.

There were three different systems of pan-Boiotian government in the fourth century, a reflection of a wider experience in this period that was anything but stable. Every decade or so, there were major changes of external pressures and internal arrangements. In the period from the end of the Peloponnesian War to the Peace of Antalkidas in 386 B.C., Boiotia broadly resisted Spartan attempts at aggrandizement and aligned with Athens. In response, Sparta pursued a policy of breaking apart the koinon and realized a major victory with the dislocation of Orchomenos in 395 B.C. But Sparta could not achieve any further gains through force, and high politics were therefore invoked, with a common peace in 386 B.C. underwritten by Persia, and with the dismantling of the Boiotian federation a principal aim. Atomized, Boiotia was swallowed in pieces by Sparta, a process that reached a dramatic climax in 382 B.C. with the seizure of the Kadmeia by the Spartan commander Phoibidas. No enemy force had ever before been inside the walls of Thebes.

The occupation was particularly significant because the Kadmeia was in all periods the cultic, social, and defensive heart of Thebes. It is not a naturally spectacular akropolis but rather a rocky dais, difficult to distinguish from the low hills that surround it on three sides and obscure the view of the site from all but northern approaches. Other than in periods of unusually large population, the hill would have been home to the majority of Thebans; it housed major religious centers and was also the political center of the polis, hosting assemblies, perhaps containing federal treasuries, and, before the battle of Chaironeia, providing a base for federal meetings. The Kadmeia was therefore very different from the akropoleis of the other major mainland poleis such as Athens, which did not use its akropolis for habitation or as the principal center of expressly political activity in the historical period. When the Spartan garrison was installed, it would have disrupted the social, political, and religious behavior of the polis and is likely to have had a significant effect on the day-to-day activity of Thebans.

Politically, Boiotia had been broken apart, so when the exiled anti-Spartan leadership led a countercoup and retook the Kadmeia in 379 B.C., Thebes by necessity could construct any new regional polity only piecemeal, from the center outward. The first stage of this was achieved during the 370s, first by winning control of Tanagra, then by disbanding the polis of Thespiai, and by destroying Plataia and exiling (or perhaps, in Theban eyes, repatriating) its population to Athens. That the Theban position at the end of the 370s was still fragile has sometimes been obscured by the spectacular nature of the victory over the Spartans at Leuktra in 371 B.C. After that victory, the relative domestic security it permitted led to a wholesale reinvention of the region.

In 374 B.C. there were five major poleis in Boiotia: Thebes, Tanagra, Thespiai, Plataia, and Orchomenos; between 363 and 338 B.C. there were only two, Thebes and Tanagra. The dismantling of the polis system between 373 and 364 B.C. (when Orchomenos suffered the first of two fourth-century enslavements (*andrapodismoi*) was not simply punitive but was designed to facilitate Theban territorial domination over all Boiotia. In physical terms, the destruction of the poleis cleared the ground for the sophisticated fortification program that extended over a large part of the region, built to house and to withstand the latest weaponry, constructed in uniform ashlar masonry.[2] The scars of the Spartan occupation of Boiotia are visible at locations of the most impressive surviving fortifications. Kreusis, Siphai, Chorsiai, and (less certainly) Eleutherai were all points where Sparta had found Boiotian defenses lacking; they now became part of a regional defensive system coordinated from Thebes.

While Thebans were belligerently forcing the creation of a new regional vision within Boiotia, they were also leading Boiotian forces abroad with the aim of undermining the bases of power of those who had previously threatened the cohesiveness of the region. Boiotians oversaw the foundations of Megalepolis and Messene, together with the refoundation of Mantineia, which as a group bisected the Peloponnese and denied key economic and strategic territory and routes to the Spartans. The design was to contain Sparta at home by limiting the territory from which it could draw men and other resources. The same strategic design lay behind the naval expedition made by Epameinondas in 364/363 B.C., meant to impede Athens by limiting its ability to exploit the Aegean and the Black Sea.[3] If Athens was limited to Attica, Sparta to Lakonia, and Thebes to control of Boiotia, Thebes had arguably the best foundation for predominance on the mainland.

The expansionism of the 360s also brought Boiotia into regular direct contact with the northern mainland. Boiotians became heavily involved in the politics of Macedon, Thessaly, and Phokis, and the relationship with the northern mainland came to a head in the Third Sacred War between 356 and 346 B.C. Phokis, using the wealth of Delphi to supercharge its military resources, posed a significant threat to Boiotia in its entirety; at its strongest it controlled most of the territory in the Kopais basin. The incursions by a hitherto-unthreatening neighbor highlighted in the strongest terms that Thebes had not found the solution to regional territorial integrity. The weakening of the polis system served to undermine regional defense, even with the scheme of elaborately constructed fortifications. Financial resources lay at the root of the problem: while Phokis was using its sacred gold mine to hire mercenaries on a grand scale, the best Boiotian forces were leased to Asia and Egypt as mercenaries.

Boiotia could not end the Third Sacred War, and it was only the intervention of the ever-advancing Philip II of Macedon against the Phokians that brought matters to a close. Phokis endured terrible repercussions for its boldness and sacrilege, and the outcome meant that Boiotia and Macedon were now effectively neighbors. A few years of uneasy peace followed before the defeat of Boiotian and Athenian forces by Philip in August 338 B.C. at the northwestern border of the region. The battle of Chaironeia is often cited as a historical watershed in Greek history as a whole, but the defeat marked a greater direct change in Boiotia than in any other region. With the formation of the League of Corinth, Philip followed the example of Sparta in the early part of the fourth century by breaking apart regional federations. At the same time, Philip diluted Theban predominance within Boiotia by allowing Orchomenos, Plataia, and Thespiai to re-form. He also followed the Spartan example of installing a garrison on the Kadmeia.

After Philip had hamstrung Thebes in this way, and with the other major poleis in Boiotia able to act as a bulwark against a revival of Theban power, the destruction of Thebes was an unnecessary and, for Alexander, probably an undesirable event early in his rule. In the autumn of 335 B.C. the young king was campaigning in the far north when rumors of his death caused Thebes to revolt. That there should be an attempt by exiles returning from Athens to liberate the Kadmeia after three years of occupation is made more intelligible when it is viewed as an exact duplication of the successful eviction of the Spartan garrison in 379 B.C., and also in light of the significant physical change that the garrison would have made to the normal functioning of the community.[4] The move is also intelligible in the context of the reversal of Theban control in the region. All around them, the fabric of their domination over Boiotia was being undone in similar fashion to Sparta's loss of large parts of the Peloponnese in the 360s. Thebes needed to reassert itself quickly to stymie these changes; that the policy failed so spectacularly should not hide the rational calculation behind its formation.

The brutality reportedly meted out at Thebes by Macedonians, Boiotians, and Phokians is understandable. Every major community in the region (except perhaps Tanagra) and the Phokians had suffered because of Theban predominance in the fourth century, and many of those taking part would have only very recently (re)settled in the region. Furthermore, it is likely that the devastation was compounded by the arrival of the Macedonians after a season of hard fighting in the north. The chance for all parties to work off old grudges was irresistible, and the opportunities provided by the wealthy and unplundered polis must also have been a motivation for thoroughly ransacking the city. Theban loot was spread around, and people and goods were dispersed at least as far as Anatolia.[5]

Although the situation in which the re-forming poleis found themselves in 335/334 B.C. was in many ways unprecedented, the confederation of exiles that was formed in the years after the destruction of Thebes was part of a long-standing pattern of returning exiles remaking the region politically. The first koinon was formed in 446 B.C. under the direction of groups who had been exiled as a result of Athenian domination of the region over the previous decade. The second koinon, focused on the spectacular return from Athens of the Theban exiles led by Pelopidas in 379 B.C., again brought a new, pragmatic vision of regional political and spatial organization, based on the dominance of a single central polis, probably inspired by the relationship between Athens and Attica. The implementation of the first system was designed against Athenian domination, the second against Spartan domination, and had the rebellion of 335 B.C. been successful, a band of exiles would have again had the opportunity to re-form the koinon, this time in opposition to Macedonian domination. Instead, with the destruction of Thebes, the third koinon was formed by a different group of exiles out of exogenous Macedonian support for an endogenous anti-Thebism. Where the first two organizations had been created by small bands of exiles leading a reinterpretation and reshaping of the existing social and political landscape, the third was the work of a collection of groups with very different experiences, desires, and visions for the region.

To think of Boiotia after 338 B.C. as merely a landscape in which exiles resettled and communities were re-formed is, of course, too simple and ignores the diverse experiences of those settling after the battle of Chaironeia and the complicated social negotiations of change and integration that must have taken place. Much of this is hidden in the adoption and metamorphosis of traditional patterns of dialogue and interaction in the region (and as a region), which seem to have helped the communities manage the transition peacefully. The memory of Theban hegemony was powerful, and embedded hostility toward Thebes is likely to have aided political coalescence, as, for instance, when Boiotia unified against Athens in the Lamian War in the belief that if Athens were successful, Thebes would be restored. Although eventual Macedonian victory in that war meant a short delay, it was only a few years later, in 316 B.C., that Cassander restored Thebes for his own symbolic and strategic benefit. That a Macedonian leader was responsible for instigating Theban restoration less than two decades after another had destroyed it demonstrates both the power of the Macedonians and the unpredictability of the period.

In the following years, Boiotia was carved up and courted by other successors of Alexander, and although Thebes was fragile in its reconstruction, it was still treated with suspicion by its neighbors. Despite this, Thebes was eventually readmitted to the koinon, probably in 287 B.C. The lion of Chaironeia, standing as a monument to the battle of 338 B.C., stands also as an emblem of Theban reintegration, looking back regretfully not just across the region but across the fourth century.[6]

Theban restoration was feared on a political level but was also practically undesirable because previously Theban land had been profitably plowed by members of other communities since 335 B.C. Indeed, the availability of resources to those re-forming communities might have helped achieve a relatively peaceful integration: Theban land was available until 316 B.C., direct Macedonian support, particularly for Plataia, was not negligible, and there was also fertile land provided by the partial drainage of Lake Kopais. Land use and availability had been important features of the fourth century, as the number of people living in Boiotia reached its highest level in any period of history, perhaps around 165,500.[7] The land would have been rigorously exploited, and in Thebes, at least, freshwater fish were eaten in larger amounts than previously, probably as a result of the resources of the Boiotian lakes being available to Thebes and perhaps more fully used to supply the demands of the large population.[8] In the Hellenistic period, however, the diet returned to something more similar to that of the Bronze Age, with a greater part made up of meat and dairy products.[9] From the fourth-century demographic peak, there was a general progression toward depopulation, though not to abnormally low levels of density.[10]

Demographic fluctuations were just part of a process of almost constant change that make presenting any fixed picture of what "Boiotia" was, at any point in the fourth century B.C., impossible. But it is clear that Boiotia at the end of the century must have been a fundamentally different place from Boiotia before the battle of Chaironeia, which was in turn very different from Boiotia at the end of the Peloponnesian War. At the close of the fourth century B.C., Boiotia can be considered a paradox akin to the ship of Theseus: it had retained names, customs, and community locations, but with few parts that had not been intrinsically remade. This experience was even more unusual because the renovation that took place in the last third of the century was overseen by a power from outside the region with little history of direct interaction with any of the communities affected. The development of a relatively stable and successful Hellenistic koinon from this century of turbulence and manhandling was in large part due to the guile and inventiveness of the new Boiotians, whoever they were.

In antiquity Boiotia was generally either maligned or ignored, and although it is too late to persuade Xenophon that he would be enriched by a deeper knowledge of Boiotia, this book hopes to make a small contribution to persuade would-be Xenophons to consider again the experiences of the region in its most turbulent period. By looking across the fourth century as a whole, it is possible to engage with more of the processes that accompanied this unparalleled period of political upheaval, warfare, physical reorganization, and social change. More widely in Greek history, without knowledge of the internal dynamics of Boiotia, the century can be only partially understood. Whichever way it is considered, the fourth century is arguably *the* Boiotian century, and the chapters within this book hope to further elucidate some of the processes that made it so.

CHAPTER 1

Thespiai and the Fourth-Century Climax in Boiotia

ANTHONY SNODGRASS

Thespiai, like Plataia, was a city regularly out of step with each trend in the Classical history of the Boiotian League and was joined only very intermittently by other Boiotian poleis; these two, like a pair of reverse weather vanes, pointed persistently in the opposite direction to the way that the wind was blowing. Of the two, Thespiai was comfortably the larger in both population and territory, but it lacked the comfort zone of a common frontier with Attica. A partial Thespian substitute for this juxtaposition with Athens could be seen in its possession, on the northern shore of the Gulf of Corinth, of Kreusis and, during its periods of control over Thisbai, Siphai, and Chorsiai, of their respective harbors too; this made Thespiai into a natural stepping-stone between the Peloponnese and central Greece, with a sea route bypassing (unlike the inland and the more tenuous coastal routes) the territories not just of Athens but of its ally Plataia as well. These geographical factors were reflected in Thespiai's policy: although it was intermittently in Athenian alliance, it is recorded at other times as siding with Sparta, as adopting cults from Corinth,[1] and as joining in the leadership of an expeditionary force sent to help Syracuse (Thuc. 7.19.3).

But, closer to home, geography made it an even bolder stance for Thespiai than for Plataia to detach itself from Boiotian League policy and to express opposition to Thebes—a stance, too, more open to charges of folly. We can trace this Thespian divergence back to at least the time of its commitment of 700 hoplites to the defense of Thermopylai in 480—a vastly greater sacrifice proportionately than the one represented by the 300 Spartans, and one that should be judged (as it almost never is) as part of modern analysis of the whole strategy behind the Thermopylai campaign. Many later instances of such deviation emerge from the pages of Thucydides and Xenophon, as we shall see; they can even find a later reflection in Strabo's report (9.2.5) that in Augustan times, Thespiai and Tanagra, alone of all Boiotian cities, preserved reasonable prosperity in an otherwise desolate landscape of urban decay.

Some of the more abrupt switches of political stance at Thespiai may confidently be put down to its internal political factions and, more specifically, to the apparently rather even balance between them. Most Boiotian cities, most of the time, were classified (by Athenians at least, like Thucydides at 5.31.6) as being controlled by oligarchic regimes throughout the fifth century. As J. A. O. Larsen showed long ago in an article that is still a classic,[2] the label "oligarchic" was then extended by Athenians to those constitutions where voting rights were confined to those of hoplite status. The "oligarchies" of fifth-century Boiotia, thus defined, could not indefinitely suppress the growth of more democratic feeling in the cities. Thespiai provides an example of the consequent frictions.

The elimination of a great part of the hoplite class of Thespiai at Thermopylai (and, one might add, the service rendered by the 1,800 surviving Thespian light-armed troops at Plataia [Hdt. 9.30.1]) could very easily have opened the possibility of wider participation in the government of the city once the Persians were gone and the city was rebuilt. No ancient authority confirms that this opportunity was taken, save perhaps when the Athenians, during their brief decade of dominance in Boiotia, exiled prominent oligarchs and imposed democratic institutions on certain of the cities. But that policy was anyway overturned after 447/446, and by the time the Peloponnesian War began, the sources give a picture of a concerted, Theban-led, pro-Spartan policy and of dominantly oligarchic politics on the part of the Boiotian League.

Yet there seems to have been a lasting undercurrent of dissident opinion at Thespiai. This is seen in the sinister sequel to the battle of Delion in 424: of the "not quite five hundred" hoplites who fell on the Boiotian side in this victory, we know from epigraphic evidence that at least a hundred and possibly very many more were Thespians;[3] for their city, it was a repetition, on a smaller scale, of Thermopylai. The following year, the Thebans took advantage of this circumstance to dismantle the walls of Thespiai, "having long wished to do so," according to Thucydides (4.133.1), on grounds of suspected pro-Athenian sympathies. For a city whose contingent had just fought to the death to keep the Athenians out of Boiotia, this has always seemed an outrageous response. But it may also reflect Theban realpolitik, a recognition that the internal affairs of Thespiai were so evenly balanced that the loss of "the flower of its youth" from the hoplite class would tip its policies back in the direction of democracy and, worse still, of pro-Athenian sentiment—a hint, perhaps, that fifty years earlier, too, developments in Thespiai might have taken a similar democratic direction after Thermopylai. The unusual feature of the internal struggle in Classical Thespiai, between pro- and antidemocratic elements, is how long the near equilibrium of forces persisted.

Thus we hear from Thucydides (6.95.2) of an uprising of the demos in Thespiai already in 414, only a decade after the Delion episode. Again in 378, after the change to a more democratic regime at Thebes, Xenophon (*Hell.* 5.4.46) uses the same one-word term, "demos," for the Thespian faction that (on this occasion literally) came out in support of that change. Politically, the boot was now on the other foot for the whole league. Yet, true to form, Thespiai was before long irrevocably committed to the opposite side; Agesilaos of Sparta saw to that, suppressing political factions, rebuilding the city's (this time, short-lived) fortifications, and sealing his action by installing a garrison and making Thespiai the prime base for Spartan operations over the next six years.

But (again true to form) the Thespians had backed the wrong horse—the favorite, but one destined to fall at the last fence. In a very densely argued article, Christopher Tuplin showed that Thespiai's punishment for its mistaken choice was meted out by the Thebans in at least two stages.[4] First, by about 373 the city was deprived of its independent status within the league and incorporated as an appendage to Thebes (Xen. *Hell.* 6.3.5; 6.4.10: Diod. 15.46.6; cf. Isoc. 14.9). Second, in the period of the battle of Leuktra in 371, something more drastic took place. The city of Thespiai was, at least according to the Athenian rhetorical sources (Isocrates and Demosthenes), "destroyed" and its population dispersed. They do not make clear whether this meant flight or deportation to Attica or elsewhere (as in 480 and, for some of the activists, in 414), with the land reallocated to Theban or pro-Theban Boiotians, or whether the Thespians were merely deprived of their urban center and left to live on their landholdings. But the city's walls will surely have been destroyed once again.

This obscurity, perhaps intentional given the rhetorical nature of the two main sources, impedes all our efforts to establish links with the archaeological evidence from the survey of Thespiai and its territory. But whatever its exact ramifications, the same state of affairs was alleged to persist for decades. Isocrates in his *Archidamos* of 366 (6.27) and Demosthenes repeatedly in the 350s (16.4, 16.25, 16.28) continued to use the same language for the plight of Thespiai as "ruined" and "destroyed." The one thing they conceded, if only by silence, was that the city escaped the dire fate of Orchomenos—wholesale massacre of its male citizens and enslavement of the rest—in 364 (cf. Diod. 15.79). Even in the middle and later 340s, Demosthenes (5.10; 6.30; 19.21, 37, 42, 102, 325) could still accuse Philip of Macedon of making political capital with other Greeks by an (as-yet-unfulfilled) promise either to "settle" or to "fortify" Thespiai and other towns.

Yet there is documentary and other evidence for a very different picture of these years. Once, Thespiai had accounted for two of the eleven districts that provided the Boiotian armed forces (the same proportion as Orchomenos and its satellite towns) under the constitution of the fifth and early fourth centuries. This unexpectedly large contingent makes sense when we remember that the outlying towns of Thisbai, Siphai, and (probably) Chorsiai were at certain periods incorporated into the polis of Thespiai. Only when the entire league was dissolved under the King's Peace in 386 or soon after was this local Thespian hegemony (like the greater Theban one incorporating Plataia) annulled by autonomy for the Boiotian towns. This is enough to suggest that both after 480 and again after the further blow at Delion in 424, Thespiai could recover with remarkable speed from demographic setbacks; another such may have had to be overcome after the battle of the Nemea in 394, when the Thespian contingent is once again singled out (Xen. *Hell.* 4.2.20) for its heavy losses. Regardless of what it was to suffer in the period of Theban ascendancy, Classical Thespiai was a big place. The requirement under the fifth-century league's constitution of 2,200 hoplites and 200 cavalry implies a city whose total free population, already in five figures at the time of Thermopylai and Plataia, had grown (doubtless including Thisbai and the other incorporated towns) to a figure approaching 20,000.

Under Theban ascendancy, during and after the triumph over Sparta, the "Theban League" from 378 to 338 saw the complete absorption by Thebes of the military quotas of Orchomenos and Thespiai, as well as of Plataia, confirming the orators' evidence for the loss of Thespian political independence. Yet for fourth-century Boiotia, the picture in demographic terms is a positive one indeed. The prime figure that we have for a fifth-century mobilization of the league's army had been the pan-Boiotian force of 7,000 mustered for Delion (possibly exemplifying a "two-thirds" rule, with mobilization of two-thirds of the nominal paper strength prescribed by the league's constitution, as first suggested by P. A. Seymour).[5] But the fourth-century figures, even for actual mobilization, are at times higher than this. The 6,000 hoplites that Epameinondas led out at Leuktra do not make a fair comparison with the Theban paper strength of 4,000 under the fifth-century constitution, since they included a non-Theban element. For the forces later mobilized by the league, Diodoros offers figures of 7,000 (that is, 12,000 minus the Athenian force of 5,000 under Demophon) for the hoplites alleged to have taken part in liberating Thebes from its Spartan garrison in 379 (Diod. 15.26.4) and, by far the highest, the 13,000 that he reports (Diod. 16.30.4) for an invasion of Phokis during the Sacred War, in the year 354. This last figure may seem high, but it is perfectly compatible with the league's paper strength of 11,000 hoplites under the fifth-century constitution and indeed with the 10,500 said to have later taken the field against the Gauls in 279 (Paus. 10.20.3), suggesting a successive rise and fall in population between those two outer limits.

These figures apply to Boiotia as a whole; and if any credence at all is to be given to Diodoros' highest figure for the Sacred War, when Orchomenos had been emptied of its people only a decade before, it is inconceivable that an army of 13,000 hoplites could have been raised without a major contribution from Thespiai—which must therefore have made yet another strong demographic recovery from whatever exact disaster had been visited on it in 371. This supports one of the alternative conclusions advanced in the same article by Tuplin,[6] that even the second, severer punishment inflicted by the Thebans on Thespiai could have amounted merely to a *dioikismos*, a dispersal of the population to its rural lands and perhaps also to its second-order settlements (in Thespiai's case we know of Eutresis, Askra, and Kreusis) or, indeed, its formerly subordinated cities, now also under Theban control. Only the civic center of Thespiai itself need have remained at least temporarily in ruins and, of course, permanently unfortified as justification for the florid language of the Athenian orators. Note that Demosthenes in the 340s twice (6.30; 19.102) refers, perhaps inadvertently, to Philip's empty promise to fortify, not to resettle, Thespiai. It is conceivable that this was in fact what all the talk of "destruction," "ruin," and "leveling" had amounted to: the demolition of the city's walls.

Yet a community of citizens in ancient Greece could function effectively without a fortified city or acropolis, or even without an urban nucleus of any kind. Of relevance here is the evidence of the Thespian grave and votive reliefs: although they decline from their peak in the later fifth century, they maintain a steady level throughout much of the fourth century, and, remarkably, it is the quarter century between 375 and 350 that sees them at their richest in this era.[7] Such open display of private wealth fits well enough with the regime of "hoplite oligarchy" that we know to have prevailed in fifth-century Thespiai and the league as a whole; it is more surprising in the context of the

"Theban League" with its ostensibly democratic temper. Was it simply that Thebes was prepared to leave the Thespians to their own devices socially, confident that the lack of a civic center would deprive them of any capacity for an oligarchic coup or any other concerted political action?

Thespian inscriptions can seldom be precisely dated—we rely largely on letter forms and dialect. Yet one stone tells us that a Thespian won the Olympic boys' wrestling around 350,[8] and sometime between the 360s and the 320s B.C. Thespiai hosted no fewer than four statues by the greatest sculptor of his day, Praxiteles (Paus. 9.27.3 and 5; *IG* VII 1831), three of which (of Aphrodite, Eros, and the courtesan Phryne) stood in the sanctuary of Eros and, as Albert Schachter has observed,[9] must have required a temple to house them. Next, the fact that Thespiai sent official delegates (*hieromnemones*) to the Panhellenic sanctuary at Delphi in 340, as well as later, confirms that by then, at any rate, the city was exercising its normal functions.[10] Finally, Thespians are said to have joined in that ultimate act of retribution, the destruction of Thebes by Alexander in 335 (Diod. 17.13.5; cf. Justin 11.3.8).

Everything brings us back to the central discrepancy facing us: was Thespiai a political desert for the central years of the fourth century, unwalled and under not just military and political but also economic domination, its citizens in exile, and its lands appropriated by Thebans and their supporters, as a first reading of our fullest source, the Athenian orators, might suggest? Or was it a participant, however indirect and subdued, in the greatest climax of demographic and military growth that Boiotia was ever to experience? Between these strongly contrasting images of fourth-century Thespiai, it is fair to ask the archaeological evidence to help us adjudicate, and for the rest of this chapter, I will try to make it do so.

I must admit at the outset that the evidence is largely derived from surface survey, which produces mostly small, worn potsherds that (like the Thespian inscriptions) may not enable a dating, at times even to the nearest century. Stylistic categories whose recognition is based on decorative motifs may well go unidentified, without a fortunate line of breakage. What the survey of the city of Thespiai and part of its territory does provide is quantity: literally millions of sherds on the modern surface that, if judiciously sampled, can provide a firm basis for inferences, not just on the presence or absence of human occupation but about its density and extent at given periods. Within the city, we have assigned over 14,600 pieces to twenty-five different periods, ranging from the Middle Neolithic to the twentieth century A.D.; as the pie chart (Figure 1.1) shows, the biggest single component—if not by all that

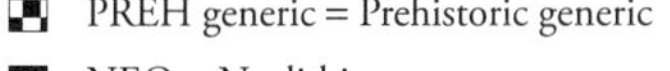

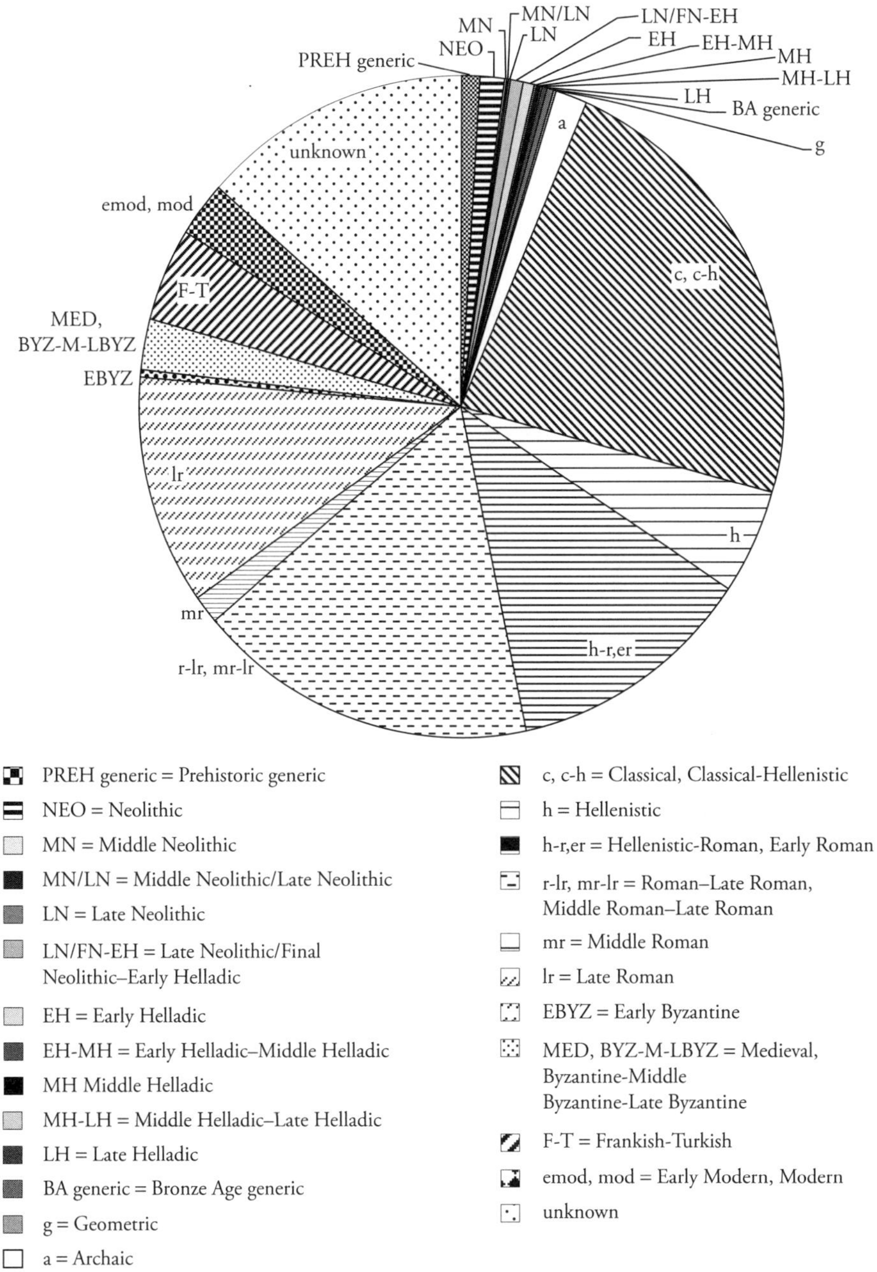

MN
MN/LN
LN/FN-EH
LN
EH
EH-MH
MH
MH-LH
LH
BA generic
g
NEO
PREH generic
a
unknown
emod, mod
F-T
MED,
BYZ-M-LBYZ
EBYZ
c, c-h
h
lr
mr
h-r,er
r-lr, mr-lr
PREH generic = Prehistoric generic
NEO = Neolithic
MN = Middle Neolithic
MN/LN = Middle Neolithic/Late Neolithic
LN = Late Neolithic
LN/FN-EH = Late Neolithic/Final Neolithic–Early Helladic
EH = Early Helladic
EH-MH = Early Helladic–Middle Helladic
MH Middle Helladic
MH-LH = Middle Helladic–Late Helladic
LH = Late Helladic
BA generic = Bronze Age generic
g = Geometric
a = Archaic
c, c-h = Classical, Classical-Hellenistic
h = Hellenistic
h-r,er = Hellenistic-Roman, Early Roman
r-lr, mr-lr = Roman–Late Roman, Middle Roman–Late Roman
mr = Middle Roman
lr = Late Roman
EBYZ = Early Byzantine
MED, BYZ-M-LBYZ = Medieval, Byzantine-Middle Byzantine-Late Byzantine
F-T = Frankish-Turkish
emod, mod = Early Modern, Modern
unknown

Figure 1.1. City site of ancient Thespiai: apportionment of surface pottery (n=14,600+) among twenty-five different periods.

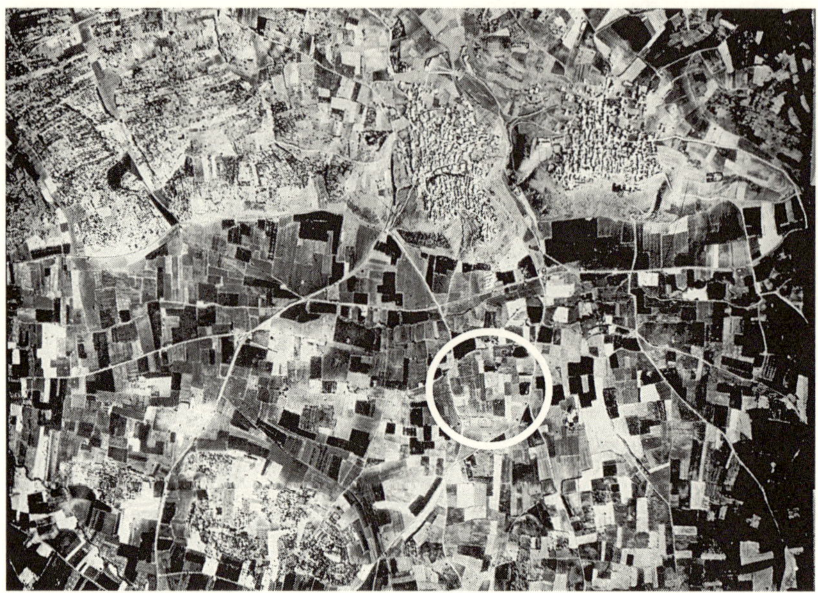

Figure 1.2. Aerial photo of the site of ancient Thespiai, with the twin modern villages of Thespiés (left) and Leondári (right) at the top. The enclosure formed by the Late Roman Kastro appears as a rough polygon due south of modern Thespiés.

much—is the "c, c–h" sector on the right, broadly the "Classical Greek" one, with over 20 percent of the total, but representing about 2 to 2½ percent of the total time span. Two separate categories, "Classical" and "Classical to (Early) Hellenistic," are merged here, as they will be on the distribution map presented later in this chapter.

A word is in order here about the site of ancient Thespiai (Figure 1.2). The visitor surveying the apparently featureless swathe of arable land on which the ancient site lies may be tempted to share John Fossey's view that "There can be no site in Boeotia more depressing than Thespiai."[11] This fertile, well-watered terrain has been cultivated fairly continuously over the last seven thousand years, except for the millennium or so in which it housed a major urban center. Long-term, intensive cultivation is deadly to the survival of ancient architecture. Historically, an unusual and abiding quality of this polis site, commented on by the early travelers, was its complete lack of natural defensive features. It seems that at times, this problem was addressed by an equally unusual provision: refuge in an external acropolis, the enigmatic Keressos, to which the urban population could withdraw in an emergency. There is not space here to speculate on the location of Keressos, but it is important to note that the Thespians had recourse to it as late as 371 B.C. (Paus. 9.4.2), in the aftermath of the battle of Leuktra. This was a time when the city's fortifications were once again out of use, as mentioned earlier, and similar factors may have applied to its only previous appearance in documented history, the occasion of the repulse of the invading Thessalians under Lattamyas, repeatedly but variably dated within the Archaic era by Plutarch (*Moralia* 866E = *De Herodoti malignitate* 33; *Life of Camillus* 19). This event very probably antedated the building of the first city wall at Thespiai, and it seems likely that one of the aims of fortifying the city was to circumvent the need for flight to Keressos.

Well before the end of antiquity, the extent of habitation on the ancient site had begun to shrink, and this process was to end only at the time of the trusty Colonel Leake's report that between his two visits, in A.D. 1802 and 1806, the very last handful of inhabitants left the ancient site, moving up to the hilltop village (modern Thespiés) to the north.[12] Nevertheless, at least one massive monument to the city's ancient past survived until 1891: the Late Antique fortification circuit surrounding a small, polygon-shaped area of some twelve hectares, the "Kastro," in what seems to have been the heart of the ancient city. But the French epigraphist Paul Jamot had found that the *spolia* from earlier antiquity that had been used to build this wall included many inscribed blocks, and that was felt to justify its total destruction,[13] leaving only a discontinuous line of rubble, although by then the local farm tracks, diverted around the wall, had long since perpetuated the outline of the polygon, so that modern aerial photographs bring out its location clearly enough (see Figure 1.2).

The wall is recorded as having been "built of very solid masonry of a regular kind"[14] in "large squared blocks";[15] similar observations can be made about the contemporary or slightly earlier final wall circuit at Plataia.[16] A *terminus post quem* for its construction can found by searching through the lists of those inscriptions recorded as having been detached from the walls by Jamot in 1890 or 1891: from a vital footnote in one of several later publications by A. Plassart, we learn that all the inscriptions that he records there with the provenance "*Kastro*, 1890" and "*Kastro*, 1891" were in fact recovered from the fortification itself.[17] It is immediately clear that some of these are of Roman Imperial date; among the latest of these is a statue base with an inscription eulogizing a figure whom Plassart could identify as Vettius Florius Praetextatus, a Roman notable who was appointed proconsul of the province of Achaia by Julian the Apostate and who is commemorated in nearly identical terms all over Greece. Plassart duly noted its provenance as "*Kastro*, 1891."[18] Vettius

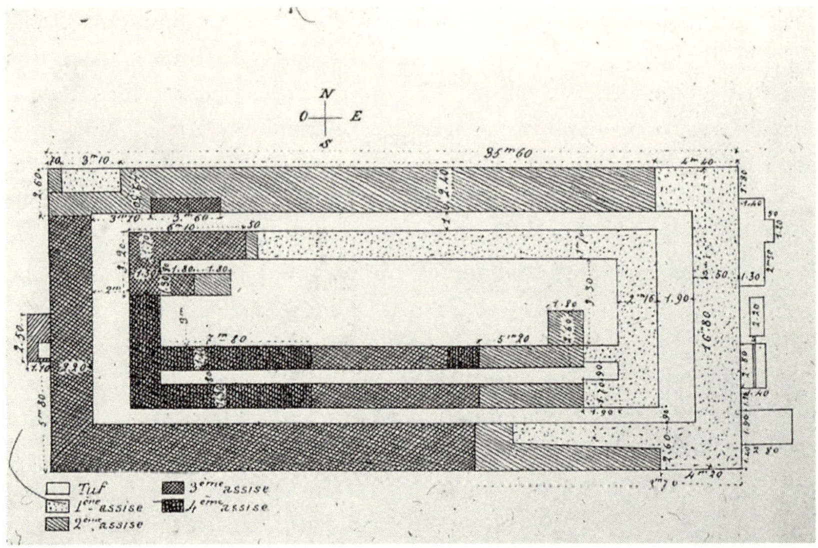

Figure 1.3. P. Jamot's unpublished plan, retrieved by Christel Müller from the archives of the École française d'Athènes (C. Müller 1996), of the temple that he excavated within the Kastro at Thespiai in 1890.

served in Greece in the 360s of the Christian era; he rose to even higher things at Rome before his death in the 380s, but the absence here of any mention of his later titles indicated to Plassart that the inscription is of earlier date than that; between the years A.D. 361 and 369 is perhaps the safest guess. At all events, the wall should belong after that date.

There are, however, grounds for thinking that the Kastro location had contained, for centuries past, the civic heart of Thespiai. The egregious Jamot also excavated (but did not publish) the foundations of a temple in the middle of the circuit; his architect's plan, preserved for over a century in the École française d'Athènes, has now been published (Figure 1.3).[19] The temple's proportions are compatible with an Archaic date, and if it can really be associated, as Jamot held, with a mid-sixth-century B.C. Doric capital of appropriate dimensions that he found nearby, then it is definitely Archaic, as well as of very substantial size (more than thirty-five meters long). Much more recently, in 2008, we found, again within the Kastro, a set of three joining inscribed sherds of Roman date, presumably from an official measuring vessel and naming the office of *agoránomos*.[20] All this suggests that in Archaic, Classical, and Imperial Roman times alike, the hub of the city's administration was to be

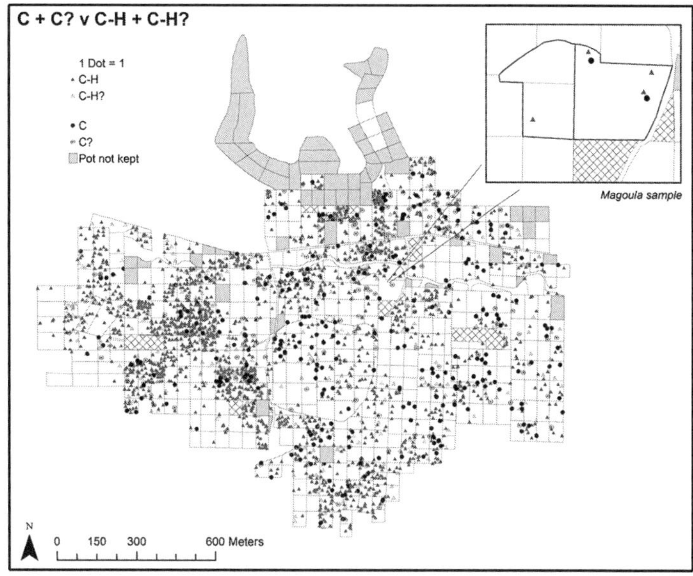

Figure 1.4. Distribution of "Classical" (black dots) and "Classical to Hellenistic" (light gray dots and triangles) pottery within the city site of ancient Thespiai.

found near here—explaining too the choice of this location for the fortified Late Roman or Early Byzantine refuge that the Kastro represents.

The remains of the Kastro still provide the best orientation point for looking at the distribution of the Classical Greek ceramics (Figure 1.4), sorted into the same categories of "Classical" (black dots) and the much more numerous "Classical to Hellenistic," often specified as "Classical to Early Hellenistic" (indicated by triangles). Several things emerge: the scatter is patchy; its main bias is toward the western half of the city site; it has an extension to the north, across the little Kanavaris River, which rises just outside the site and flows eastward across it; and finally, although the less common "Classical" makes a proportionate showing within the Kastro itself, the much more prolific "Classical to Hellenistic" makes a rather poor one. What can be inferred from this distribution?

There is a little more to be said about the pottery classes. Our ceramic experts—and five different specialists have successively studied this material—can distinguish not just the two classes we have named but also an earlier overlapping class, "Archaic to Classical," and, by further refinements at the later end, "Late Classical," or occasionally "fourth-century to Hellenistic." The easily recognized class of fine, black glazed tableware dominates each of these

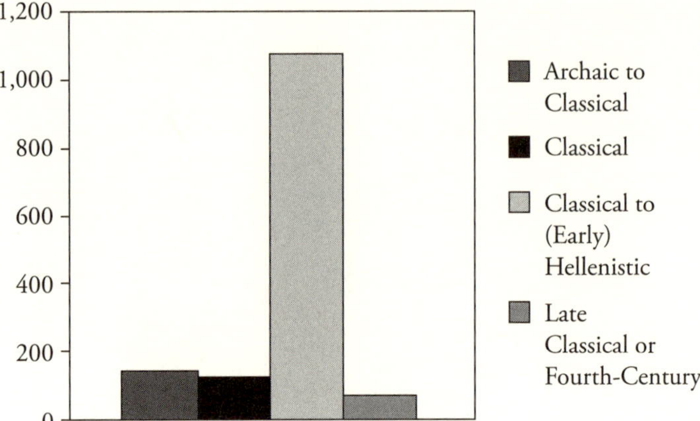

Figure 1.5. City site of ancient Thespiai: apportionment of broadly Classical Greek pottery among four subperiods.

categories, alongside some characteristic but still less closely datable cooking and storage wares. Figure 1.5 gives the proportions of each. Unsurprisingly, given its much more generous chronological scope by comparison with the other three classes, "Classical to Hellenistic" greatly exceeds the rest in quantity, reaching a proportion of over three-quarters of all Classical Greek material. The problem is that the categories of pottery, and especially the ubiquitous black glazed wares, do not lend themselves to a simple separation of the fourth-century material from that of either the fifth or the third centuries B.C.

To maintain some impartiality (and shorten the discussion), it is probably best to make a few entirely arbitrary and crudely mathematical assumptions, setting aside several factors that might otherwise privilege the fourth-century element. First, since the relatively small "Archaic to Classical" category spans four centuries, let each century be nominally credited with a quarter. Second, let the straight "Classical" category similarly be halved between the fifth and fourth centuries that, together, are largely covered by it. Third, and most important, the huge "Classical to [Early] Hellenistic" category can, on the same principle, be divided into three parts: it spans the fifth, fourth, and third centuries, and it is not impossible that it divided fairly evenly among them, for all that the fourth century is the only one that falls entirely within the category and may therefore have generated more than its share of those finds most securely allocated to it. Fourth, the small "Late Classical or fourth-century" category could theoretically spill over into Hellenistic so

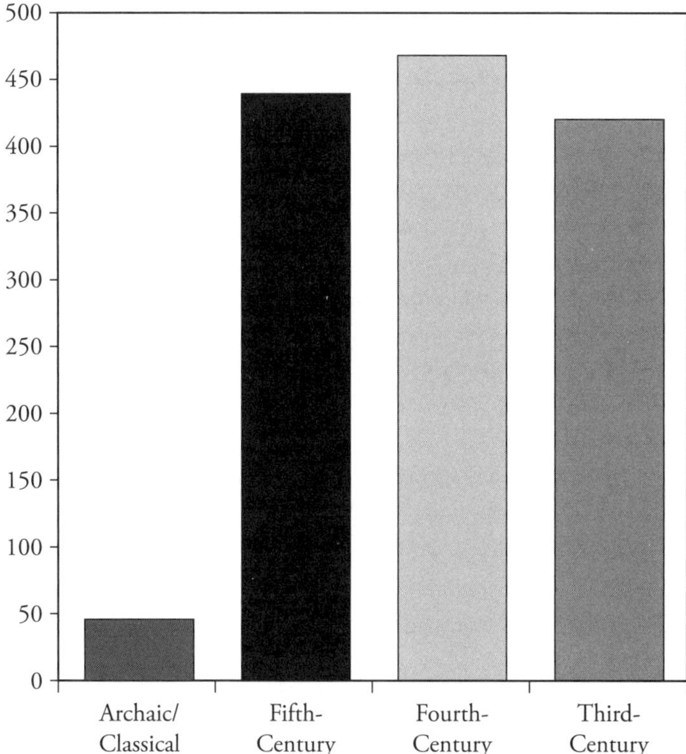

Figure 1.6. The pottery classifications of Figure 1.5, redistributed according to possible absolute dates.

heavily as to divide equally between the fourth and third centuries, the latter period being then reinforced by the definitely Early Hellenistic (a small class). Even then, when we have made every possible allowance to the disadvantage of the fourth century and to the benefit of the preceding and ensuing centuries, the tally for fourth-century Thespiai is still found to exceed those for either the fifth or the third centuries (Figure 1.6). In the absence of proof, everything supports a belief that the population of fourth-century Thespiai, that is, of the *astu* proper, over the century as a whole was at least as high as, and in all likelihood higher than, at any time before or after. This generalization probably holds good for Boiotia as a whole in the rest of both earlier and later history, extending down to the present day.[21]

A further spatial refinement may be possible. We saw that the area of the later Kastro, which there are strong grounds for concluding was already the location of Thespiai's agora and administrative functions and of a major temple, has produced disconcertingly few finds of the prolific "Classical to Hellenistic" class. Two quite separate lines of explanation offer themselves for this state of affairs. First, there is the taphonomic and archaeological argument that the sherds of this period were simply swamped by the overwhelming mass of the Roman, and especially the Late Roman, material that is precisely concentrated within this fortified hub of post-Classical times, and so are systematically underrepresented in the samples. Second, there is a possible historical and political line of explanation: could the Theban reprisals against the city in the 370s have taken the form that the public and civic buildings of Thespiai were destroyed and kept derelict, but with no lasting obstruction to citizens who sought to revive domestic occupation elsewhere in the urban center? The personal reputation of Epameinondas for clemency notwithstanding, this would have been a surprisingly softhearted attitude on the part of a city soon to visit on Orchomenos the direst communal penalty known to Greek polis warfare.[22] Also, there had been more than a century of prior existence to take into account for the Classical polis, when no such severe conditions were imposed on it, which strengthens the case for the alternative, taphonomic explanation.

But our survey has also covered extensive tracts of Thespiai's own traditional rural territory. Figure 1.7 shows the coverage of the years 1985 to 1991, during which the city site and an additional sector to the south were surveyed. For the countryside, the story can be briefly told, and it closely matches that of the urban center. Pottery of the very same ceramic phase, the "Classical to Hellenistic," is easily the most fully represented in the entire seven-thousand-year history of the landscape and is found especially as the commonest component in what has been called the "small rural site phenomenon."

This refers to a feature discovered by survey after survey all over Greece, that of small but dense accumulations of material, usually a few hundred meters apart, often covering less than a hectare, showing several classes of find that one would associate with dwellings: fine wares, storage and cooking pottery, roof tiles and other building materials, lamps to indicate nighttime occupancy, and sometimes loom weights, pointing to the presence of resident women. Whatever one's exact understanding of the nature of these sites and the status of their occupants—and one reviewer has described my colleagues and me as "hypnotised by their idea that their sites . . . must have been inhabited permanently by people"[23]—one thing is clear: they too reach their all-time peak of frequency in Classical Greek times.

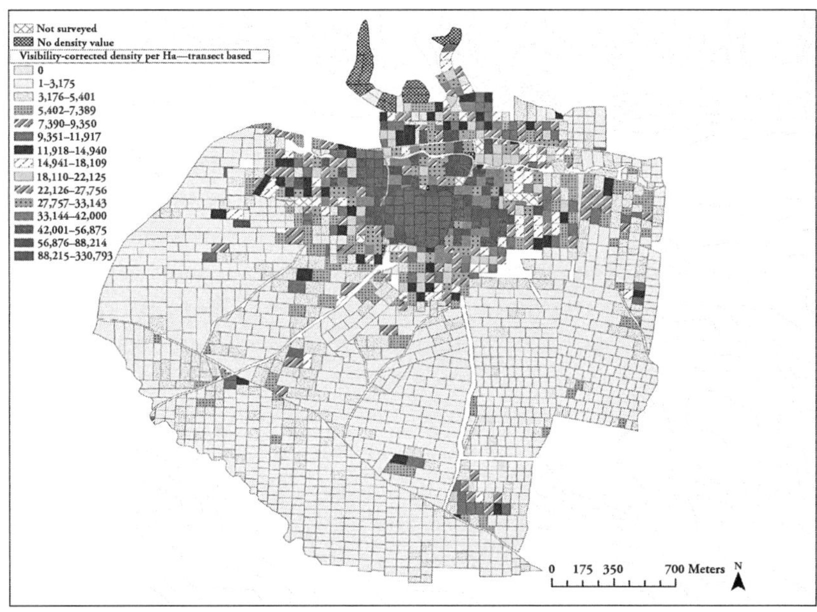

Figure 1.7. The city site of ancient Thespiai with its southern hinterland, showing the graded densities of surface pottery.

In a few cases, as with the city site itself, greater chronological precision is possible. Thus a dating of "fourth century B.C." or "late fifth to fourth century B.C." is sometimes given, not to mention the more frequent "fourth to third centuries." These categories are at their commonest in the rural sites LSE 3 and LSE 6, with their heavily predominant Classical occupation.[24] Finds of coins on the small rural sites were very rare indeed, but two sites (LSE 1 and THS 17) produced examples of fourth-century date.

More remarkable still, however, is the overwhelming prevalence of pottery of the broadly Classical era in the material scattered across the whole landscape, away from the small rural sites.[25] Here the time span "G[eometric]–H[ellenistic]" turns out to account for over three-quarters of all the material, of all periods, ever deposited in these "fully off-site" locations. In other words, the landscape around Thespiai was very much more intensively used in the broadly Classical Greek era than ever before or since. The purposes behind this activity can only have been agricultural: without wishing to reopen a long-standing debate here, I will reiterate our own firm conviction, first set out in Bintliff and Snodgrass 1988, that this ceramic scatter is the result of the spreading of manure and other fertilizing material, in which potsherds had become embedded, on the farmland.

So a demographic climax, including and probably centered on the fourth century B.C., is visible in three separate types of location: the city itself, the small rural sites lying to its south, and, more loosely, the open landscape lying between those sites. As is shown in the summary table in Bintliff, Howard, and Snodgrass 2007,[26] the rural sites are most numerous (though not most extensive in area) in the same period that sees the urban center at its largest. Nothing that happened politically in either the fifth or the fourth century, it seems, did much to disrupt this. To the question whether abandonment and desertion, extending over, say, thirty to forty years, such as the Athenian orators portray, could escape detection, hidden within this evident demographic climax, the honest answer is that theoretically such a thing cannot be excluded. But the pottery throughout the entire Classical era remains overwhelmingly of local manufacture, even within the city itself, without the slightest hint of any change of landownership. The epigraphic and artistic evidence that I have previously mentioned is already an argument against such belief in a deserted city. The historical evidence for Thespian populousness, too, tells its own story.

At its greatest extent, the *astu* seems to have covered some ninety-five hectares of settlement occupancy (excluding cemeteries, which can also be detected). A very conservative estimate of population density, at 125 people per hectare, would give a total urban population of some 12,000. Add to these the several thousand living in second-order settlements like Askra and Eutresis, and we are already approaching the predicted total free population of about 20,000 mentioned earlier, even without taking into account the inhabitants of Thisbai, Siphai, and Chorsiai at those times when they were absorbed into the city of Thespiai.

One notable feature of the city can be located with some confidence, even though today it displays no trace of architectural evidence in situ: the theater, mentioned by Pausanias (9.27.5). There is only one natural physical location for a Greek theater at Thespiai: the roughly semicircular scoop in the hillside, possibly enhanced by human activity, below the modern village of Thespiés and at the outermost edge of the ancient inhabited area (it is clearly visible in Figure 1.2, top center, between the two projecting spurs over which modern Thespiés extends). There is only very indirect supporting evidence for its existence in the stone seating blocks occasionally found on the ancient site. In 1883 P. Stamatakis, then the ephor, recorded the striking fact that he collected together, from across the entire site, 150 seating blocks that he believed to belong to a theater.[27] These he stored at a location south of the river, by the Varváka fountain, thus dissolving any significance that their present-day distribution could have had. This collection, apart from a single example that we found nearby, has today almost entirely disappeared, but three other specimens survived in 2007, in a steep gully immediately to the west of the natural scoop in the hillside where we locate the theater, and a fourth in the courtyard of a village house just above it.

It remains to deal with a topic so far only alluded to, the fortifications of ancient Thespiai. We learn from Thucydides (4.133.1) that in 423 B.C. the Thespians had a city wall that the Thebans had "long" wanted to destroy; it had perhaps more likely been of Early Classical rather than Archaic construction. Then Xenophon (*Hell.* 5.4.41) says that one of the things that Agesilaos did on occupying Thespiai in 378 was to rebuild its fortifications. Taking this statement at face value, one would conclude that he did no more than restore the circuit on its original line; the Theban "destruction" may have amounted to a systematic slighting of the walls at intervals around its course, and Agesilaos needed a speedy reconstruction before his return to Sparta. At least according to Diodoros, the Thebans, though repeatedly successful in defeating this and the other Spartan garrison forces in the open field, were to make at least two unsuccessful attacks on these fortifications, which must therefore have been quite substantial (15.33.5–6; cf. 27. 4, perhaps misdated before the arrival of Agesilaos). An unexpected continuation of this story occurs much later, during the campaign of 87 B.C. in the course of Rome's First Mithridatic War. Appian (12.5, 29) reports that Mithridates' general Archelaos advanced on the now pro-Roman Thespiai and besieged it—clearly implying that it still had an effective fortification circuit. An inscription records that soon afterward the Thespians awarded a statue and a golden wreath to the commander of the Roman force that had halted the advance of Archelaos, Q. Braetius Sura.[28] This comes close to proving that Archelaos' siege was unsuccessful. Finally, there is the additional but historically unrecorded case of the Kastro wall, where a dating rests on the epigraphic and archaeological sources in combination. But how far are our findings in the field compatible with the earlier historical data?

First, in the course of our survey, we began to notice the widespread occurrence of large, ugly, flattish conglomerate slabs of fairly regular size, measuring up to 1.40 by 0.90 by 0.30 meters when unbroken. The greatest concentration of these blocks was beside the Kastro wall, but here they had most probably occurred as *spolia*, as suggested by the fact that their scatter goes far beyond the Kastro's vicinity. The greater number are located south of the Kanavaris

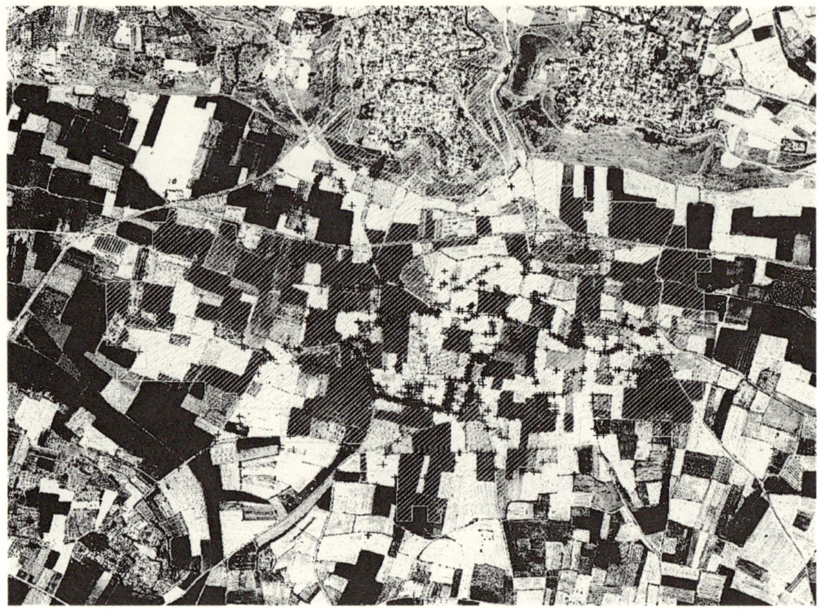

Figure 1.8. Aerial view of ancient Thespiai as shown in Figure 1.2, with the present locations of the large, rough-hewn conglomerate blocks shown as gray crosses. The cross-hatched shading represents the area covered by the grid of the city survey.

River, although there are certain exceptions to which I will turn presently (Figure 1.8). The size and coarseness of these blocks are most readily compatible with use either in fortifications or as invisible, buried foundations; their later use in the Kastro wall, for a start, confirms their defensive capacities.

Our hypothesis is that their distribution in part records, in an extremely rough and haphazard way, the outline of a fortification circuit. This distribution extends a long way eastward—at least four hundred meters—from the northeastern corner of the Kastro, as if to enclose three of the major springs, then doubtless perennial, that lie in this direction. To the west of the Kastro, they are neither so extensively nor so densely scattered, hardly occurring beyond a distance of two hundred meters; but once again, there are enough of them to suggest a function entirely separate from that of the Kastro fortification. This whole hypothesis may appear to rest on flimsy support, but it receives some reinforcement from a find that came to light during the winter of 1986/87, just after the city survey was completed. A farmer, evidently plowing deeper than in previous generations, turned up three exceptionally large specimens of the conglomerate blocks in a field a little to the south of the Kanavaris River. These he placed in a row, end to end, on the field bank that lined his property—certainly no longer in situ, but arguably not far, in arrangement or in distance, from their original placement. Encouraged by this evidence, we searched along the continuation of this field bank, which runs in a southwesterly direction and serves to divide an upper field (to the south) from a much lower one to the north. A substantial number of further blocks were visible, concentrated in this bank, and the break of the slope suggested that it could represent an original wall line. The bank runs continuously from a distance of about three hundred meters to one of about one hundred meters from the midpoint of the north wall of the Kastro, as if aiming to run tangentially to it, if not actually to join its line (Figure 1.8, center). If this latter was indeed the case, then the Kastro itself would have preserved in part the line of an earlier wall, but the very small compass (about twelve hectares) enclosed by the Kastro wall can hardly allow of this applying to more than one short stretch.

In short, I presume that these blocks are the faint surviving traces of a wall line, presumably that destroyed in 423 and rebuilt, probably on the same line, by Agesilaos. The assumption here is that this fortification must antedate a second wall, to which I will turn next. Meanwhile, I note that the scatter of conglomerate blocks, unlike the Kastro circuit, is easily extensive enough to mark, however approximately, the skeleton of a proper city-wall perimeter, capable of accommodating a city population of 10,000 or more, but not exceeding the length of circuit that such a community could man.

But another wall was found in 2006 that ran in a completely different alignment: north-south instead of roughly east-west, on both banks of the Kanavaris rather than just to its south, and extending steeply uphill to the north. This lay largely outside the grid of the detailed urban survey, hence the delay in its discovery. It was clearly laid out with the intention of taking in the high ground to the north, in the manner of the city circuits of many other Greek cities. At Thespiai the two systems could hardly have formed parts of one and the same concept for the city defenses, and logical considerations alone suggest that the construction of this second wall would have made little sense without the prior existence of the Classical fortification, around the main settlement to the south of the Kanavaris. There is further evidence to confirm that this was indeed the true sequence.

The first sign of the new wall's presence was a straight, hundred-meter-long line of conglomerate blocks, on average slightly smaller than those of the other wall, on a field edge to the north of the Kanavaris, where they masqueraded

Figure 1.9. Google Earth image showing, as a crop mark, the line of the north-south-running wall first discovered in 2006, crossing the field at an acute angle to its eastern boundary and apparently incorporating a series of evenly spaced towers on its outer (western) side, with a broad parallel ditch beyond.

as a field boundary. Their alignment at first seemed easily explained by recent displacement for agricultural purposes, but then we found that a line closely similar to theirs could be followed much farther, in both directions but especially northward, that is, away from the main ancient site, to the point where its design and purpose were more fully clarified. At a distance of more than one hundred meters farther north, a few half-buried blocks on the same alignment appeared to be in situ and suggested a wall thickness of up to five meters. A Google Earth image from 2012, taken after a change in cultivation, adds further detail: the wall shows up as a clear crop mark, at a slight angle to the line of blocks in the field bank and to its west, with a series of rectangular towers set at intervals of very roughly twenty meters along its outer face, and with a parallel line farther west again, undoubtedly marking the course of the defensive ditch (Figure 1.9).

From this point, the ground begins to slope upward very much more steeply, climbing through a dense conifer plantation; above that, it is transected by a bulldozed track, made only in the 1990s, that runs around the southwestern edge of the modern village of Thespiés. Here, in the cutting made by the track, a wall composed entirely of mud bricks was revealed in the autumn of 2006, in part founded directly on the conglomerate bedrock and evidently of a lesser thickness than in the stretches discovered below. By the time it reached this level, the wall had begun to curve sharply around to the northeast, abandoning the more or less straight course that it had followed on the plain below, as if aiming for a new destination. This brings us to the very edge of the modern village of Thespiés, and local informants have told us of further ancient constructions in mud brick coming to light within the village. Just below its highest point, fittingly marked by the village water tower, there was evidently a corner where the wall turned eastward again; eventually, it must have returned southward to rejoin the fortification on the other side of the river, but no further traces in situ came to light.

The upper sections of the new wall show signs of hasty construction, and pottery found close to it suggests a likely Hellenistic date. Historically, the obvious opportunity (and *terminus post quem*) for such a construction would be after the destruction of Thebes in 335 B.C. As mentioned earlier, Diodoros and Justin include the name of Thespiai among the allies who joined eagerly in Alexander's assault on Thebes. Another authority, Arrian (*Anabasis* 1.9.10), specifically states that Plataia and Orchomenos had their walls rebuilt at this time, and in both cases there is substantial surviving evidence from the right period;[29] but nowhere is there a specific mention of a refortification of Thespiai. This could possibly be because, in Thespiai's case, the rebuilding had already taken place; as I have mentioned, it had evidently been the subject of a promise by Alexander's father, Philip, and there had been time for him to fulfill this undertaking between 343 (when we hear that he had not yet done so) and his death in 336. At the very least, Thespiai was involved in events that led to a rebuilding of fortifications of at least two other cities whose circumstances closely paralleled its own. It is possible that this construction project was maintained, in functioning form, long enough to be used against Archelaos two centuries or more later; but equally, the rather makeshift appearance of its upper sections could be interpreted as a sign of hasty preparation in the face of the advance of Archelaos. A purely schematic plan, incorporating the few likeliest stretches located for each of the two walls, will give an outline of the general conclusions drawn (Figure 1.10).

To return for a moment to the theater: so neatly does the extension wall of the city enclose it that one might see the two building projects as having been conceived in awareness of each other; and certainly a Greek theater, designed as it was to concentrate a large part of the community in a vulnerable location, would be best sited within such defenses as there were, as was usually the case. But the dominant factor here may have been no more than a

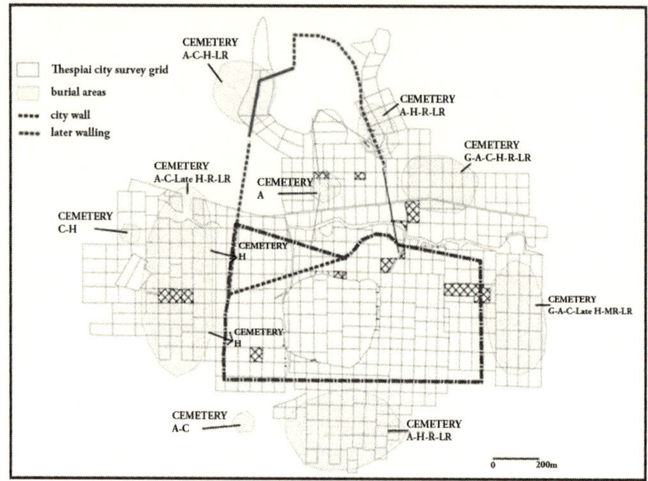

Figure 1.10. Schematic plan of the city site of ancient Thespiai, showing the conjectural or definite lines of the fifth-century B.C. (dark gray) and the Hellenistic (light gray) lines of fortification.

simple convergence of topographical needs between a theater that required a steep hillslope and a fortification that needed to run along the crest of the slope. For the dating of the theater, in any case, only analogy with other surviving theaters in Boiotia provides even a loose a priori argument. Almost all of these show their prime development within the Hellenistic age: at Orchomenos; at Chaironeia, where the originally rectilinear, rock-cut theater was converted to one approaching the standard semicircular form; at the theater, vestigial today, in Thespiai's own territory at the Sanctuary of the Muses; and at the sanctuary of the Kabeirion. Only the theater at Tanagra may be earlier, while the extant traces of the theater at Plataia are probably of Roman Imperial date. A Hellenistic date for the building of the theater at Thespiai is thus a reasonable conjecture, perhaps bringing it into at least the same general era as the extension wall that encloses it. But it should be noted that this theater (unlike, presumably, the fortification) survived until at least the late second century A.D., and it did so in such a condition that Pausanias, rather unusually for him, picked it out as one of the sights to visit in Thespiai.

Finally, there is the much smaller enclosure of the Kastro, so baffling to the early travelers who could see that it was far too small in area to encompass Classical Thespiai. Visitors to the site before 1891 record this as a feature of substance, which makes one regret its loss even more. We now know that it belongs at the earliest to the fourth century A.D.—possibly even to the time of Justinian, whose activity in building fortifications all over central Greece (though not specifically here) is attested.

So in retrospect, notwithstanding all the limitations of survey archaeology to illuminate historical periods, it is something to be able to say that for each of the attested Thespian fortifications, we have possible identifications on the ground. But what broader lessons can we draw from this inquiry? The first and simplest one is not to trust what orators say. To the obvious point that Isocrates, Demosthenes, and their like had political axes to grind we may add the often neglected factor of geography. I doubt very much whether they or their rivals ever traveled to Thespiai to check their reporting; then, as now, it lay off the main arteries, whether of the favored Athenian invasion routes into Boiotia, of the pre-1970s road from Athens to central Greece, or of the new National Highway. Autopsy by either speakers or listeners might have revealed a different reality. By contrast, the testimony of the historians Thucydides, Xenophon, Diodoros, and Appian, at least in the matter of the fortifications, has nowhere been controverted outright and perhaps to a limited degree has been reinforced, despite the fact that only Xenophon is at all likely to have seen the city for himself. In short, archaeological evidence has shown, to different degrees, its capacity to reinforce, to supplement, or to call into question the testimony of documentary sources.

CHAPTER 2

The Autonomy of the Boiotian Poleis

JOHN MA

In 446 B.C. the Athenians sent a punitive expedition into Boiotia against an uprising led by anti-Athenian exiles. The expeditionary corps (1,000 elite Athenian hoplites, reinforced by allied contingents) was large, if not overwhelming; it was led by the formidable Tolmides. The expedition took Chaironeia, one of the cities held by the exiles; the population was enslaved, and the town was garrisoned. A force of Boiotian exiles, coming forth from Orchomenos, their ranks swollen with Lokrian and Euboian exiles and local Boiotian partisans, caught up with the Athenian force on its return route along the western shore of the Kopais marsh. At the subsequent clash, which took place in the basin of Koroneia, by the temple of Athena Itonia, the Athenian contingent was overwhelmed with severe casualties (including the general), and many Athenians captured alive. In exchange for their men, the Athenians evacuated Boiotia; the exiles returned, and "all the other Boiotians became autonomous again," as Thucydides notes at the end of this small piece of narrative in the Pentekontaeteia, characteristically terse yet detailed and intriguing.[1]

Hence the Boiotians, in Thucydides' understanding, had been autonomous before the Athenians defeated them at Oinophyta and took over Boiotia, Phokis, and Opountian Lokris. The last gave hostages; the walls of Tanagra, the Boiotian frontier city, were demolished. The exact modalities of Athenian domination over these regions is unclear (garrisons, tribute, oaths of allegiance, tampering with local constitutions, redrawing local landscapes of settlement hierarchy, levying "allied" contingents?), but the Boiotians were "under the Athenians," as Thucydides portrays the Thebans remembering this period. Just as Athenian domination ended Boiotian autonomy, the end of Athenian domination brought back autonomy, and the victory at Koroneia was remembered and referred to as the liberation of the Boiotians.[2] The Boiotian exiles, having escaped the territory under Athenian domination, could be considered as living as autonomous communities, strictly speaking; and when they drove out the Athenians, the "other Boiotians," too, returned to a condition of being autonomous, enjoying self-rule under their own laws.

Autonomy: in practice, what was this condition, as extinguished in 457 and re-created in 446? The inhabitants of the region, Boiotia, shared an identity as Boiotians, reflected in different ways; they were organized in settlements of different sizes and resources that related to one another through structures of integration and of power.[3] Some settlements were endowed with statehood, controlling their territory and capable of state agency in their interactions with communities perceived as peers. This interaction notably occurs in the form of interpolis war: these are the Boiotian poleis whose victories and defeats are recorded on dedications of weapons at Olympia, set up during the sixth century; Perikles' comparison of the Boiotians to holm oaks, which knock each other down in their fall, refers to this level of local warfare.[4] Interaction could also take more collaborative forms, as suggested by the shared emblem of the "Boiotian shield" on coins struck by a wide series of poleis, big and small, from the late sixth century onward.[5] In this period collaboration must have taken institutional forms, even though these are obscure for the Archaic period and do not seem to have reached the full "federal" horizon of state-like practice. At some point after 446 B.C., the Boiotian communities endowed themselves with remarkable federal institutions, described precisely in a famous passage by a fragmentary historian of the fourth century.[6]

Other settlements were integrated within the territory controlled by a big site; in the precise political terminology that developed to describe hierarchized sites, they were komai, villages, existing within the chora, territory, of the polis, a statehood-endowed urban center. Askra and Kreusis were secondary sites in the extensive territory of Thespiai; Aspledon, Kyrtone, and Chorsiai were such sites in the territory of Orchomenos. Finally, some settlements were recognized as poleis and showed the signs of polis-hood but were subordinate to larger poleis.[7] Thespiai, in the early fifth century, led a group of communities, "those with the Thespians," which almost certainly designates smaller poleis: Eutresis and Thisbai (mentioned as being "with" Thespiai in the description of the Boiotian constitution and its territorial districts) and also smaller poleis such as Chorsiai and Siphai (not even mentioned in the constitutional sketch).[8] Chaironeia was a small polis but somehow belonged to a bigger polis, the prestigious "Minyan" city of Orchomenos, to which it "paid contributions" in 424 (*xunetelei*) and perhaps much earlier.[9] The polis of Tanagra had its own dependent poleis, Mykalessos (the site of the awful massacre of 413 B.C.) and probably an obscure settlement called Pharai. Plataia, though not politically part of the Boiotian League in the Classical period, controlled settlements along the Asopos valley that were poleis (and passed under Theban control after the temporary destruction of Plataia in 427). Most important, Thebes before 480 ruled over a vast territory, probably including the settlements of Haliartos and Akraiphiai—which may have been dependent poleis—as well as a scattering of small sites near the urban center of Thebes, which may have been dependent poleis or nonpolis settlements (many of these were synoikized into Thebes in 431 B.C.).

A conspectus of this hierarchized landscape of settlements raises two questions. The first is that of the difference between a komê (a small settlement without self-government and integrated within the territory of a polis) and a dependent polis (a small settlement not integrated within a bigger settlement's territory, enjoying some form of self-government but politically controlled by the bigger settlement to which it paid dues). The answer, beyond issues of size and population, must lie in questions of polis-hood as status, a symbolic "handle," a fiction heavy in practical consequences that matters because it inflects community interaction and the range of negotiated, accepted behavior. The second question is that of historical origins: what were the processes that led to the emergence of the landscape of poleis and their komai, big and small poleis related through unequal power structures, and general regional identity? The answer to that question must lie in the interaction of big and small sites in the early Iron Age (Hesiod provides an arresting snapshot of the dynamics between the lords of the big site that was or would become Thespiai and the landowners of Askra in their own ecological niche)[10] and in the lost political history of Archaic Boiotia: victories by bigger poleis over the smaller ones leading to subordination and the payment of defeat taxes, or the success of smaller poleis in maintaining independence. There may have been other processes than violent conflict for the establishment of dependency links, notably economic relations, mediated through symbolic forms.[11] Finally, large-scale political history had its impact on the Boiotian landscape—the attraction or opposition of the powerful, populous, well-resourced, and well-integrated neighboring region-polis south of Mt. Parnes (it is clear that conflict and competition with Peisistratid and Kleisthenic Athens favored a Theban-led effort at Boiotian consolidation and affirmation),[12] the meddling of the adventurous hegemonic power that was Archaic Sparta, competition with Thessaly and Phokis (notably over Delphi and hence supraregional structuration), and the settlement of relations in the aftermath of the Persian Wars, before the conquest of the region by Athens. The Boiotian landscape of poleis was produced by a dynamic human and political ecology of settlements, bounded regionally in ways that made the interaction reinforce shared experience and identity. Boiotia fits within a broader Hellenic world of poleis whose relations were shaped by history and power—for instance, in Arkadia, in Thessaly, or, indeed, in the southern two-fifths of the Peloponnese, under the control of a Spartiate power elite but integrating a large number of communities and individuals within differentiated relations to the central polis.

So we can revisit our initial question: in view of this complex landscape, in what way were all the Boiotians autonomous before 458 or after 446, when the region created a remarkable formal structure of political representation and common action? A good number of Boiotian poleis were dependencies of larger poleis; in addition, the post-446 careful structure of representation was overshadowed by the power of the largest, most prestigious, most central polis, Thebes, where the assemblies of the league took place. Therefore, many Boiotian poleis were not autonomous in the sense of being totally free from control, and all Boiotian poleis had to deal with the preponderance of Thebes within the region. But all the Boiotian poleis taken together were autonomous in that they were collectively free from external control by Athens, irrespective of local power arrangements and relations within the autonomous regional unity of Boiotia. All the Boiotian poleis participated in this autonomy as the constituent parts whose sum made up Boiotia, especially since Boiotia itself was a statehood-endowed formation; in fact, the need to express and assert this general autonomy may have been one of the stimuli to the formalization of state institutions at the regional level. This level of autonomy was clearly compatible with the subordination of some poleis to others. The Thespian control of a scattering of smaller poleis, the Orchomenian rule over Chaironeia (this lapsed in the late fifth century), the Theban takeover (after 427) of the poleis that had once belonged to Plataia—all these relations existed within the federal structures of representation and governmental action. This situation hints at the negotiations and bargains that must have occurred when the conception and the implementation of the federal structures took shape; it also shows the rootedness of hierarchical structures in the Boiotian political landscape.

Challenging Autonomy: The Spartans and (in) Boiotia

In 395 B.C., at the beginning of the conflict that turned into what we term the Corinthian War, Lysander led the Spartan army into Boiotia from Phokis. The expedition ended with defeat before Haliartos (not far from the site of the Boiotian victory in 446), Lysander's death in the confused battle, and a humiliating withdrawal under truce by the Spartan contingent. The incident was the first event in a generation-long history of Spartan military interventions and presence across Boiotia, ending with the unexpected outcome at Leuktra in 371 B.C. It also marked the first moment of Spartan power politics in Boiotia with the deployment of a particular Spartan strategy, namely, the claim to protect the autonomy of local cities against bigger powers, and hence the first appearance of this recurrent theme in fourth-century high politics, the autonomy of the Boiotian cities.[13] The strategy had already been applied to the case of Elis, shortly before the invasion led by Lysander;[14] it would form a central element of the Spartan system of hegemony created by the King's Peace (an element that the Athenian-led reaction would have to work its way around). Before Lysander had begun his expedition, he had called on the Haliartians "to revolt and to become autonomous." During his march toward Haliartos, Orchomenos had rallied to him, almost certainly in response to a similar invitation to "become autonomous"; Lebadeia had resisted, almost certainly in the aftermath of the same invitation (Lysander stormed it).[15]

The alternatives (accepting the invitation to "become autonomous" or being stormed and sacked by a Spartan army) bear the mark of paradox and chutzpah so characteristic of Spartan foreign policy in the age of Agesilaos.[16] What matters here is that Lysander could consider Haliartos as not being autonomous. In the light of the nature of the Boiotian League at that point (still the same formation as that created in 446 B.C.), how was this conception justified? Haliartos was part of a Boiotian League that was very much autonomous, as shown by its foreign policy (its choices and actions had caused the Spartan invasion and had played a major part in provoking the Corinthian War). As such, Haliartos could be considered, by the Thebans and by its own citizens, as autonomous already by the time Lysander's proclamation came; the Lebadeians probably took the same view. Furthermore, Haliartos was not a dependent polis belonging to another polis, although it probably had been in that status in the late sixth and early fifth centuries: it was a fully nondependent polis in the workings of the federal constitution between 446 and 386 B.C. In the Spartan view, therefore, it could only be its very belonging to the Boiotian League that constituted lack of autonomy. Likewise, the Spartans must have viewed, or affected to view, the Chalkidian League as incompatible with the autonomy principle.[17]

The Spartans did not articulate their argument in 394 B.C. in the case of the Boiotian League, but it presumably took the same form that it would when the Spartans intervened in the Chalkidike, namely, that the preponderance of one particular big polis, Thebes, did not allow other Boiotian poleis to enjoy autonomy in the league. Two connected paradoxes are detectable here. First, the Spartans did not apply this reasoning to the relationship between Sparta and the perioikic cities; this may have been a case of chutzpah and doublethink or an implicit claim that this relationship, at least in the eyes of the Spartiate political elite and perhaps of the Spartan members of the perioikic cities, was not one of dependency and semi-integration but one of hegemony and alliance.[18] In fact, the objection was raised by Epameinondas and indeed was gleefully applied by him and those powers that succeeded Thebes in gradually amputating the perioikoi from Sparta and generally deconstructing the Spartan system. The second paradox is that the Spartan propensity for seeing regional leagues as instruments for the domination of a single city did reflect, consciously or not, their own situation, namely, the inescapable dominance of Sparta over its regional landscape. The Spartan reading of regional situations was dominance-aware because the structuration of Lakonia, the southern Peloponnese, and indeed the whole Peloponnesian League was dominance-centered. These two paradoxes are not the only ones linked to the workings of autonomy.

Ambiguities and Paradoxes of Autonomy

Autonomy was ambiguous. It could designate the political independence of a whole group of communities organized in a formation that gave it advantages of scale and pooled resources at the price of compulsory collaboration to varying degrees of consent or coercion (if one wishes to be typological about it, one can call this "autonomy 1"). Or it could mean the freedom of every polis as a statehood-endowed unit (say, "autonomy 2"); this is what Agesilaos meant when he told Tissaphernes about "the cities in our part of Greece being autonomous."[19] The situation suited Sparta because it prevented any pooling of resources by individual cities to resist Spartan military dominance; this system of divide and rule worked in the Peloponnese and was applied on a vast scale in Agesilaos' time through the application of autonomy 2. The ambiguity explains various moments in the high political history of the short fourth century (404–338 B.C.). The first was the reluctance of various powers (Thebes, Athens, Argos) when they were faced with Antalkidas' terms, namely, the adoption of a binding clause to preserve the autonomy of the poleis in Greece, because they all realized that the Spartan-style interpretation of autonomy (autonomy 2) would deprive them of some advantageous hierarchical arrangement.[20] The second was the realization of this fear when the Spartans imposed their interpretation at the time of their dominance. In 386 B.C. the Spartans won the peace by explicitly closing down any leeway for the Thebans to exploit the ambiguity and impose a general interpretation of autonomy as autonomy 1.[21] This maneuver was repeated in 375 and, for the last time, in 371; it lay at the heart of Spartan attempts to curb and control Boiotia in the years between 394 and 371.

But autonomy was also a tragic paradox. If autonomy was to be the autonomy of every Boiotian city (for instance, Thespiai) in the Spartan interpretation (autonomy 2), it meant breaking up the Boiotian League and hence stripping the Boiotian cities of any capacity to meaningfully resist outside interference. Such interference was above all constituted by the presence of Sparta itself, which garrisoned the Boiotian cities (Thespiai had a harmost, the infamous Sphodrias, and the tombstone of a Spartan has been found),[22] supported pro-Spartan oligarchies,[23] and levied troops to serve as spear fodder in Spartan-led expeditions (Boiotian troops fought under Spartan leadership against Mantineia immediately after the King's Peace and at Olynthos).[24] Autonomy as the autonomy of every Boiotian city gave statehood markers to all communities (including, almost certainly, the subordinate poleis within the ambit of big poleis such as Thespiai, which lost control of its dependent poleis and the structures of dependency and unequal relations that made up "greater Thespiai"—and perhaps tried to make up for this development).[25] But this arrangement also marked the end of autonomy as the possibility of freedom for the whole of the Boiotians, which had direct consequences for every Boiotian city.

But the paradox does not stop there. If autonomy was to be autonomy of the whole of the Boiotians (autonomy 1), this was possible only if there was a strongly coherent federal formation to express and protect this autonomy. Coherence entailed finding ways of integration; in the face of Spartan interference, this role was taken on by the big central polis of Thebes, which seems to have regarded its historical destiny as the incorporation of Boiotia under its leadership.[26] However, this process could be considered (and indeed was considered, more or less tendentiously) as brutal domination. Rather than espouse Xenophon's view of a Theban inclination to hubris, we should locate the cause in three factors. The first was the inspiration of strong hegemonic models of political success (the Athenian Empire, the Spartan formation), whose legacy determined the aims and means of fourth-century high politics. The second was purely practical, namely, the presence of local recalcitrance because of the diversity of actors in the Boiotian landscape, including sizable poleis with their own hierarchical structures—Thespiai, Orchomenos, Plataia. In these conditions, creating a federal formation was a no-omelet-without-broken-eggs proposition, involving violence in the reduction of centrifugal tendencies justified as autonomy 2 but allowing for the interference of an outside power, Sparta. The third factor was historical—the legacy of the past of violent competition between big and not-so-big Boiotian poleis during the Archaic period, which meant that political interaction took the form of war and that Thebes would behave with the same ruthlessness and self-interest that it had applied in earlier campaigns. The result of these three factors was that the Theban effort to reaffirm autonomy 1 in the face of Spartan interference ended up fulfilling the very claims by which the Spartans had promoted autonomy 2, namely, that the Boiotian League did not allow for autonomy because it violated the autonomy of all the constituent member poleis in favor of the dominance of a single polis.

Especially after 379 B.C., in the face of Spartan opposition in collaboration with some larger Boiotian communities, the Theban attempt to foster the autonomy of all of Boiotia could take only the concrete form of hierarchization under single leadership, so that Xenophon speaks of the Thebans "capturing" Boiotian cities or fearing the loss of surrounding cities (*perikoikides poleis*)[27] as if the integration of the Boiotians under Theban leadership was in fact creating a situation where a big city was dominating other, dependent cities, and the league was merely the vehicle for unequal structuration into relations of centralized dependency. The creation of the conditions for the autonomy of all of Boiotia was a violation of autonomy 2 for all Boiotian cities *singulatim*, as could be seen from the functioning of the Boiotian League institutions that expressed the dominance of Thebes or the violent destruction of recalcitrant Boiotian cities. Concretely, the brutality and hierarchizing that were needed to affirm autonomy 1 made autonomy 2 more attractive and viable. Even after the restoration of the recalcitrant cities of Thespiai and Orchomenos after 338 B.C., their citizens harbored a passionate hatred of Thebes and participated in the sack of Thebes when it was captured in 335 B.C.: a sign of the deep failure of the Theban project of leading Boiotia to autonomy and even hegemony, and of the contradiction between different understandings of *autonomia*.[28]

Resolving the Paradoxes of Autonomy: Toward Hellenistic Boiotia

In the decades before 338 B.C., individual autonomy of Thespiai or Orchomenos meant collaborating in the Spartan system of domination; membership of Thespiai or Orchomenos in the Theban-led Boiotian League amounted to loss of their individual autonomy as the price for participating in the general autonomy of Boiotia, autonomy of the type enjoyed by the whole of Boiotia before 458 and after 446 B.C. (notwithstanding local situations of dependency). The latter situation is, however, particular to the specific circumstances of Classical Boiotia, especially in the fourth century, when Theban preponderance, already latent in the post-446 landscape, grew immensely. But it should be obvious that membership in a federal structure in itself does not amount to necessary loss of autonomy, and in spite of the Spartan reading of autonomy 1 (a reading both tendentious and colored by Sparta's own regional politics), a regional league should be sharply distinguished from relations of unequal structuration between big polis and dependent polis if dependency and autonomy are to have any meaning.

The solution that emerged from the violent history of fourth-century Boiotia solved the paradoxes of autonomy in ways that were intellectually consistent (at the price of a fiction of political equality), institutionally coherent, and humane:[29] they simply amounted to the consistent working-out of autonomy 1. The post-338 Boiotian League did not allow for the dominance of any one polis; nor did it allow for any situation of formal dependency between poleis, so that Chorsiai, Thisbai, and Thespiai, poleis that showed extreme variation in size, resources, potential, and historical ambitions, were all equal members of the confederacy, with the same rights, duties, and possibilities, regulated constitutionally (in the structures of decision making and governance), performed institutionally (for instance, in the federal army), and displayed ideologically (in monuments and festivals). This situation was the result of remarkable restraint, political courage, and imagination on the part of all the Boiotian poleis after the terrible and paradoxical vicissitudes of autonomy in the fourth century.

These vicissitudes were the result of ambiguities in the way autonomy can be understood; these ambiguities, in turn, were the result of the dynamic interaction of multiple self-interested power actors, such as Sparta, Thebes, Thespiai, and Plataia. But the history of fourth-century Boiotia shows how autonomy really mattered for the polis and was an essential part of it to the point of determining structuration within the polis and between poleis. Finding the place of autonomy and working out the practical consequences of this political idea in troubled times determined the political history of Boiotia until the solutions proposed in the Hellenistic period. Those solutions make sense in the light of the fourth century, just as to understand the fourth century, it is necessary to continue the story down into the third and second centuries.

CHAPTER 3

Toward a Revised Chronology of the Theban Magistrates' Coins

ALBERT SCHACHTER

The so-called Boiotian or Theban magistrates' coins are a series of silver staters bearing on the obverse the so-called Boiotian shield and on the reverse an amphora, more often than not accompanied by one or more smaller symbols, and the abbreviation of a personal name. Such abbreviations are also found, together with the head of the young Herakles, on the reverse of a series of obols, with the shield on the obverse; and on the reverse of bronze coins together with one or more additional symbols, the obverse carrying in all cases the head of the young Herakles. Most but not all of the names on the obols and bronze coins are matched by names on the staters.

None of these coins identifies itself as having been issued by any particular mint, but since it has been possible to recognize in several of the abbreviations the names of well-known Thebans of the first half of the fourth century B.C., it is agreed that the coins were minted at Thebes, and it is further assumed that this was in effect a federal coinage. It is agreed also that the people whose names appear on the coins were either magistrates of some kind or private individuals, but at any rate they were charged with the responsibility of getting the coins minted.

This was roughly the state of affairs from Imhoof-Blumer to Martin by way of Babelon, Head, and Kraay.[1] Further than this it was not possible to go because there was really nothing much to go on. But all this has changed: in 1972 Robert Hepworth began a study of the staters, and by meticulous analysis of about 1,700 known specimens he was able to work out a relative chronology, showing which of the reverse varieties bearing magistrates' names were struck on a common obverse die.[2]

Hepworth identified about 160 obverse dies, 47 of which were used to strike two or more magistrate dies each; on average, about four magistrates' issues would be linked by several common obverse dies,[3] but he found that toward the end of the series obverse dies were being used to mint between seven and fourteen issues.[4] Unfortunately, but understandably in view of the complexity of the subject, Hepworth did not go closely into the question of the obverse dies but focused instead on the reverse varieties, of which there are 97, which he illustrates.[5] It is not clear how many dies were used for each reverse variety.

The analysis of the dies showed that forty-one of the forty-five magistrates were linked. The issues fall into four main groups; the obverse-shield dies in each group were used only within that group. Comparing the relative wear of the common obverse dies allowed Hepworth to establish a relative chronology within each group. In all cases the magistrates' names were consecutive. Relative chronology within the four groups was worked out by a variety of methods: "composition and wear in the larger hoards; artistic style; script; flan type; the axial relationship of the dies."[6] Most of the magistrate issues were successive: eight in Group A, seven in Group B, four in Group C, and twenty-two in Group D. Four issues are not die-linked to any other magistrates, but the position of three can be fixed with relative certainty between Groups C and D.[7] The fourth, if it is not a fake, is tentatively placed by Hepworth at the end of the series.[8]

Hepworth concludes that each magistrate was appointed to run the mint for a fixed, probably annual, term. He posits several breaks in the series and concludes that it might have covered more than fifty years, from around 395/390 to 335 at the latest.[9] It is generally assumed that the series of magistrates' coins must have ended in 338, after the battle of Chaironeia, or in 335, when Thebes was destroyed.[10]

The first name in the series—(A1) ΔΙΩ—is in the Attic-Ionic alphabet, which was adopted formally in Athens in 403/402 B.C. but was in fact in use in Athens well before that date.[11] But nine, if not more, issues, covering at least eighteen years, can be identified as using the epichoric Boiotian alphabet, usually not exclusively. A5 (HIKE) has five varieties, all epichoric, while C1 (HIΣME) and possibly D15 (HIΣM)[12] and C3 (ΠΤΟΙ) have only one issue each, all in the epichoric alphabet. One variety of A4 (ΕΨΕ) is in the epichoric alphabet, the other three (EXE) in the Attic-Ionic (Figures 3.1 and 3.2). In A6, there are three varieties each in epichoric (ΔΑΜΟ) and Attic-Ionic (ΔΑΜΩ);

Figure 3.1. Issue A4, epichoric alphabet (BCD Lot 482). Courtesy of Classical Numismatic Group, Inc., www.cngcoins.com.

Figure 3.2. Issue A4, Attic-Ionic alphabet (BCD Lot 483). Courtesy of Classical Numismatic Group, Inc., www.cngcoins.com.

in B2, there are three epichoric (KLEES) and two Attic-Ionic (ΚΛΕΕΣ) varieties; in B3, four are in the epichoric (ΨARO) and one in Attic-Ionic script (ΧΑΡΟ); in B6, there is one of each (ΠΟΘΙ, ΠΥΘΙ), as is the case with the die-isolated ARKA/ΑΡΚΑ (which is placed between Groups C and D; see below). It is possible also that two of the five varieties of A2 ANTI, which have a reversed "N," should be regarded as being in the epichoric alphabet. What emerges from this is that there must have been at least two engravers involved, one or more of whom used the epichoric alphabet.

The second conclusion was pointed out by Hepworth: since both epichoric and Attic-Ionic forms appear throughout at least the first three of his four groups, and the epichoric forms cover so long a time, there is no question of there having been a single date for the adoption in Boiotia of the Attic-Ionic alphabet.[13] There are in fact other signs that the epichoric alphabet was used, at least sporadically, until the middle of the 360s.[14] The magistrates' coins show that the adoption of the new alphabet, even in official documents (for what are coins if not official?), was a fairly long-drawn-out process, depending at least in part on the availability of scribes, masons, and engravers who were familiar with the new forms.[15]

When Hepworth published the results of his work in 1998, he promised further articles on hoards and other aspects.[16] Previously, in 1986, he had argued

Figure 3.3. Epameinondas (BCD Lot 544). Courtesy of Classical Numismatic Group, Inc., www.cngcoins.com.

that the series must have begun much earlier than previous scholarship had believed, and he had reiterated the identification of several of the magistrates with well-known Thebans.[17] He had also revived an idea first mooted by E. S. G. Robinson,[18] that the Epameinondas issue belonged precisely to 364 B.C. because the unique additional symbol of a rose—actually a rosette—on the reverse of two of the five Epameinondas varieties represented the naval expedition of that year, which, to quote Hepworth, "detached Rhodes and several other states from the Athenian alliance."[19] The rose would have been a punning reference to the establishment of an alliance with Rhodes (Figure 3.3).[20]

In addition to dating the Epameinondas issue to 364, Hepworth, who accepts that issues seven and eight of Group A—FAΣT and ANΔP—stand for (W)astias and Androkleidas, political rivals in Thebes, argues that Androkleidas' issue, being the last in the group, fits well with the known facts of the coup of 382, and that he must have held political office "in (or shortly before) 382 B.C.";[21] that the break in the sequence before Group B "might then fall in the period of Spartan occupation of the Kadmeia between 382 and 379 B.C.";[22] and that the third magistrate of Group B—ΨARO/XAPO—should be identified with Charon, a leading figure both in the insurrection of 379 and in the years to come.

Hepworth's work in establishing the relative chronology of this series is groundbreaking, and if I disagree with him on the absolute chronology, this in no way diminishes the magnitude of his achievement. Without his analysis, it would not have been possible to do anything at all with these coins. All of us who work in Boiotian history are deeply indebted to him.

Toward a Revised Chronology (1)

There are several points that weaken the case for Hepworth's dating. The first is that it does not take account of the two issues C1 and D15, HIΣME and HIΣM, respectively. It is fairly safe to guess that these abbreviations represent the name

Hismeinias, and others have already made this connection. Although Hismeinias is a fairly common name in ancient Boiotia,[23] especially in Thebes in the first half of the fourth century B.C., only two men called Hismeinias stand out. One was the prominent pro-Athenian or rather anti-Spartan who was active until the coup d'état of 382; the other, possibly his son, was a close associate of Pelopidas, who was active during the period of the Theban hegemony.

There were—even if we allow for no chronological breaks between groups—at least eight years between the issues of Androkleidas and Hismeinias I, which, on Hepworth's reckoning, would take us down to about 374 B.C. If the two magistrates Hismeinias I and II were the men of that name active before the coup and after the insurrection of 379, respectively, then the issue of Hismeinias I cannot date to 374 because he—the first Hismeinias—was executed by the Spartans in 382.[24]

Next, the equation of C3 ΨARO/XAPO with Χάρων is not possible; if it were, the *o* in the Attic-Ionic form would not be an omicron but an omega, as it is, for example, in A6 ΔAMO/ΔAMΩ, which also has both epichoric and Attic-Ionic varieties. What the abbreviation stands for is probably a name beginning with Χαροπ-.[25]

Then there is the matter of the symbol of the rose. Hepworth based his date of the Epameinondas coins—364 B.C.—on the symbol of a rose that appears in two of the five Epameinondas varieties. This symbol is unique on the coinage, an argument in favor of Hepworth's dating. In fact, however, the symbol on the Theban coins in no way resembles the rose that is depicted on coins of Rhodes. Instead, the Theban symbol is a rosette, or, less definitely, a floral device, of a kind commonly found as a decorative or apotropaic feature in figurative art and jewelry.[26] To identify Epameinondas's symbolic floral device with the rose of Rhodes is certainly tempting but by no means certain.[27]

A few observations on the symbols that appear on many of the coins of the series may be pertinent at this point.

Of the forty-five (if one includes ΞENO) issues, eighteen have no symbols at all on their coins;[28] the number of different symbols in issues with multiple variations ranges from one to five. Of the symbols themselves, the club, either alone or in combination, and a bunch of grapes on a branch are the most popular (on nine and seven varieties, respectively), followed closely by leaves (six) and wreaths of one sort or another (five). Several symbols appear only once in the series.[29] Some of the same symbols appear also on other Boiotian coins of the first half of the fourth century: the club, the bunch of grapes, the ivy wreath, and the ivy.[30] Moreover, several symbols that are used only once in the magistrates' series turn up elsewhere, both in Boiotia and in Euboia.[31] The club seems to have been most popular in coins of Group A, while the bunch of grapes on a branch is found exclusively on issues D10 to D16, that is, in seven successive years.[32]

Whatever the symbols mean, one thing should be clear from all this, and that is that they are not tied to individual magistrates, nor are they exclusive to the magistrates' coinage. The symbols were, perhaps, a kind of hallmark, identifying individual workshops. This would coincide with the conclusion reached by Christophe Flament concerning the various symbols and initials found on coins of mints in the northern Peloponnese.[33]

Finally, as I have noted, it is generally assumed that the series would have lasted until 338 or even 335. This assumption has to be squared with the fact that from as early as 355, the cost of the Third Sacred War was already taking a heavy toll on Theban resources. After the battle of Neon, the Thebans, in the mistaken belief that they and their allies had won the war, sent Pammenes, their most experienced commander, and 5,000 men, a large proportion of their fighting force, off to fight for the satrap Artabazos against the king. Clearly the Thebans needed the money. The Phokians, on the other hand, recovered with the aid of funds acquired by looting the sanctuary at Delphi and were back in the field the next year.[34]

When it came to finding money to pay for the war, the Thebans were simply not able to keep up with the Phokians. The strain on their exchequer must have been considerable. It has to be remembered that unlike the Spartans, who, at their peak, had benefited from the labor of subject peoples, and the Athenians, who had lived off the tribute of their allies and the revenues of silver mines in Laurion and the north, the Thebans had relatively little to fall back on. They had no substantial mineral resources and no subject peoples to exploit and could not always depend on support from all their fellow Boiotians. They were unable to sustain long military campaigns. The expeditions of Epameinondas and Pelopidas were short-term forays, extended raids rather than full-scale invasions. For major undertakings and in times of great need they looked to others for help: the Boiotian fleet was probably paid for by the Persian king and the contributions of allies,[35] and twice, if not three times, in the 350s and 340s the Thebans hired out troops to Persian paymasters.[36] This is a sign of their growing desperation and inability to prosecute the war against Phokis. Moreover, from 354 B.C. until the end of the Third Sacred War, much of western Boiotia—including Orchomenos, Koroneia, Chorsiai, and Tilphossaion—was for much of the time in the hands of the Phokians, and there could have been little if any expectation of financial help from them, or even from Lebadeia and Chaironeia, which, although they remained loyal to the Thebans, were virtually cut off from them, not to mention the fact that Haliartos and Thisbai were under constant threat of attack.[37]

Whatever money the Thebans may have gained in 355 for sending the force under Pammenes to Artabazos—and it is not certain that any great amount was forthcoming—it was not enough. Over the next few years they appealed to their allies and friends, with indifferent success, to judge from a Theban inscription that dates from about 354 to 352 B.C. It lists donations of money "for the war that the Boiotians were fighting concerning the sanctuary at Delphi against those who were committing sacrilege against the sanctuary of Apollo Pythios." The donations were made over three archon years, probably successive. In the event, the contributions collected did not amount to very much, rather less than half a talent.[38]

The end result of this would seem to have been that from the mid-350s until at least the end of the Sacred War, if not longer, the Thebans may have found it increasingly difficult to issue much silver coinage, and it is unlikely that the minting of magistrates' coins could have gone on uninterrupted as late as the battle of Chaironeia or the destruction of Thebes. It is more likely to have petered out gradually, with sporadic rather than annual issues near the end. Indeed, Hepworth has pointed out that "both the die-link and hoard evidence suggest that ΑΣΩ(Π) [D22] was the final issue and may have been preceded by a short period when the mint was dormant following the penultimate magistrate (ΔΑΜΟΚΛ [D21])."[39] It is possible, although one cannot be certain, that the final issue of Group D—ΑΣΩ(Π)—was minted in 350 or 349 B.C.[40]

In regard to the beginning of the series, a date toward the end of the fifth century seems to be most likely.[41] We therefore have a maximum range of between fifty and sixty years for the magistrates' series, ending at some time during the Third Sacred War, c. 356–346 B.C.[42] The scheme I am about to propose leaves the initial and final years of the series open within limits but anchors the whole around two crucial issues that can be dated, I believe, with something approaching certainty.

Toward a Revised Chronology (2)

A study of the list of the magistrates' abbreviations according to Hepworth's scheme shows that fifteen of the forty-five of them can be identified with the

Figure 3.4. Kabirichos (BCD Lot 539). Courtesy of Classical Numismatic Group, Inc., www.cngcoins.com.

Figure 3.5. Klion (BCD Lot 531). Courtesy of Classical Numismatic Group, Inc., www.cngcoins.com.

names of Thebans known from other sources, and indeed, most of them already have been. The most obvious identification is that of the abbreviations ΕΠΠΑ/ΕΠΑΜ(Ι) of D2 with Epameinondas. From the point of view of dating, however, the most profitable match is that of Epameinondas' immediate predecessor, KABI (D1), with Kabirichos, the eponymous archon of 379 B.C., who was killed during the liberation of Thebes (Figure 3.4).[43]

Kabirichos is not a common name, and I argue that Kabirichos the eponymous archon was the same as the minting magistrate of D1, and that, accordingly, the coins issued in his name were minted in 379 B.C. Epameinondas, whose coins follow those of Kabirichos, would then have been the minting magistrate of 378 B.C.

As I have noted, Hepworth suggested that the coins minted under Androkleidas, A8, the last in this group, were issued in 382 B.C., the year of the pro-Spartan coup d'état. But if the Kabirichos and Epameinondas issues date to 379 and 378, this would not be possible, because the Androkleidas and Kabirichos issues are separated by over a dozen years, and there are only three years between 382 and 379.

A far more likely candidate for 382 is Klion (Figure 3.5). The Myron-Karditsa coin hoard, found in Thessaly in 1914 and published by J. N. Svoronos two years later, contains 1,596 coins, of which 1,078 are Boiotian.[44] Of these, 523 are magistrates' coins. All but 19 of these belong to Hepworth's

Groups A, B, or C. The remaining 19 were minted by Klion. Klion's coins were minted in three varieties, but the Myron-Karditsa hoard contained coins from only one, the first of these (ΚΛΙΩ). It was this conjuncture that led Hepworth to conclude that Klion's year followed immediately the final year of Group C, when the magistrate was ΔΑΙΜ.[45]

Moreover, Hepworth tentatively placed the ΑΡΚΑ issue between ΚΛΙΩΝ and ΚΑΒΙ and put ΠΟΛΥ—if genuine—together with ΚΛΙΩΝ and ΑΡΚΑ.[46] This would fit neatly into the period of the Spartan occupation and pro-Spartan government at Thebes, from mid-382 to the end of 379 B.C.

The pro-Spartan coup d'état took place during the summer of 382 B.C., that is, around mid-August, about two-thirds of the way through the Boiotian calendar year (which began at the winter solstice).[47] I think that it is reasonable to hypothesize that 382 B.C. was Klion's year, and that the Myron-Karditsa hoard was deposited by somebody fleeing the coup. On the whole, Boiotian coins did not circulate widely outside Boiotia, so it is likely that a hoard of coins consisting largely of Boiotian coins would have belonged to a Boiotian—specifically a Theban. We know that about three hundred Thebans fled to Athens;[48] others may have fled north, where they also had friends.[49]

It will be appropriate at this point to pause and consider the question whether the magistrates' coinage was a federal or a local, Theban, one. Under the terms of the King's Peace of 386, the Boiotian federation was dissolved and remained that way until the liberation of Thebes at the end of 379. At that time, the Thebans revived the federation, but it was a federation in name only.[50] The Thebans kept control of the government of the country, naming most if not all of the boiotarchs and negotiating with foreign powers in the name of all Boiotians. Individual poleis were attached to the Thebans, as they had been in the past, by a series of bilateral agreements, whereby they consented to merge their affairs with those of the Thebans, agreeing Θηβαίοις συντελεῖν or συντελεῖν εἰς τὰς Θήβας and thereby giving up their αὐτονομία, which had been restored to them by the King's Peace.[51] Proxeny decrees might have been issued in the name of the Boiotoi, but when it came to serious business, it was the Thebans who signed the documents. This will explain the confusion before the battle of Leuktra, when the Thebans insisted on ensuring that when they signed the proposed treaty, they were doing so on behalf of the Boiotoi. We see this process operating also in a treaty published in 2012, according to which the Histiaians agreed to submit to the military hegemony of the Thebans—not the Boiotians.[52]

If the magistrates' coinage had been a federal coinage, it would simply have stopped when the federation was dissolved in 386, but instead it continued to be issued. There was, on the other hand, a different, overtly federal, series of coins that probably did stop in 386. These are the so-called BO-IΩ staters, with a kantharos and BO-IΩ on the reverse. Seventy-seven of these, including examples of the whole issue, were found in the Myron-Karditsa hoard.

This series of coins had previously been dated after 338 by Head, to the years 378–371 by Lilika Kisseoglu, and to 379–371 by Colin Kraay, according to whom there were some seven issues in this series.[53] The author of the sale catalog of the BCD collection of Boiotian coins[54] dates the series 395–387 B.C., basing his opinion partly on lot 496 of the collection, a stater of Wastias (A7; Hepworth 1998: 38) where there are traces of an earlier abbreviation, BO-IΩ, under the FA-ΣT.[55] Some of this series, therefore, will have been in circulation shortly before or even at the same time as the FA-ΣT issue.[56] As Hepworth points out, "it is by no means certain that the BO-IΩ issue must entirely pre-date the magistrates—some overlap is possible."[57] Indeed, I would date the series between the end of the fifth century and 387 or 386 B.C., the year of the King's Peace.

Since the two series of coins overlapped, and since the magistrates' series continued to be issued after the dissolution of the federation in 386, it is difficult to avoid the conclusion that the magistrates' series was a purely Theban coinage, and that the magistrates were all Thebans. Day-to-day operation of the government of the polis was in the hands of a small inner cabinet, consisting of an elected committee of three polemarchs and their secretary, the hipparch, with an eponymous archon selected by lot. This was the Boiotian norm.[58] Whoever was responsible for overseeing the minting of coins for a given period would have been chosen from or by this group of magistrates. It does not follow, of course, that a magistrate would have taken charge of the mint in the same year as his term of office in government.[59]

I return now to the remaining dozen or so identifiable magistrates' names, which fall into two groups, those known to have been active before the coup d'état of 382 and those active after the liberation of Thebes at the end of 379 B.C. In four of the issues—three silver and one bronze—the abbreviated form of the magistrate's name can plausibly be identified with a known eponymous archon: KABIrichos (D1), KRATtidas (D17), WERGOteles (D19), and HAGEIsinikos (*IG* VII 2418).[60] But it does not follow that the magistrate responsible for minting was invariably the eponymous archon. Practice and circumstance may well have changed over the years. It is difficult, for example, to believe that Epameinondas, who follows Kabirichos in the series, was a mere figurehead at any time, let alone in the immediate aftermath of the coup d'état of late 379. He had a position of some authority in the newly formed government of the polis: not only was he a person of considerable prestige, but it was he who, together with Gorgidas, led Pelopidas and his fellows to the demos, presenting them as heroes. He might have been one of the newly organized board of polemarchs, hastily put together to fill the vacuum created by the dissolution of the pro-Spartan government.

We can now look at the other Thebans whose names can be matched to those on the coins. First are those prominent before the coup d'état of 382, namely, Antitheos (A2), Wastias (A7), Androkleidas (A8), Amphitheos (B5), and Hismeinias I (C1).

All these men except Wastias are named in one or more sources as members of the pro-Athenian faction at Thebes during the early years of the fourth century B.C. Antitheos, Amphitheos, and Wastias are known only in the context of events leading up to the Corinthian War.[61] The magistrate whose name appears on the reverse of Issue 2 of Group A, would then be Antitheos. The next name identifiable from the coins is Ϝαστίας (A7), called Asias (20.1) or Astias (20.2) by the Oxyrhynchos historian.[62]

Androkleidas (A8) was one of the three hundred Thebans who fled to Athens after the coup of 382. He was assassinated there by agents of Leontiadas and his colleagues.[63] The magistrate of B5 could have been Amphitheos.[64] Hismeinias I (C1) was said to have been the richest man in Thebes.[65] He was one of the polemarchs in 382, one of the other two being Leontiadas, his political enemy.[66] After the coup of 382, Hismeinias was seized and put to death.[67]

Next, let us look at the magistrates in office after 378. The names of most of these men are found in Boiotian proxeny decrees passed during the 360s. These include three men who served as eponymous archons; if their terms of office as archon and minting magistrate coincided, this would have a considerable effect on the chronology of the archon years, but there is no certainty either way.

A Timolaos (D7) is one of the boiotarchs in two of the proxeny decrees.[68]

Theopompos (D8), with Melon and Damokleidas, was among the twelve exiles who returned to Thebes with Pelopidas;[69] the returning exiles are called τοὺς περὶ Δαμοκλείδαν καὶ Πελοπίδαν καὶ Θεόπομπον (the followers of Damokleidas, Pelopidas, and Theopompos), which appears to place Theopompos among the leaders of the enterprise.[70] He killed the eponymous archon

Kabirichos in 379 B.C.[71] He is probably the Theopompos who is commemorated with two others in a joint monument set up at Thebes, probably after the death of Epameinondas,[72] and he might have been the Theopompos who was a proxenos of the Phokians, possibly shortly after the battle of Leuktra.[73]

Hismeinias II (D15) was possibly the son of Hismeinias I (C1).[74] He accompanied Pelopidas on his unlucky expedition to Thessaly in 368 and was imprisoned with him there.[75] In 367 he went with Pelopidas to the court of Artaxerxes II.[76] He might have been a boiotarch in both years. It may be this Hismeinias who was *hieromnemon* at Delphi in 340/339.[77] He was almost certainly the rogator in the proxeny decree honoring Timeas the Lakonian,[78] and he was probably the father of Thessaliskos,[79] who was set free by Alexander after the battle of Issos.[80] The retention of the aspirate *H* on the coins could be regarded as a conscious anachronism, but not necessarily.

In 2009 Helena Vlachogianni published a new proxeny decree, which she dated to the period 366–364.[81] The eponymous archon in this decree, Krattidas, is undoubtedly the same person as the KPAT on issue D17, and indeed the editor alludes to this issue.[82]

A Diogiton (D18) was one of the boiotarchs in the proxeny decree *IG* VII 2408 (for a Byzantine), and possibly also in 364, when he and Malekidas (also in *IG* VII 2408) were sent to Thessaly after the death of Pelopidas.[83]

Wergoteles (D19) is the archon (as Ergoteles) in two Boiotian proxeny decrees, one in honor of Timeas son of Cheirikrates, a Lakonian,[84] and the other in honor of the Carthaginian Nobas.[85]

A Damokleidas (D21) was, with Melon and Theopompos, among the twelve exiles who returned to Thebes with Pelopidas.[86] He was also one of the boiotarchs at the battle of Leuktra.[87]

For ΑΣΩ(Π) (D22) there are a number of possible candidates whom we know about: three men called Asopodoros, two—or perhaps only one—called Asopichos, and one called Asopoteles.[88]

Hepworth suggests that the issue of ΞΕΝΟ, if it is not a forgery, belongs to the end of the series.[89] The name that springs immediately to mind is that of Xenokrates, one of the boiotarchs at Leuktra,[90] who is honored in the epigram *IG* VII 2462 as having been selected to offer the trophy to Zeus.[91] If this was so, he would have been of a certain age when the coins were minted, but not necessarily much older than his fellow boiotarch of 371, Damokleidas (D21).

The last magistrate whose name can be matched to the initials on a coin is Hageisinikos, the third of three eponymous archons in the inscription that

Figure 3.6. Hageisinikos (BCD Lot 526). Courtesy of Classical Numismatic Group, Inc., www.cngcoins.com.

lists donations, in three archon years, to the Boiotoi in support of their war against the defilers of the sanctuary at Delphi, which has been dated c. 354–c. 352.[92] The coin on which his initials appear—ΑΓΕΙ (Figure 3.6)[93]—is one of five bronze issues that do not have a silver counterpart. This suggests that, as the situation became direr for the Thebans in their prosecution of the war, the mint ceased to put out silver coins regularly. Hepworth, as noted earlier, believes that there may have been a short period between the last two issues of Group D when the mint was dormant.[94]

He also observes that during the final issues of Group D, the obverse dies show signs of "intensive activity—perhaps to finance military campaigns—and the stretching of state resources to the limit."[95] It may also be noted that the final issue of Group D—ΑΣΩ(Π)—has three varieties, a relatively high number for Group D, except for the issues of Epameinondas, which had five, and ΕΥϜΑΡΑ/ΕΥΑΡΑ (D14), which had four. If I am correct in assigning Epameinondas' coins to 378—or possibly even 377 as well—they may be connected with the so-called Boiotian War of 378–375, during which the Thebans had to face repeated Spartan invasions and relied, at least at first, on assistance from the mercenary forces of the Athenian Chabrias.[96] And issue D14—ΕΥϜΑΡΑ/ΕΥΑΡΑ—with its four varieties could, if the Epameinondas issue belongs to 378 or 378/377, have been minted in 365 or 364 and have been contemporary with the construction of the Theban fleet.[97] Finally, the unusually high number of varieties in the issue of ΑΣΩ(Π), the last of Group D, might perhaps have been made possible by the so-called gift to the Thebans by Artaxerxes III of three hundred talents in 350 B.C.[98]

We may also note that the early issues—the whole of Group A and the first three of Group B—have more reverse varieties than the later ones, between two and seven, to be precise; could this have been connected with the Corinthian War? And could some, at any rate, of these issues, as well as those of Epameinondas, ΕΥϜΑΡΑ/ΕΥΑΡΑ, and ΑΣ-Ω(Π), have covered more than one year? A rough count of the magistrates' staters found in the Myron-

Karditsa hoard shows a fair correlation between the number of varieties in Groups A, B, C and the relative number of specimens of these issues.

* * *

To summarize the argument, then: the series began toward the end of the fifth century and ended during the Third Sacred War. Of the magistrates whose names are the same as those of prominent Thebans during that period, one—KABI for Kabirichos—can be fixed with reasonable certainty to 379 B.C. His immediate successor, Epameinondas, would have served in 378 (possibly also in 377), and a case can be made out for Klion's having served in 382. The others fall easily into two groups, those known to have been active up to 382 and those known to have been active after 379. I have avoided attaching them to specific years.

No doubt new names will appear as more inscriptions turn up. These, if past experience is any guide, will belong to the later rather than the earlier part of the range. And again, since all the names identified so far are those of men who held or had held some form of public office—polemarch, eponymous archon, boiotarch—we might expect new additions to follow the same pattern.

If the dating I have proposed is correct, why did the Thebans stop minting this series of coins? The reasons are more likely to have been practical and economic rather than political.

Boiotian coins did not, on the whole, travel very far. They were produced mainly for local or at most regional use. The Boiotians had no silver of their own and commonly resorted to restriking the coinage of other mints on the Aiginetan standard. Quite a few of the examples of magistrates' coins illustrated by Hepworth show signs of having been restruck.[99] For foreign transactions, the Boiotians would no doubt have relied on much more widely acceptable coinage, probably that of Aigina.[100] And if, during 356, they were in the market to hire mercenaries for the coming war, payment in Aiginetan coinage would have been a more attractive incentive.

In addition to this, of course, there are the obvious signs that the Theban treasury was in increasing difficulty during the Third Sacred War. The mint would have continued to function for a few more years, producing some silver but eventually only bronze coinage. Eventually, when the Thebans became seriously strapped for funds, it ceased to operate altogether.

Then there is the question of cost. The privilege of advertising oneself as the responsible minting magistrate cannot have come without expense. What led these men to take on the office—vanity, a sense of civic duty, peer pressure, or a mixture of these? But even more intriguing than why the series ended is the question of why it began in the first place, and how it happened that having begun under one political regime, it continued through at least two others. To these questions, as to many others, I have no answer.

As far as I can tell, nothing proposed in this chapter violates what we know from other sources, although, to be sure, the redating of the Theban magistrates' series has serious implications for the deposit date of the Myron-Karditsa hoard: 382 B.C. is at least fifteen years earlier than the earliest date so far given to it.[101] But one thing at least is clear, and that is that we have not heard the last about the Theban magistrates' coins.

Appendix: Theban Magistrates' Coins, Relative Chronology

Silver coins (staters): the relative chronology has been established by Robert Hepworth (see Hepworth 1989 and 1998).

Group	*Issue No.*	*Number of varieties*	*Abbreviation*	*Possible name*
A[a]	1	2	ΔΙΩ	
	2	5	*(?)ΑΝΤΙ (1)[b]	Ἀντίθεος
	3	5	ΤΙΜ/ΤΙΜΙ	
	4	4	*ΕΨΕ/ΕΧΕ	
	5	5	*ΗΙΚΕ	
	6	7	*ΔΑΜΟ/ΔΑΜΩ	
	7	4	ϜΑΣΤ	Ϝαστίας
	8	2	ΑΝΔΡ	Ἀνδροκλείδας
B[c]	1	2	ΘΕΟΓ	
	2	5	*KLEE/*KLEES/ΚΛΕ(Ε)Σ	
	3	5	*ΨARO/ΧΑΡΟ	
	4	1	ΠΕΛΙ	
	5	1	ΑΜΦΙ	Ἀμφίθεος
	6	2	*ΠΟΘΙ/ΠΥΘΙ	
	7	1	ΕΥΓΙ	
C[d]	1	1	*ΗΙΣΜΕ	Ηισμεινίας Ι
	2	1	ΟΝΑΣ[B*]	
	3	1	*ΠΤΟΙ	
	4	1	ΔΑΙΜ	
	–	3	ΚΛΙΩ/ΚΛΙΩΝ[e]	

Appendix (*continued*)

Group	*Issue No.*	*Number of varieties*	*Abbreviation*	*Possible name*
	–	2	*ARKA/APKA[f]) or vice	
	–	1	ΠΟΛΥ[g]) versa	
D1[h]	1	1	ΚΑΒΙ	Καβίριχος
D1/2	2	5	ΕΠΑΜ/ΕΠΑΜ(Ι)/ΕΠΠΑ	Ἐπαμεινώνδας
D2	3	1	ΘΕΟΤ[B*]	
	4	1	ΔΙΟΚ	
	5	1	ΑΓΛΑ	
D2/3	6	2	ΚΑΛΙ/ΚΑΛΛ(Ι)	
D3	7	1	ΤΙΜΟ	Τιμόλαος
	8	1	ΘΕΟΠ	Θεόπομπος
	9	2	ΟΛΥΜ[B*]	
	10	1	ΦΙΔΟ[B*]	
	11	1	ΑΡΙΣ[B*]	
	12	1	ΑΠΟΛ	
	13	1	ΦΙΛΟ	
	14	4	ΕΥϜΑΡΑ/ΕΥΑΡΑ	
	15	1	(*)ΗΙΣΜ	Ηισμεινίας II
	16	2	ΛΥΚΙ[B*]	
	17	2	ΚΡΑΤ	Κραττίδας
	18	1	ΔΙΟΓ	Διογίτων
	19	1	ϜΕΡΓ[B*]	Ϝεργοτέλης
	20	1	ΑΝΤΙ (2)	
	21	1	ΔΑΜΟΚΛ	Δαμοκλείδας
D3/4	22	3	ΑΣΩ(Π)	Ἀσωπόδωρος/ Ἀσωποτέλης/ Ἀσώπιχος
	—?	1	ΞΕΝΟ (a fake?)[i]	(Ξενοκράτης)

Silver coins (obols):
There are obols with the following abbreviations:[j] ΕΠ, ΘΕ, ΙΣ, ΚΛΕ, ΚΟ.
Bronze coins:
(a) Matching magistrates on silver staters:
C2: ΟΝΑΣ: the bronze reads ΟΝΑΣΙ.
D3: ΘΕΟΤ.
D9: ΟΛΥΜ: the bronze reads OLYM-ΕΠΙ.
D10: ΦΙΔΟ: the bronze reads ΦΕΙΔΟ, and see the next item.
D11: ΑΡΙΣ: one bronze issue reads ΑΡΙΣ-ΦΕΙΔΟ.
D16: ΛΥΚΙ: the bronze reads ΛΥΚΙΝΩ.
D19: ϜΕΡΓ: one bronze issue reads ΣΑ-ϜΕΡΓ.

(*continued*)

Appendix (*continued*)

(b) Bronzes only:
ΠΥΡ-ΡΙ.
ΦΑ-ΡΑΙ.[k]
ΛΑΑΝ-ΘΕ: two names.[l]
ΘΙΩΝ: alone and together with Α, Η Λ, ΙΜ.
ΑΓΕΙ: alone and together with Α, ΑΡ, Η; perhaps Ἀγεισίνικος, the third archon in *IG* VII 2418, and so c. 352.

Notes: * before an abbreviation=epichoric script. [B*]=bronze coins of this magistrate exist. See Head 1881: 69–71.

[a] Hepworth 1998 63–64.

[b] Two of five varieties have the "N" reversed, perhaps therefore epichoric.

[c] Hepworth 1998: 64.

[d] Hepworth 1998: 64–65.

[e] Hepworth 1998: 65: "The Boiotian issues in the Myron hoard were clearly completed mid-way through the ΚΛΙΩ(N) issue, before either of the two ΚΛΙΩΝ varieties were in common circulation. This fortunate end-date for the Myron magistrates allows us to place the ΚΛΙΩ(N) issue immediately after the last issue in Group C (ΔΑΙΜ)."

[f] Hepworth 1998: 66: "Like ΚΛΙΩ(N) the ARKA issue is not die-linked to any other magistrate. *Termini post* and *ante quem* are established by the absence of ΑΡΚΑ from the Myron hoard and its presence in the Thessaly 1978 hoard whose linked magistrate sequence ends seven issues after those of Myron. It seems logical to place both the unlinked issues together and ARKA is therefore tentatively positioned between the ΚΛΙΩ(N) and KABI issues."

[g] Hepworth 1998: 67: "The other unlinked issues—ΞΕΝΟ and ΠΟΛΥ—should be regarded as probable forgeries until any further specimens appear, preferably from a certain hoard provenance. However, if ΠΟΛΥ—known from only a single museum example—is genuine, it would probably belong on stylistic grounds to the same period as the ΚΛΙΩ(N) and ΑΡΚΑ issues. ΞΕΝΟ is more difficult to place—perhaps at the very end of the series."

[h] Hepworth 1998: 65–66.

[i] But see above, nn. 8 and 89–91.

[j] Head 1881: 69 and 1911: 352.

[k] Is it possible that the obols bearing the abbreviation ΦΑ and attributed to Pharai (Head 1911: 347) belong here?

[l] *LGPN* 3B lists ΛΑΑΝ s.v. Λάανδρος (1).

CHAPTER 4

Boiotian Democracy?

P. J. RHODES

Thanks to Thucydides and the *Hellenica Oxyrhynchia* we know that the Boiotian federation and its constituent cities in the late fifth and early fourth centuries had what the citizens would have described as an oligarchy based on fair laws, *oligarchia isonomos*.[1] There was a property qualification for full citizenship.[2] In the individual cities the qualified citizens were divided into four groups that took turns acting as a probouleutic council, and final decisions seem to have been made by ratification of the *probouleumata* by the other three groups rather than by an assembly of all the qualified citizens. The federation was based on eleven electoral units,[3] each of which supplied one of the principal officials known as boiotarchs and sixty members of a federal council that was also divided into four groups; there seems to have been no federal decision-making body larger than that council.[4] As far as we know, external affairs were always the responsibility of the federation, not of the individual cities. This federation was dissolved in 386 after the making of the King's Peace.[5]

In 382 Thebes was occupied by Sparta, and in Thebes and the other cities pro-Spartan regimes were set up that Xenophon describes as tyranny in the case of Thebes and *dynasteiai*, rule by narrow cliques, in the case of the others.[6] How far there were changes in the formal constitution we do not know, but it is highly unlikely that the requirement of a property qualification for full citizenship was abolished. In 379/378 Thebes was liberated,[7] and after that the federation was revived. Thebes joined Athens' Second League as Thebes, but ongoing negotiations perhaps concerned a claim to join as Boiotia.[8] Plutarch has boiotarchs already in 378,[9] but Isocrates claims that at first the Thebans assured the Spartans that they would not disturb "any of the previous agreements,"[10] and, if Pelopidas was boiotarch in thirteen years and 371 was the only year in which he was not boiotarch, his first year and perhaps the year when the federation was formally revived will have been 377.[11]

Modern scholars have regularly described the revived Boiotia as democratic,[12] although I have expressed doubts.[13] I welcome this opportunity to examine the question in more detail.

Certainly the liberated Boiotia was ambitious: Xenophon, in the nearest he comes to mentioning the revival of the federation, says that "the affairs of the Thebans were rekindled [ἀναζωπυρεῖτο]"; Diodoros has the Thebans in an encounter with Agesilaos "for the first time not inferior to the Spartans" and says that after their victory at Tegyra in 375 they "were filled with presumption, became more renowned for their courage, and had clearly established themselves as men who would contend for the leadership of the Greeks"; Plutarch writes of the liberation of Thebes and of Pelopidas' part in it that "the change in the situation made the deed more glorious, for the war which undid the reputation of Sparta and stopped them ruling land and sea arose from that night."[14] But, of course, what gave Thebes/Boiotia its new momentum was not the form of government but enthusiasm arising from indignation at the Spartan occupation and pleasure in putting an end to it, coupled with the presence of ambitious men who were eager and able to build on this.

No ancient text unambiguously describes the new Boiotia as democratic.[15] Xenophon in describing the ambitions of Thebes after its liberation writes that from Thespiai and the other cities the demos had fled to Thebes from the *dynasteiai* which had been set up.[16] The *dynasteiai* were probably set up at the same time as the pro-Spartan regime in Thebes;[17] the migrations to Thebes presumably took place after its liberation; but those who fled were fleeing from the pro-Spartan *dynasteiai* to a city that had overthrown its own pro-Spartan *dynasteia*, and Xenophon's use of the word "demos" in this context need not mean either that they were the poorest men or that Thebes now had a constitution that gave political rights to its poorest men. I see no reason to suppose that the property qualification for full citizenship was abolished in the new Boiotia;[18] Pausanias' account of the decision leading to the destruction of Plataia in 373 perhaps suggests that full citizens were hoplites.[19]

The new federation had an archon, eponymous but probably without significant powers,[20] and not eleven but seven boiotarchs. Many scholars have argued that the seven boiotarchs corresponded to seven electoral units (with Orchomenos and Thespiai eliminated);[21] but down to the destruction of

Thebes in 335 all identifiable boiotarchs were Theban, and more probably the boiotarchs did not represent constituencies but were simply elected, and an assembly meeting in Thebes and dominated by Thebans (see discussion later in this chapter) overwhelmingly elected Thebans. R. J. Buck rejected electoral units but argued that the boiotarchs did not always number seven and that not all were Thebans, but he seems mistaken on both of those points;[22] some have thought that until 335 all boiotarchs had to be Theban.[23]

In the federation there was now an assembly, but there is no sign of a council or of four groups.[24] For the cities there is hardly any evidence before 335: inscriptions perhaps (but the dating is uncertain) record enactment by the polis in Lebadeia and by the demos in Thebes,[25] while Xenophon (unless he has simply been careless) attests a council in Thebes.[26] It is reasonable to assume that external affairs were again formally the responsibility of the federation, and when texts refer to assemblies in Thebes that were dealing with external affairs, they ought to be referring to the federal assembly rather than to the assembly of Thebes, but we cannot be sure that the proprieties were always observed, particularly in matters concerning cities within Boiotia that were opposed to Thebes.

Inscribed decrees of the federation name the archon at the beginning and the boiotarchs at the end, have the enactment formula ἔδοξε τôι δάμοι (resolved by the demos), and (as was the case in many parts of the Greek world) normally do not name the proposer.[27] Buckler claims that the boiotarchs performed *probouleusis* for the federal assembly (and compares an incident in 421/420 when they took the lead before the federal council but failed to explain their plans fully), but although this is plausible and, if correct, is a pointer away from democracy, it goes beyond the evidence; the naming of the boiotarchs at the ends of the decrees need not mean that they acted in that capacity.[28]

Otherwise, characterization of the new dispensation as democratic seems to depend simply on the use of an assembly and of the word "demos" to refer to it. However, assemblies were widespread in the Greek world and were not limited to democracies: to go no further, in Athens an assembly (of the Five Thousand) was envisaged under the regime of the Four Hundred in 411 and seems to have existed under the intermediate regime of 411/410; the Three Thousand in 404/403 were "to have a share in affairs," which again suggests that assemblies of them were envisaged; and there were assemblies under the oligarchic regimes of 321–318 and 317–307.[29] The words used to refer to an assembly varied with locality as much as with political regime, and although states that were oligarchic often in fact preferred another word, that preference was not necessarily a result of their being oligarchic,[30] and the word "demos" in enactment and motion formulas was widespread and (for instance) continued to be used in Athens in 321–318 and 317–307. The existence of an assembly and the use of the word "demos" are not enough to prove that Boiotia and its cities were democratic. The factors that mark out a city or other unit as oligarchic rather than democratic are the membership of the assembly, from which the poorest men were excluded under Athens' oligarchic regimes, and its powers (frequency of meetings and the range of business discussed; whether lay members of the assembly were allowed to make speeches and put forward proposals). I have argued above that there is no reason to think that the property qualification for citizenship that existed in the earlier Boiotian federation was abolished after 378. Except in one case, inscribed decrees do not name proposers, and we cannot tell what the rights of lay citizens in the assemblies were; the decrees of the federation in this period that we know of concerned foreign affairs, and we do not know what other matters were brought before the federal assembly. In practice the main effect of using a federal assembly, meeting in Thebes, rather than a representative federal council was that the assembly was dominated by Thebans at the expense of men from the other cities.

The fact that boiotarchs could be called to account (e.g., Epameinondas and Pelopidas for not being in Thebes to leave office at the end of 370; Epameinondas' being accused of favoring the Spartans in 369) is not a sign of democracy, since accountability of officials was a widespread principle in Greece, and the character of the regime was reflected not in the principle but in how the principle was applied.[31] In connection with the first of those cases, Pausanias refers to the jury as appointed by lot; that may be careless writing rather than authentic tradition, but even if it is correct, we must remember that allotment too was not limited to democracies but could also be used by oligarchies to choose between men considered equally eligible.[32] There is no justification for Buckler's assumption that "The size of these courts is unknown, but they probably involved hundreds of jurors, as did the Athenian courts."[33] Again, a story told by Plutarch in which Pelopidas prosecuted an opponent for making an illegal proposal may indeed reflect a copying of Athens' *graphe paranomon*,[34] but that institution could as well have been copied by an oligarchy based on the rule of law as by a democracy.

After Chaironeia, Philip of Macedon is said to have exiled or executed the leaders of the opposition to him, to have reinstated men exiled earlier, and to have entrusted the city to a council of Three Hundred.[35] This again does not help us pronounce on the character of the previous regime, nor do the accounts of the revolt against Alexander in 335. Arrian mentions the return of the (new) exiles, who in the assembly won the confidence of the *plethos* and proclaimed freedom <and autonomy> and escape from the severity of the Macedonians; Diodoros writes that the leaders of the revolt met as a *synedrion* and made a *probouleuma* about the war, all agreeing that they should contend for autonomy, and this proposal was ratified by the *plethos*.[36] Clearly the assembly suppressed by Philip reasserted itself, but I do not think that we can conclude more than that.

According to Diodoros, Thebes' final crushing of Boiotian Orchomenos resulted from a plot involving dissident Thebans and the three hundred *hippeis* of Orchomenos to change the constitution "in Thebes" (presumably in the Boiotian federation) to an aristocracy, and when the plot was disclosed, the demos in the *ekklesia* (presumably the federal assembly) voted to destroy the city.[37] That there were men who wanted a narrower regime does not prove that the existing regime was democratic. Outside Boiotia, the federal Arkadia supported by the Thebans, with its citizen body of the Ten Thousand, seems to have been a moderate oligarchy.[38] For the constitution of the new Messene we have no pre-Hellenistic evidence, but E. Meyer thought that the original constitution was "oligarchic-timocratic."[39] In Sikyon an oligarchy survived when the city joined the Thebans; Euphron, in order to make himself tyrant, set up a democracy and claimed that this would be more securely anti-Spartan and pro-Theban; but at a later stage a Boiotian governor was associated with the revived oligarchy, and Euphron was opposed to them both.[40] In 366, when Epameinondas attacked Achaia, he originally avoided exiling the leading men and changing the constitutions; when the Arkadians objected that this would favor Sparta, the Thebans sent governors who did exile the leading men and set up democracies, but this backfired, and the leading men returned and attached the Achaian cities to Sparta.[41] Justin writes of the *stasis* in Herakleia Pontike that ended with the establishment of Klearchos as tyrant in 364 that both the Athenian Timotheos and Epameinondas were invited but refused to support the upper class against the *plebs*; but even Buckler, who cites this as evidence for a democratic Boiotia, remarks that "Epameinondas' interest . . . was no more altruistic than Timotheos'. . . . Herakleia was so divided against itself that it could not serve his plans."[42] In all of this I see no sign that the Boiotians supported democracy in principle; in the Peloponnese their main concern seems to have been to support regimes opposed to Sparta. Similarly, although other federations, such as that of Arkadia, which the Boiotians supported, were established in the fourth century, Thebes was overwhelmingly supreme in the post-379 Boiotian federation, and it is unlikely that the Boiotians supported federalism in Greece in principle. H. Beck has written, "Thebes' foreign policy was not determined by ideological concepts, but was subject to power politics."[43]

So there is no clear evidence that the revived Boiotia was considered democratic at the time, or that in the membership and powers of the federal and city assemblies it would appear democratic to us, or that as a matter of policy it supported democracies elsewhere in Greece. There was, of course, a spectrum of regimes from the narrowly oligarchic to the emphatically democratic, not a sharp division between obvious oligarchies on one side and obvious democracies on the other. In the earlier federation, which is agreed to have been oligarchic, the members of the federal council seem to have received a payment to cover their living expenses.[44] But, insofar as moderate regimes can be placed on one side of the line or the other, Boiotia after 378 no less than Boiotia before 386 is best characterized as an *oligarchia isonomos*.

CHAPTER 5

Diodoros 15.78.4–79.1 and Theban Relations with the Bosporus in the Fourth Century

THOM RUSSELL

Under the year 364/363, Diodoros places a speech by Epameinondas, in which he exhorted the Thebans to strive to challenge the Athenians at sea and to extend their dominance on land to "mastery of the sea." In response, the Theban demos voted to construct a hundred triremes and dockyards to accommodate the shipbuilding; Epameinondas himself embarked on a voyage around the Aegean, and he was received at Byzantion, Rhodes, and Chios, three founding members of the Second Athenian Confederacy (Diod. 15.78.4–79.1).[1]

Epameinondas' language in the Ephoran epitome preserved by Diodoros is not sheepish, speaking of the acquisition of "hegemony at sea" (ἀντέχεσθαι τῆς κατὰ θάλατταν ἡγεμονίας) or of a naval empire, literally an "*arche* at sea" (τὴν τῆς θαλάττης ἀρχῆν). What Epameinondas did and what he achieved on this voyage remain unclear. Modern views tend to polarize between two extremes: on the one hand, that Epameinondas achieved nothing; on the other, that his voyage detached these key members of the Second Athenian Confederacy and sparked the Social War—seven years earlier than indicated by Diodoros. In what follows, I explore the evidence for Epameinondas' trip to the Bosporus and try to come to a middle ground between these extremes. This confusing episode has been subject to a great deal of discussion, and epigraphic discoveries have altered dramatically our understanding of the impacts of the Theban voyage. My aim here is modest. It is not to offer a wholesale reinterpretation of Epameinondas' voyage, but rather to view the episode from a slightly different perspective, and to focus on only one aspect of the voyage: Epameinondas' reception at Byzantion, which occupied one of the most economically and strategically significant sites in the Mediterranean. I consider how his trip affected Theban relations with the Bosporus in the long-term, and what this might suggest about the nature of the Theban hegemony after Leuktra. Attempting to gauge Epameinondas' success in terms of the rhetoric preserved in Diodoros may be misguided; probably, the naval *arche* at sea was not a genuinely held ambition, and Epameinondas had no real intention of ever forming a naval hegemony on the model of the Second Athenian Confederacy or the Delian League. Instead, talk of thalassocracy was Theban propaganda designed to play on Athenian weakness and exploit localist ambitions by providing an incentive for key allies like Byzantion to begin acting in their own interests. From this perspective, Epameinondas' expedition, even if it did not result in the creation of a Theban naval *arche*, should not be called a failure.

This is most clearly illustrated in the case of Byzantion, whose control of the Bosporus made it crucial for Athens' supply of grain from the Black Sea. It has often been thought that, prompted by Epameinondas' visit, the Byzantines revolted from the Second Athenian Confederacy, allied themselves with Thebes, and launched attacks against Athenian grain ships. Despite some modern uncertainties, the evidence, I suggest, compels us to accept Byzantion's revolt as highly likely. Moreover, exploration of Theban relations with the Bosporus in the years following Epameinondas' visit reveals that he may have had considerable long-term impacts in the region. In response to Epameinondas' visit, and possibly on his urging, the Byzantines embarked on a policy of territorial aggrandizement, annexing several neighboring communities, and perhaps used their newly acquired power to levy a transit toll on Pontic trade. The mere insinuation of Theban power could awaken local ambitions and entice away from Athenian influence members of the Second Athenian Confederacy on whose loyalty Athens depended to secure her grain route. Epameinondas succeeded, effectively, through clever diplomacy in wresting from Athenian control the Bosporus strait, and persuaded his new allies to begin to obstruct Athenian shipping from the Black Sea. Although it is hard to call this the "*arche* at sea," τὴν τῆς θαλάττης ἀρχήν, that Epameinondas speaks of in Diodoros' epitome, it does constitute a lasting achievement of Epameinondas' mission and, with other recent evidence, prompts us to reconsider the ramifications of Thebes' short-lived "naval policy." By fomenting discontent throughout the Aegean and offering an alternative to Athenian hegemony, Epameinondas was recognizing that the end of Greek bipolar politics had arrived and adapting to the new situation. The episode thus provides useful evidence of the nature of the Theban "hegemony" after Leuktra, and of the breadth and flexibility of Epameinondas' vision.

Much of this episode is obscure because our principal source is a condensed summary of Ephorus. It is not even certain that the hundred triremes were ever actually built, for Diodoros tells us only that the Thebans voted to build them.[2] It is also likely that this Theban naval policy was a reaction to increased Athenian imperial operations in the Aegean, specifically, the recent Samian cleruchy, which conjured up sour memories of the fifth-century empire.[3] If so, then it was directed as much toward the Persians as it was toward the Greek poleis that Epameinondas visited; a Theban fleet in the Aegean would help show Artaxerxes II that a resurgent Athens could not challenge Thebes' guardianship of the peace.[4]

Despite the Thebans' lofty ambitions, however, it is often thought that Epameinondas' short-lived naval policy achieved very little. The Social War, under the usual chronology, did not break out until 357, caused by the revolts of precisely these three poleis: Byzantion, Chios, and Rhodes, joined by Kos (not a member of the Second Athenian Confederacy).[5] On this chronology, the allies could not have revolted in 364/363, or, if they did, they were quickly reconquered by the Athenians. The accepted outbreak of the Social War in 357 effectively makes Epameinondas' voyage nonimpactful, with the possible exceptions of the revolts of Byzantion and Keos.[6] The Thebans' putative naval policy, meanwhile, was nipped in the bud by the premature death of Epameinondas at Mantineia in 362.

All this is good reason to believe that Epameinondas' successes were limited, and the ancient evidence likewise supports this view. Isocrates implies that Epameinondas achieved nothing.[7] Plutarch says so explicitly, claiming that Epameinondas fought on sea "in a manner not befitting his excellence and reputation."[8] Yet high ambitions there were. Aeschines (2.105) could speak of Epameinondas hoping to transfer the Athenian Propylaia to the Theban Kadmeia, while Isocrates spoke of an attempt by the Thebans to rule by land and by sea (5.53). It may be that our alarmist Athenian sources exaggerate the extent of Epameinondas' goals and the vigor of his rhetoric.[9] Perhaps this was precisely the point. If Epameinondas wanted to cause alarm in Athens, and wanted the allies to think that Thebes was on the cusp of establishing an *arche* at sea, Byzantion was a good place to begin. Distinguished precedents existed for an imperial mission to the straits or through them into the Black Sea. Thrasyboulos, in 389 during the Corinthian War, began his brief revival of Athenian imperial institutions at the Bosporus by reestablishing the 10 percent tax collected on Pontic trade in the fifth century.[10] Perikles' enigmatic "Pontic expedition" took him through the straits in a show of Athenian imperial strength.[11] Indeed, it was here that the Athenian Empire was born.[12] No doubt talk of Epameinondas' intent to visit the city, as well as other key founding members of the Second Athenian Confederacy, caused considerable consternation in Athens.

It would be wrong to minimize the significance of the other locations visited by Epameinondas. Chios remained a ship contributor during the fifth century, attesting to its wealth, while, as we will see, the diplomatic ripples of Epameinondas' trip were felt throughout the Aegean. Yet Isocrates (5.53) singles out Byzantion when describing Epameinondas' expedition, and the city was one of the jewels in the Delian League's crown, paying 15 talents between 454/453 and 450/449, rising to 18T 1,800 drachmas by 433/432, and reaching a height of 21T 3,420 drachmas in 430/429.[13] Byzantion and, with greater relevance, the Bosporus strait were surely among the primary goals of Epameinondas' expedition, for it was on Byzantion's loyalty that the Athenians depended to secure their Pontic grain route.

Epameinondas' mission, of course, did not take him only to Byzantion, and a growing body of evidence has cast new light on the expedition, suggesting that its ramifications may have been considerably more far-reaching than previously thought. Justin (16.4.3) mentions an appeal by Herakleia Pontike to Epameinondas, made presumably while Epameinondas was present in the Bosporus.[14] Epameinondas' visit to Rhodes may have been commemorated on a Theban coin whose type carried the name Epameinondas, the Rhodian *rhodos*, and a Theban shield.[15] From Knidos, near Rhodes, an inscription published in 1994 reveals that Epameinondas had been accorded proxeny by the Knidians.[16] The trip probably also provoked the revolt of the island of Keos and the murder of the Athenian proxenos there, although the Keans were swiftly subdued and reincorporated into the Confederacy.[17] Traces of Epameinondas' diplomatic overtures can therefore be discovered all around the Aegean, and it is highly likely that a spate of Boiotian proxeny decrees should also be connected to the Theban naval policy. These include federal proxeny grants to a Byzantine (*IG* VII 2408), typically dated to 364/363, the year when Epameinondas was present in the city; to a Carthaginian (*IG* VII

2407); and to an Athenaios of Macedon (*SEG* XXXIV 355).[18] Two other Boiotian proxeny decrees should be added to this list: to the Lakonian Timeas (*SEG* LV 564bis) and to two men from Olynthos or Corinth (*SEG* LVIII 447).[19]

All this evidence adds up to give a strong impression that Epameinondas' trip was more successful than it is often thought to have been, and it provides good a fortiori reason to give countenance to Ruzicka's argument that the revolts that prompted the Social War, usually dated to 357, actually took place seven years earlier and were originally a response to Epameinondas' diplomatic overture.[20] Diodoros uses a curious phrase to refer to the results of Epameinondas' trip: "he made the cities *idias* with regard to the Thebans" (15.79.1: ἰδίας τὰς πόλεις τοῖς Θηβαίοις ἐποίησεν). The term *idias* here is controversial, and has often been taken to mean somewhat more than "he made the cities friendly toward the Thebans," implying instead something closer to a formal alliance.[21] If so, this leaves open the possibility that all three cities revolted from the Second Athenian Confederacy in response to Epameinondas' visit. The Social War proper, on Ruzicka's chronology, did not begin until 357, when the Athenians turned their attention toward the subjection of the revolting allies, who had begun their revolts seven years earlier.

To assume with Ruzicka that all three cities revolted and remained in a state of war until 357 may push the point too far, because only for Byzantion is there any evidence that this was the case. Demosthenes (9.34) speaks of an alliance between Byzantion and either Thebes or Philip II, but he is unclear which is meant (συμμάχους ὄντας).[22] The wording of Diodoros' account of the outbreak of the Social War (especially the expression ἔτι δὲ) might also be taken to suggest that the Byzantines were already in revolt.[23] More significantly, however, only two years after Epameinondas' visit, in an episode dated securely by archon year, the Byzantines with the Chalkedonians on the opposite bank of the Bosporus are found forcibly coercing Athenian grain ships passing south through the Bosporus in 362/361 into their own harbor and requiring the merchants to unload their cargoes, an action that forced the Athenians to send a fleet north to escort the fleets past Hieron and through the strait.[24]

What reasons lay behind the coercion of Athenian and Athens-bound grain ships by the Byzantines and Chalkedonians? Apollodoros maintains that the Byzantines and Chalkedonians were compelled by their own private shortage of grain.[25] Economic motives are likewise suggested by a passage of the Aristotelian *Oeconomica*, which adds several other details concerning the beaching of ships in the Bosporus. In need of food and money, on one occasion the Byzantines seized boats sailing out of (*ek*) the Pontus—thus probably laden with grain from the Crimea—and forced them into their harbor. The protesting merchants were permitted to trade only on payment of a tithe of 10 percent of their profits, a *tokos epidekatos*.[26] It is not clear when this later episode occurred, but it is at least possible that it is identical with the episode mentioned by Demosthenes in 362/361; if not, the two episodes must be roughly contemporaneous.[27] It may therefore be that the Byzantines' motives were purely economic, as implied by the sources, and they were driven by necessity. As a consequence, some commentators downplay the significance of this episode, noting that the measure was limited to emergency circumstances, and suggesting that the coercion of the grain ships reveals only that tensions existed between Byzantion and Athens, not that the two poleis were at war and that Byzantion was actually in revolt.[28]

In fact, the Athenians' reliance on imported grain and the sensitivity of the Hieron-Aegean route made a blockade of the Bosporus perhaps the most hostile action that could possibly be taken against Athens.[29] The episode no doubt conjured up memories of those dark days at the end of the Peloponnesian War when King Agis dispatched Klearchos to Byzantion to blockade the Bosporus, and when Lysander blockaded Peiraieus itself.[30] Antalkidas' blockade of the Hellespont was what compelled Athens to accept the King's Peace.[31] It was precisely this action, the seizure of a fleet of grain ships docked at Hieron in the Bosporus—Philip of Macedon's "most lawless act" (τὸ παρανομώτατον ἔργον)—that prompted the Athenians to declare war against Philip II and tear down the *stelai* containing the terms of the Peace of Philokrates.[32] Free passage of grain ships between Greece and the Black Sea was so serious that when, over one hundred years later, the Byzantines revived their 10 percent tax on Bosporus shipping and began seizing ships and forcing them to pay a toll, the action ignited a war with the Rhodians, who took it on themselves to coerce the Byzantines into restoring free passage through the strait.[33]

It is true that Apollodoros, the speaker who mentions the seizure of ships by the Byzantines, does not go so far as to refer to this episode in 362 as an act of open war. Certainly it was in his interest to exaggerate, wherever possible, the dangers facing him as trierarch; and a state of war with Byzantion would have served this purpose nicely. As such, the episode cannot be taken as evidence that a formal state of war existed between Athens and Byzantion, but this does not mean that Byzantion had not turned its back on Athens and renounced the Second Athenian Confederacy. Epameinondas' visit inspired the Byzantines to begin to take advantage of their own position at Athens' expense. Perhaps the Byzantines simply permitted pirates to act freely in the region against Athenian ships. More likely is that they provided state sponsorship to disguise the involvement of the Byzantine state, and to avoid any formal declaration of war at this stage. Although Buckler makes much of the Thebans' attempt to endanger Athens' grain supply, he fails to make the connection between Epameinondas' trip and the Byzantines' actions only a year later: the seizure of shipping in the Bosporus was, very likely, a direct consequence of Epameinondas' visit.[34]

Epameinondas' presence at the strait is thus likely to have driven a wedge between Byzantion and Athens and to have encouraged the seizure of Athenian grain ships, whether or not this constituted a revolt proper until 357.[35] However, it is possible that his successes in the region went even further. In *On the Liberty of the Rhodians*, delivered in 353 or 351, Demosthenes alludes to a Byzantine takeover of Chalkedon, the polis on the opposite Asiatic bank of the Bosporus, and Selymbria, to the west of Byzantion: "Why is there no man in Byzantion to dissuade his countrymen from seizing Chalkedon, which belongs to the King and was once held by you, while the Byzantines have no shadow of a claim to it? Or from taking Selymbria, once an ally of yours, and making it tributary to themselves, and incorporating it into the territory of Byzantion, contrary to all the oaths and agreements which guarantee the autonomy of those cities?"[36]

The seizure of Chalkedon is also mentioned by Theopompus, who criticizes the Byzantines' democratic constitution for contributing to their licentious mode of living and drunkenness, defects that, he claims, were exported to Chalkedon when the Byzantines imposed a democracy there.[37] Both episodes are typically connected to the Social War, when Byzantion could take advantage of its independence and seize control of both cities. The "oaths and agreements" broken by the annexation of Selymbria would therefore be the peace terms of 355.[38]

However, there is no reason other than a desire to connect these actions to the Social War that the episodes could not have taken place several years earlier, at the time of or in the years following the reception of Epameinondas in the city in 364/363. A crown was dedicated in Athens by the Chalkedonians in 354/353: this shows that friendly relations existed between Athens and Chalkedon, and that the Chalkedonians could, at this stage, take the decision to grant a crown independently.[39] Yet by this point the Social War had ended, and friendly relations with Athens may have been reestablished.

Furthermore, the union between the two cities might not have taken the form of a *sympoliteia* proper; other forms of union between the two cities that permitted a greater degree of self-determination to the Chalkedonians (such as a simple alliance or relationship of dependency) remain possible. Selymbria's autonomy was guaranteed by the King's Peace and by its membership in the Second Athenian Confederacy (Selymbria is included as a member on the prospectus of the League), while Chalkedon had been ceded to the King as one of the "cities in Asia" that fell to the Persians by the terms of the King's Peace.[40] Demosthenes makes the implicit criticism that the seizure of Chalkedon was a breach of the King's Peace (ἣ βασιλέως μέν ἐστιν), and it may be that the oaths and agreements that the Byzantines broke in seizing Selymbria were not in fact the peace terms that followed the Social War but the various common peace agreements of the fourth century, which upheld the autonomy of the member poleis enshrined in the original Peace of Antalkidas. If so, then the union with Chalcedon might conceivably have taken place at any time between the arrival of Epameinondas in the Bosporus in 364 and the outbreak of the Social War proper in 357. This is especially true if we accept Ruzicka's view that the Social War was a more long-term state of affairs beginning in 364 and lasting until 355. Byzantion, on this view, took the opportunity provided by the growth of Theban power and the arrival of Epameinondas in the area to revolt from Athens. This was not motivated primarily by any particular slight suffered at the hands of Athens or by the Byzantines' fear of becoming embroiled in a war against Persia on the side of Athens, though both may have been contributing factors. Instead, Epameinondas exploited petty, localist ambitions, and the Byzantines revolted to free themselves from the obligations demanded by membership in the Second Athenian Confederacy, which forced them to respect the autonomy of member poleis, including Selymbria, and to recognize the King's possessions in Asia. This prevented them from pursuing their own expansionist ambitions. Renunciation of the Confederacy's charter thus allowed them to acquire Selymbria and Chalkedon, creating a zone of control extending across both sides of the strait and extending west for about sixty kilometers, and to begin taxing ships passing between the Pontus and Greece. The reception of Epameinondas was therefore a calculated piece of realpolitik that permitted the Byzantines to engage in some opportunistic land grabbing, not necessarily a meditated act of hostility targeted specifically against Athens. I suggest that this, and not membership in any formal *arche* at this early stage, is exactly the sort of destabilizing situation that Epameinondas had hoped for, and it may be the kind of situation that Diodoros means by the term *idias*.

It would be relevant to this argument if a *sympoliteia* with Perinthos, implied by a document inserted into Demosthenes' *De Corona* (Dem. 18.90–91), could be dated to the fourth century, but the decree is certainly a later forgery.[41] It purports to preserve the honors granted by Byzantion to Athens for Athenian aid during the siege of Philip II in 340 and refers to itself as a decree passed by the *damos* of Byzantion and Perinthos (δεδόχθαι τῷ δάμῳ Βυζαντίων καὶ Περινθίων) as though the two communities were one. A *sympoliteia* later, in 202/201, existed between Byzantion and Perinthos, and this is usually taken as evidence that the insertion was made in the second century by someone who was familiar with the situation at the time of Philip V but anachronistically interpolated it back into the time of Philip II.[42] Another, tentative explanation is that in connection with Byzantion's fourth-century annexation of Chalkedon and Selymbria the city also briefly gained Perinthos, a fact that the forger was aware of. On our current evidence it remains more likely that the phrase reflects an anachronistic interpolation of the third-century *sympoliteia*, if one that might vaguely reflect the fourth-century situation. It was, after all, probably written by someone trying to make the decree reflect fourth-century circumstances.

It is probable that the Byzantines' purpose in turning away from Athens was precisely to gain control of both shores of the Bosporus and to use their dominance of the strait to seize shipping. In 362/361, we saw, the Byzantines and Chalkedonians began to seize the Athenian grain ships (though Chalkedon belonged to Persia by the terms of the King's Peace), necessitating that the Athenians send an armed convoy north to the strait. That the seizures of shipping in the strait were a state-sponsored enterprise may be supported by a difficult fragment of Ephorus, preserved in Stephanus of Byzantion. According to Ephorus, Chrysopolis, a village in Chalkedon's territory on the Asiatic coast of the Bosporus, was given "to the allies."[43] The verb does not have a subject, but the fragment apparently derives from book 23 of Ephorus' history, falling under his account of the Theban hegemony that ended at the battle of Mantineia in 362. If so, as Stylianou suggests, a plausible context in this period is Epameinondas' trip to the Bosporus; while he was at Byzantion, he gave Chrysopolis, a possession of Chalkedon, to his new allies, the Byzantines.[44] Chrysopolis was the possession of Asiatic Chalkedon, not Byzantion.[45] This may therefore have been the first stage in a local rivalry which led, in a few years, to the formal acquisition of Chalkedon by Byzantion, and which was sparked by Epameinondas' visit.

Chrysopolis, the "city of gold," was named (in one of the aetiologies given by Dionysios of Byzantion) because it had served as a toll station since the sixth century, when it was a possession of the Persian Empire. According to Dionysios, it was named either after Chryses, son of Chryseis and Agamemnon, or because the Persians, when they were in control of the region, collected gold gathered from the local poleis at this spot.[46] It had functioned as such as recently as the close of the Peloponnesian War; in 409 Alkibiades established a toll station (a *dekateuterion*) at Chrysopolis, which according to Xenophon charged the *dekate*, a 10 percent toll, on ships sailing out of the Pontus (Polybius, speaking of the third-century toll, has this tax levied on ships sailing into the Pontus).[47] The site was the penultimate elbow of the Bosporus before Byzantion, where the currents in the strait force sailing ships to skirt close to the headlands, making the site a perfect location at which to impose a toll. By ceding the site to the Thebans' new allies, Epameinondas was encouraging the Byzantines to reestablish the old customs house originally operated by the Athenian Empire at Chrysopolis and to use it to begin taxing Athenian ships sailing out of the Pontus. The undated episode recounted in the Aristotelian *Oeconomica* (1346b29), discussed earlier, reveals the probability that the ships seized by the Byzantines were forced to pay a tax of 10 percent on the value of the goods carried. The full implications of this are that the Byzantine state itself, and not state-sponsored pirates, under Theban influence and in partnership with the Chalkedonians, had revived the old Athenian *dekate* administered at the Bosporus and were turning it against Athenian ships—indeed, it was perhaps at Chrysopolis that the Byzantines were beaching Athenian grain ships in 362.

We possess, then, good reason to believe that Epameinondas achieved considerable successes at the Bosporus of a diplomatic kind. What of the Theban "*arche* at sea"? Must this remain rhetorical exaggeration? Evidence that the Byzantines had thrown in their lot with the Thebans in a formal alliance has been adduced on *IG* VII 2418 (Rhodes and Osborne 2003: no. 57), a record of contributions made over three separate Boiotian archon years to the Boiotians during the Third Sacred War, fought by Thebes on behalf of the Delphic Amphiktiony against the Phokians between 356 and 346. These funds were presumably intended to provide the Thebans with a source of funding to match that provided by the sacred treasures of Delphi, which had been seized by the Phokians and had been used to hire mercenaries. A probable but not certain date for the contributions is 354–352 inclusive.[48] Envoys, πρισγεῖες, from Alyzea and Anaktorion, poleis belonging to the Akarnanian League, brought the contributions of these two cities, while a Boiotian proxenos of Tenedos, Athenodoros, is credited with contributing a thousand drachmas. Contributions from Byzantion, amounting to eighty-four Lampsacene gold staters and sixteen Attic silver drachmas in the first archon year and five hundred Lampsacene gold staters in the third, were brought by officials called σύνεδροι.

Alyzea and Anaktorion both belonged to the Akarnanian League, which had been a member of the Second Athenian Confederacy but had allied with the Boiotian Federation after the battle of Leuktra.[49] Tenedos was not a Boiotian ally and remained a member of the Second Athenian Confederacy. This is why its contributions were brought by an individual proxenos and not by official representatives of the Tenedian polis: Athens supported the Phokians during the Sacred War, and Tenedos could not officially support the Theban side while it was still a member of the Athenian Confederacy.[50] The Byzantine σύνεδροι, however, are at the center of an old debate concerning the organization of Boiotian allies and relate to the question of the existence or nonexistence of a formal, allied *synedrion*. D. M. Lewis pointed out that the existence of these officials implies the parallel existence of a *synedrion* to which they belonged. This, he argued, must have been the organizational and institutional basis for the Theban hegemony after Leuktra.[51] Like the Athenians, the Thebans had organized their allies outside Boiotia into a confederacy, the decisions of which were taken by a *synedrion* made up of representatives from the allied poleis, σύνεδροι.

If we follow Lewis, a Boiotian *synedrion*, to which Thebes' allies outside Boiotia belonged, existed in this period, founded on the model of the Second Athenian Confederacy, and to which the Byzantines (at least) belonged in the period after Epameinondas's trip to the Bosporus—more evidence of the long-term impacts of Epameinondas' trip on Theban-Byzantine relations. Can this scenario be upheld? Plutarch did, after all, claim that Pelopidas and Epameinondas led the allies "without a common resolution or law," implying that the Theban hegemony lacked the kind of institutional infrastructure that the Second Athenian Confederacy possessed, and that it was bound together rather by the personal abilities of the two Theban leaders. In the same passage Plutarch mentions the *synedria* of the individual Theban allies, Argive, Eleian, and Arkadian: As Buckler notes, these were individual assemblies, which took counsel separately and contested Thebes' right to sole hegemony.[52] If this testimony is correct, the Thebans led their allies, who continued to meet in their own separate *synedria*, as *hegemon* purely by virtue of the *auctoritas* gained at Leuktra. The existence or nonexistence of this Boiotian *synedrion* remains an open question.[53]

Lewis adduced in connection with the *synedrion* a passage of Xenophon (*Hell.* 7.3.11).[54] This is a speech made by a man accused of killing Euphron of Sikyon in 366, where it is claimed that it was just and lawful to kill an exile who had returned home ἄνευ κοινοῦ τῶν συμμάχων δόγματος, "without a joint decree of the allies." This is taken to imply the existence of a common decision-making body of the allies, which passed joint resolutions (*dogmata*) on the model of the Athenian Confederacy. Buckler plays down the significance of this passage, arguing that there is no reason to presume that the term *dogma* means a joint decision of Thebes' allies in any technical sense. He argues instead that the trial of Euphron's assassins took place before the Theban *boule*, not in a federal council. The "*dogma* of the allies" refers, on Buckler's view, to a clause governing the treatment of exiles in the alliance among the Sikyonians, the Argives, and the Arkadians, formed after the Boiotian treaties of 370 and 369, and that the defendant was basing his argument on the assumption that such a clause still possessed validity.[55] However, as Buckler notes, the closest parallels in the *Hellenica* for Xenophon's use of *dogma* here are at 5.2.37 and 5.4.37, where the word is used to refer to a joint decision of Sparta's allies within the Peloponnesian League. It is also used in the *Hellenica* to describe decisions of the Athenian demos (6.2.2), the Athenian *boule* (6.5.33), and the citizens of Mantineia taken in their own assembly (6.5.5). In each case we are dealing with the formal decisions of constitutional bodies. Despite Buckler's claims to the contrary, a *dogma* passed by a *synedrion* more closely fits Xenophon's usage of the word than a clause governing treatment of exiles in a treaty. This passage does, then, provide some evidence for an organizational framework for Thebes' allies, but not any precise details of that framework. *IG* VII 2418 remains the sole evidence that this framework consisted of something called a *synedrion*.[56] It also does not demonstrate that the Byzantines had joined Thebes as early as 364 in response to Epameinondas' voyage, though it strongly suggests that Theban-Byzantine relations were significantly strengthened by the visit and that at some point between then and 354 they were solidified into a formal organizational structure.

Yet if these officials did belong to a Boiotian *synedrion*, why are only they called σύνεδροι, while those from the Thebans' other allies, Alyzea and Anaktorion, are termed "envoys" (πρισγεῖες, i.e. πρεσβεῖς)?[57] For what reason should some of the Thebans' allies send *synedroi* as their representatives and so belong to an allied *synedrion*, but not others? It is not the case, Jehne notes, that Byzantine envoys were regularly called σύνεδροι; in *IG* II^2 41, Byzantion's separate alliance with Athens, we find Byzantine πρεσβεῖς entertained in Athens. Jehne has therefore offered an explanation for this difficulty. He cites, perhaps too ingeniously, the Boiotian claim to have founded Byzantion, found in Constantine Porphyrogenitus.[58] In antiquity Byzantion possessed a notoriously confused and contradictory foundation tradition. Megara is cited most often and is commonly accepted by modern authorities, but also cited are Sparta, Athens, Boiotia, Argos, Miletos, Karystians, Mycenaeans, Korinthians, and "many others."[59] Jehne argues that the city's status as a Boiotian colony, or at least as an alleged Boiotian colony, allowed it to be treated as an extension of the Boiotian Federation when the city came into alliance with Thebes. This Federation had as its central organ the people's assembly, which therefore treated its members as extensions of the Boiotian *damos*.[60] Byzantion, he argues, was simply encompassed within the structure of the existing Boiotian Federation, so its envoys were called *synedroi* as a mark of its kinship connection to the Boiotians.[61]

Although this helps explain why of Thebes' allies outside Boiotia only Byzantion sent *synedroi*, it is a difficult scenario to accept. For Byzantion to have been treated as an extension of the Boiotian Federation, we would, as Lewis noted, "in effect have to believe that the Byzantines became Boiotians."[62] A contemporary Theban decree, *IG* VII 2408, which was discussed earlier, grants Boiotian federal proxeny to a Byzantine and suggests that this was not the case. Byzantion could not have been treated as a member of the Boiotian Federation any more than Carthage, Lakonia, or Macedon, for the grant of federal proxeny would lose its significance if Byzantion was already viewed as belonging to the Boiotian Federation; the Byzantine would already have been regarded as a member of the federal Boiotian *damos*. It is tempting to imagine that the Byzantine *synedroi* alternatively belonged to a local, Byzantine body, set up to accomodate Byzantion's new allies or dependencies Selymbria, Chalkedon, Chrysopolis, and Phileas. Demosthenes says (15.26) that the Byzantines made Selymbria "tributary" (συντελῆ ποιεῖν καὶ Βυζάντιον). Diodoros uses the word *synteleia* to describe the Boiotian Federation in 375/374 (15.38.4); Pausanias later used the same term to describe the Achaean League (7.11.3). However, in the inscription the various ambassadors seem to be named according to their relationship with the Thebans: ambassadors *to* the Thebans, a proxenos *of* the Thebans. It is more likely that the *synedroi* describe the

Byzantines' relationship with the Thebans in some way. Whatever the case may be, Byzantion's contribution to the Thebans during the Sacred War reveals that a very close relationship existed between the two poleis in the decade after Epameinondas' visit—either the Byzantines had formally joined a Theban *synedrion* some time after Epameinondas' visit, or the colonial connection between Byzantion and Boiotia was invoked to strengthen their relationship at this time.

What we possess, if Lewis is correct, is concrete evidence of an organizational basis for Thebes' allies outside Boiotia, including Byzantion, in the second half of the fourth century. This helps bring the aims and outcomes of Epameinondas' expedition into sharper focus. If Byzantion's membership in the Theban *synedrion* took place in the years following his reception in the city in 364/363, it may have been an outcome of close relations between Thebes and the Bosporus which had been strengthened by Epameinondas. This Theban maritime league was short lived and unsuccessful, undermined by the early deaths of both Epameinondas and Pelopidas and by the apparent failure to seduce other Athenian allies into membership. Epameinondas' aim was to impress Theban power on Athens' most important allies and to sow dissension along Athens' vital sea lanes. In this he was successful, and the ramifications of his visit were felt at the Bosporus for years afterward: in response to the visit, Byzantion revolted from Athens, began to seize Athenian shipping, levied a tax on Pontic trade at 10 percent, and breached the King's Peace by annexing Selymbria, Chalkedon, and Chrysopolis (also perhaps Phileas, and Perinthos at a stretch). Chalkedon, too, may have breached the King's Peace in response to Epameinondas' overture by joining with the Byzantines to seize shipping. It remains possible that Rhodes and Chios also revolted, and that Ruzicka's view of Epameinondas sparking the Social War is correct. But even if the Social War did not break out until 357, the ripples of Epameinondas' trip were felt throughout the Aegean. Some time between the visit and the Sacred War, the Byzantines assented to a formal alliance with Thebes, joining an allied *synedrion*.

Friendship with or control of Byzantion permitted the Athenians to secure what grain imports they required from the Black Sea in the fourth century. By successfully enticing Byzantion to revolt and encouraging the Byzantines to embark on an aggressive policy of expansion, Epameinondas threatened the Athenians' grain supply. This strategy emulated that of the Spartans in the fifth century, and his success was in turn copied by Philip II, who likewise perceived that control of the Bosporus was the Athenian Achilles' heel. If this is correct, then Thebes' brief "naval policy" was considerably more ambitious and more successful than has sometimes been thought, but its success cannot be judged in terms of traditional hegemony. Byzantion may not have belonged to a formal Theban organization until later, but nevertheless Epameinondas had succeeded in removing Athens' stranglehold on the Bosporus strait. We should not, then, discount Epameinondas' expedition as unsuccessful or non-impactful. Evidence for its far-reaching impacts at Byzantion and the strait, as well as elsewhere in the Aegean, reveals the kinds of subtle successes that could be achieved by powers in the post-Leuktra period. As Epameinondas observed, it was possible to sow disruption within larger hegemonies and to create a vacuum into which another power could insert itself. The expedition is an example of the kinds of things that could be realistically accomplished in the fractalized Greek world that emerged following the collapse of bipolar hegemonic politics after Leuktra but before Chaironeia.

CHAPTER 6

Enchanting History

Pausanias in Fourth-Century Boiotia

SAMUEL D. GARTLAND

> His "Greece" is of course a fantasy. It consisted of an enchanted past, of living myths and rituals whose apparent antiquity guaranteed their modern meanings, of ruins and monuments executed by the hallowed hands of the great.
>
> —J. Elsner in *Pausanias: Travel and Memory in Roman Greece* (2001: 18)

Pausanias' *Periegesis* is spatially structured, but it is as much an exploration of history as it is of geography. The ten books progress region by region around mainland Greece, offering a very human approach to space, where past landscapes as experienced in the present exert a strong influence on the choice and presentation of material. But Pausanias' capabilities as a historian and utility as historical evidence have long been scrutinized. The once-powerful tradition of fraudulent incompetency begun by Wilamowitz-Moellendorff that undermined attempts to recover Pausanias' historical value has long since ceded authority to subtler approaches, spearheaded by Elsner, reading Pausanias as a literary construct, a fantastic work that represents the Greece neither of Pausanias' own time nor of any other period. Whether fallacious or fantastic, both readings have contributed to continued misgivings concerning the history contained within the *Periegesis*.[1]

The response by historians to both approaches has been to restore Pausanias' reputation one passage at a time, isolating a passage and testing its reliability against other sources where possible. Piecemeal, atomized historical restoration of the *Periegesis* can be of only limited value, however, because the work is carefully planned to cohere as a whole; this is a fundamental insight on which much of the recent rehabilitation of Pausanias has been founded. The history contained within the *Periegesis* is important for our understanding of ancient Greece, as well as for our comprehension of Pausanias' scheme and methods, and as his progressions through space have been found more complicated than they seem at first, so are his visits to the past.[2] To realize the full potential of Pausanias' work for historians of ancient Greece, neither the isolation-verification approach to passages nor the orthodox regional/book breakdown offered by most commentaries will overcome these problems. Therefore, rather than simply assessing the reliability of a passage against other sources, it may be better to assess historical examples in Pausanias within the entirety of the *Periegesis* to fully elucidate their meaning and utility before considering the presentation of "history" in more general terms within the work. In my contribution to a holistic reading of Pausanias' historical technique, I will follow the presentation of a region and a period through the whole of the work and see whether there is something to be learned about his approach and our own use of his ancient Greece. Boiotia in the fourth ce[illegible] chapter because this is a combination of period a[illegible] several books of the *Periegesis* and touches on [illegible] Pausanias' general purpose and his perspective

[illegible] Pausanias' *Periegesis*, begins on the borders with [illegible] leutherai and Plataia over Mt. Kithairon. This is [illegible] ooks marked by a major physical break, and this [illegible] to consider whence we are arriving. In physical [illegible] ed directly from book 1.38, where Pausanias left us on the southern slopes of Mt. Kithairon with Antiope, exiled from Thebes and mother of Amphion and Zethos, who together would go on to refound Thebes, its walls, and their most characteristic physical feature, the seven gates.

At the same time as the path into Plataia begins on this road from Eleusis, the narrative also proceeds from Arkadia and the end of book 8. Arkadia was a region significantly affected by the Theban hegemony of the fourth century, and almost at the end of book 8, Pausanias summarizes the life of the Achaian League *strategos* Philopoimen and compares it unfavorably with that of Epameinondas,[4] a figure whose biography is a prominent feature of book 9, in the process acting as a transition between the books: "When Greece was in a miserable condition it was revived by Konon, the son of Timotheos, and Epameinondas, the son of Polymnis, who drove out the Lakedaimonian garrisons and governors, and brought an end to the boards of ten, Konon from the islands and coasts, Epameinondas from the cities of the interior. By founding cities too, of no small fame, Messene and Arkadian Megalepolis, Epameinondas made Greece more famous" (Paus. 8.52.4; cf. 8.11.5, 49.3).[5]

To understand the significance of this twin entrance into Boiotia, it is necessary to consider the composition of the work, as well as its presentation. Denis Knoepfler, in an enlightening analysis, argued that book 9 began to be written around the time that book 1 was completed, and that work continued on the *Boiotika* until it was perhaps finished shortly after the end of book 4 (the *Messenika*).[6] Although this explanation is based on Pausanias' discovery and use of Polybius at a late stage in the composition of the *Periegesis*, it also makes sense of the geographical continuation of the beginning of book 9 from book 1.38 and, further, the close relationship between Pausanias' accounts of Messenia and Boiotia. If we also accept that the account of Boiotia was written substantially before that of Arkadia (i.e., book 9 was written before book 8), the order in which the books were finally presented indicates careful, long-term planning. An example is the anticipation of the biography of Epameinondas at the end of book 8 just cited, but throughout the *Periegesis* biographies are advertised in advance, suggesting that the author was concerned that his work should "appear well planned."[7]

The Structure of Pausanias' Boiotia

With this careful planning of the situation of the *Boiotika* within the *Periegesis* in mind, we can observe further indications of similar care in the ordering of material within book 9. At the beginning of his account of Boiotia, Pausanias states that before 490 B.C. the Plataians had no claim to renown (οὐδὲν ὑπῆρχεν ἐς δόξαν: 9.1.3). However, there is a useful contrast with this, namely, the introduction to Orchomenos, the last major community to be considered in the *Boiotika*.[8] Pausanias announces that the only ancient things there that are worthy of memory are those that follow: "On the other side of Mount Laphystios is Orchomenos, as renowned a city as any in Greece. Once raised to the greatest heights of prosperity, it too was fated to fall almost as low as Mycenae and Delos. Its ancient history is confined to the following traditions [περὶ δὲ τῶν ἀρχαίων τοιαῦτ' ἦν ὁπόσα καὶ μνημονεύουσιν]" (Paus. 9.34.6).

What follows concentrates almost entirely on early myth, which at Plataia was deemed to warrant only a few sentences of consideration. This characterization of Orchomenos is consistent throughout the *Periegesis*, with a notable Homeric influence: the picture of a famous and wealthy city of the Minyans.[9] It is also a feature of a wider cleavage in book 9 in which events of a certain period are related in broadly discrete zones, representing choices made by the author.[10] For instance, the destruction of Orchomenos in the 360s is related not in the extensive description of that city but instead in the biography of Epameinondas, which lies within the Theban part of the book: "In the absence of Epameinondas the Thebans removed the Orchomenians from their land. Epameinondas regarded their removal as a disaster, and asserted that had he been present the Thebans would never have been guilty of such an outrage" (Paus. 9.15.3).

In fact, Pausanias' relation of fourth-century history is almost all presented during the journey around the southern and eastern part of Boiotia centered on Thebes. Although much of the Third Sacred War took place in western Boiotia, one of only two explicit mentions of the fourth century after the crossing into the Kopais basin is the battle of Chaironeia of 338 B.C.[11] The other is the biography of the Spartan Lysander, which is triggered by a memorial (μνῆμα)[12] at the site of the battle of Haliartos, fought in 395 B.C.: "In Haliartos is a memorial to Lysander the Lakedaimonian. For having attacked the walls of Haliartos, within which were troops from Thebes and Athens, he fell in the fighting that followed a sortie of the enemy" (Paus. 9.32.5).

Pausanias' decision to relate Lysander's biography at Haliartos has provoked some confusion and accusations that he was "in search of 'copy'" in an area where his usual interests were thin on the ground.[13] But throughout, the form, content, and location of biographies in the *Periegesis* are very carefully chosen, and there are other opportunities elsewhere to relate the life of Lysander.[14] More pertinent might be to consider the other major historical individuals in book 9, Epameinondas and Cassander. The three figures correspond to Pausanias' wider view of the major influences on the history of fourth-century Greece: Lysander represents Sparta, Cassander Macedon, and Epameinondas Boiotia. It is worth noting that all three figures are also closely connected with Thebes, its rise as a major power, its hegemonic ascendency, and its later regeneration after destruction.

The first and shortest account is that of Cassander.[15] Pausanias relates his supervision of the return of the Thebans and also that he rebuilt all the ancient walls that had been destroyed by Alexander in 335 B.C.:

> On this occasion the Thebans were removed from their homes by Alexander, and straggled to Athens; afterwards they were restored by Cassander, son of Antipater. The Athenians were the most eager in their support of the restoration of Thebes, and they were helped by Messenians and the Arkadians of Megalepolis. My own view is that in building Thebes Cassander was mainly influenced by hatred of Alexander. . . . In the time of Cassander all the ancient circuit of the Theban walls was rebuilt, but fate after all willed that afterwards the Thebans were again to taste great misfortune. . . . The lower city of Thebes is all deserted today, except the sanctuaries, and the people live on the akropolis, which they call Thebes and not Kadmeia. (Paus. 9.7.1–6; cf. 7.6.9)

This echoes a passage related only shortly before on the foundation of Thebes' walls by Amphion and Zethos:

> When they reigned they added the lower city to the Kadmeia, giving it, because of their kinship to Thebe, the name of Thebes. What I have said is confirmed by what Homer says in the Odyssey:
>
> > "Who first laid the foundation of seven-gated Thebe,
> > And built towers about it, for without towers they could not
> > Dwell in wide-wayed Thebe, in spite of their strength."
>
> Homer, however, makes no mention in his poetry of Amphion's singing, and how he built the wall to the music of his lyre. (Paus. 9.5.6–7)

This focus on the foundation (and refoundation) of Thebes and its fortifications is important because Pausanias uses the gates of the Kadmeia to support the unique structure of book 9, in which he returns to a single hub (Thebes) three times to begin explorations of the surrounding territory.[16] The Bronze Age walls were real, but the narratives that surrounded them were constructions of the early Iron Age, a product perhaps of the migrating Boiotoi attempting to make sense of the monumental landscape they had inherited.

The fourth-century destruction and restoration of Thebes were events of such magnitude that they became additions to the mythology, postscripts to the Thebaid and the Persian Wars. When Pausanias came to survey the walls, they were severely dilapidated, and he was perhaps able to use only three of the "gates" (the Neistan, Elektran, and Proetidian), while the other four were merely place names or in disrepair, further complicating the recovery of this enceinte-palimpsest.[17] The history of the fortifications of the Kadmeia and their effect on the *Boiotika* is an excellent example of the way in which mythical and historical experience could become embedded in the physical landscape. The gated walls of Thebes were invested with myth and with history, and because of this, even in a ruinous, semivisible state they had enough substance to structure much of the progression through book 9.

The spatial form of the *Boiotika* is undeniably articulated around Thebes, and much of the region is treated "as if it were part of the Theban countryside."[18] In the Bronze Age and the Archaic period Thebes appears to have been the dominant polis in the southern part of Boiotia, but only in the middle decades of the fourth century was the sort of spatial hegemony over the entire region implied by Pausanias' arrangement of book 9 achieved. But the extent to which Thebes dictates the form of book 9 has its limits. For instance, a site such as Orchomenos is able to resist because of both a physical separation (it is situated at the northwest corner of Lake Kopais) and its own ancient traditions, which emphasize the independence and wealth of the Minyans.[19] Also, although the fourth century is the focus of much of Pausanias' attention in the *Boiotika*, events of the period are not explicitly prioritized in Pausanias' historical summary of the region (chapters 5 to 8).[20] Instead, the reader is left with the impression that Pausanias is keen on emphasizing that the events of the fourth century, though undoubtedly significant, are part of a cyclical pattern of destruction and renewal that can be understood only within a long span of Theban and Boiotian history.

Epameinondas, Messene, and Sensible History

This selectivity and emphasis of pattern come from Pausanias' intimate control of his material. Because of the idiosyncratic selectivity of the author, the *Periegesis* has been read as a "hegemonic" version of Greek history.[21] But the *Periegesis* is also a work in which hegemony and historical agency are themselves of central concern. For instance, biographies tend to begin at the point when a figure gains the ability to wield power, and the narratives of cities generally focus on periods when the community is at its most prosperous or is most widely involved in the wider history of Greece. This interest in power and its exercise naturally draws Pausanias toward Epameinondas, and it is through him that fourth-century Boiotian history is predominantly related.[22] His biography is the longest in the *Periegesis*, and he is given credit for masterminding the victory at Leuktra. Throughout the *Periegesis*, Epameinondas stands for the agency of Boiotia and the centrality of Thebes in Greek affairs, and this centrality is situated chronologically between the dominance of Sparta and that of Macedon. The biography is also situated in the middle of the period in which Pausanias considers Greece to have produced "good men" (ἀνδρῶν ἀγαθῶν, 8.52.1). Furthermore, after Epameinondas' death in 362 B.C., the representation of Boiotian activity becomes predominantly passive and narrated in books other than book 9, implicitly suggesting that the agency of Thebes rested solely on his leadership.

In support of this, Pausanias almost entirely ignores the other great fourth-century Boiotian leaders, Pelopidas and Pammenes. Despite receiving a full treatment in Plutarch's *Lives*, Pelopidas is mentioned only twice in Pausanias, both times as a grateful recipient of Epameinondas' attention. He is saved from death at the battle of Mantineia (385 B.C.) by Epameinondas' heroism and is also released from captivity in Thessaly because his captors learn that Epameinondas is at the head of a relief force. Pammenes, the friend of Philip II and military leader of Thebes in the 350s, receives even shorter shrift, being mentioned only once, when he is left by Epameinondas to protect the Arkadians at the new foundation of Megalepolis (8.27.2).

The biography of Epameinondas concludes with an epigram in which his role in the foundation of Megalepolis and Messene is emphasized:

> By our counsels Sparta was shorn of her glory,
> And holy Messene finally receives her children.
> With Theban arms was Megalepolis crowned,
> As well as all of Greece, in freedom and independence.
> (Paus. 9.15.6)

The verse is strikingly nonpersonal, and the common good of the achievements is emphasized. In many ways this text encapsulates much that is of interest to Pausanias and fits well with the portrayal of Epameinondas as the benefactor of Greece and all-around ἀνὴρ ἀγαθός elsewhere in the *Periegesis*.[23] Messene and Megalepolis stand as Epameinondas' greatest achievements, and according to Pausanias, members of both communities were present at the reconstruction of Thebes by Cassander.[24] Messenians are also present in Pausanias' narrative of the mythical Argive invasion of Thebes.[25]

The interactions between Messene and Thebes serve as indicators of an intricate scheme that becomes visible only when the *Periegesis* is viewed in its entirety. At the same time they serve to highlight the importance of the senses in affecting the experience of events and consequent behavior. An excellent example is the dramatic description of the foundation of Messene in 369 B.C.:

> As Epameinondas considered the spot where the city of the Messenians now stands most convenient for the foundation, he ordered enquiry to be made by the seers if the favour of the gods would follow him here. When they announced that the offerings were auspicious, he began preparations for the foundation, ordering stone to be brought, and summoning men skilled in laying out streets and in building houses, temples, and ring-walls. When all was in readiness, victims being provided by the Arkadians, Epameinondas himself and the Thebans then sacrificed to Dionysus and Apollo Ismenios in the accustomed manner, the Argives to Argive Hera and Nemean Zeus, the Messenians to Zeus of Ithome and the Dioskouri, and their priests to the Great Goddesses and Kaukon. And together they summoned heroes to return and dwell with them. . . . the most summons from all alike was to Aristomenes. For that day they were engaged in sacrifice and prayer, but on the following days they raised the circuit of the walls, and within built houses and the temples. They worked to music, but only from Boiotian and Argive flutes, and the tunes of Sakadas and Pronomos were brought into keen competition. (Paus. 4.27.5–7)

The foundation of Messene is an affair stage-managed by Epameinondas, and among a wealth of interesting information, Pausanias tells us that the new polis was built to music, but only that provided by Argive and Boiotian *auloi*. More than this, we are told that the tunes of Pronomos of Thebes and Sakadas of Argos were played in competition with each other, an obvious echo of the legendary conflicts of the Thebaid, which Pausanias elsewhere considers the greatest of the wars fought by Greeks against Greeks.[26] This musical competition of these mythical foes was engaged in against the backdrop of the nascent Theban-Argive alliance, struck in the aftermath of the battle of Leuktra (8.6.2). The combination of Epameinondas and the famous *aulete* Pronomos mirrors their statues, which are presented juxtaposed on the Kadmeia (9.12.6). It is likely that Pronomos was active into the fourth century, and that his statue was erected on the Kadmeia shortly after his death, perhaps in the late 390s or 380s; it would therefore have been in place only a few years before the foundation of Messene.[27]

The reference to *auloi* and Pronomos becomes more significant when it is considered in light of Pausanias' reproach of Homer for not mentioning the music of Amphion and its importance in the foundation of Thebes (9.5.7, quoted earlier). Elsewhere, in book 4, Pausanias (while reflecting on the Messenians' own later use of visual deception) praises Homer for his sensitivity to stratagems involving the manipulation of senses, suggesting perhaps that he was paying particular attention to sensory aspects of his sources (4.28.7–8). Pausanias is involved in imagining historic landscapes but, more important, how events were experienced in past landscapes. In this scene the music evokes mythical rivalry and nascent alliance between the Argives and the Thebans, a changing relationship represented visually at Delphi at the same time.[28] The musicians are matched in their art by the architects and builders brought in by Epameinondas to form the fabric of the city that would have to be able to withstand the foreseeable assaults from Lakonia but would also stand as a visible monument to the end of Spartan domination of Messene.[29] "Around Messene is a wall, the whole circuit of which is built of stone, with towers and battlements upon it. I have not seen the walls at Babylon or the walls of Memnon at Susa in Persia, nor have I heard the account of any eyewitness; but the walls at Ambrossos in Phokis, at Byzantion and at Rhodes, all of them the most strongly fortified places, are not so strong as the Messenian wall" (Paus. 4.31.5).[30]

The comparison of the walls at Messene with other great fortifications is based on their visual impact. The walls were built to the same standard as the impressive fortification system erected in Boiotia at the same time, but at around 9.5 kilometers they were far longer than any Boiotian fortification of the period. Pausanias judges their strength by the impression they make on the viewer, a factor that must have been part of Epameinondas' considerations when he was founding a new settlement on such a scale. For a Theban, whether Amphion or Epameinondas, great cities and strong walls were built to music.[31]

The foundation of Messene was able to occur as a result of the Theban defeat of Sparta in battle, and in another detail not given in any other extant source, Pausanias narrates the stage management of the collection of the dead at Leuktra in order that the magnitude of Spartan defeat be plainly visible. Despite considering it the greatest battle ever fought between Greeks, Pausanias does not supply any narrative of the fighting itself. Instead, the focus is clearly on the actions and responses of the participants before and after the battle, with the implication that an important aspect of the victory was the visible demonstration of its significance and the clear perception of its magnitude by those taking part:

> The victory of Thebes was the most remarkable ever won by Greeks over Greeks. On the following day the Lakedaimonians intended to bury their dead, and sent a herald to the Thebans. But Epameinondas, knowing that the Lakedaimonians were always inclined to cover up their disasters, said that he permitted their allies first to take up their dead, and only when these had done so did he consent to the Lakedaimonians' burying their dead. Some of the allies took up no dead at all, as not one of them had fallen; others had only a few men killed. So when the Lakedaimonians proceeded to bury their own, it was immediately proved that those who had lain unburied were Spartans. (Paus. 9.13.11–12)

A parallel in visual effect can be made with Pausanias' famous description of the statue of Zeus at Olympia. Here Pausanias explores the difference between supplying information and conveying experience, arguing that it is most important to focus on the experience of the viewer: "The measurements, in height and breadth, of the Olympian Zeus are known, but I shall not commend those who made the measurements, for even their records fall far short of the impression made by a sight of the image" (Paus. 5.11.9).

Another visually focused narrative is the account of the last great stand of the Messenians before their centuries of exile (4.20), where a subtler but no less significant link is made between Boiotia and Messenia. In brief, a herdsman (a slave of a Lakonian) seduced the wife of a Messenian guardsman at Eira and conducted an affair with her. He was able to conduct this affair only because their house was outside the walls, and therefore he could monitor when her husband left for the town walls on guard duty, leaving his wife unattended. The fall of Eira came when a moonless and stormy night unexpectedly drove the guards from the walls of the settlement and back into their homes. Hidden in the bedchamber, the herdsman learned of the undefended walls from the returning guardsman and was able to slip away to his master's army and inform it of the opportunity to attack. The Spartans then took the settlement, and so began the Messenians' long exile.

A "moonless and stormy night" (ἐν ἀσελήνῳ νυκτὶ καὶ οὕτω χειμερίῳ, 4.20.7) is a rare combination used in only a few instances in extant Greek literature, and even fewer in relation to besieging and city taking.[32] The most famous is perhaps the seizure of Plataia in book 3 of Thucydides.[33] There are many similarities between the two accounts: the dark and stormy night, the desperate resistance to the Spartans, and even perhaps the poor state of the defensive fortifications at each site.[34] In these accounts perception is impaired, with a moonless night rendering blind those who should be watching, the wind too loud to hear over, and the rain obscuring all senses further.[35]

> When they [sc. the Plataians] had completed their preparations, having watched for a stormy night of wind and rain, which was at the same time moonless, they left, led by those responsible for the endeavour. First, they crossed the trench that was encircling the town, then they came to the wall of the enemy unnoticed by the guards, who were not able to see them in the darkness, nor to hear them over the howling wind which drowned the noise of their approach. They were keeping far apart from one another to prevent being noticed on account of their weapons clattering together, and were also lightly equipped, with only the left foot shod, to guard against slipping in the mud. (Thuc. 3.22.1–2)

In Pausanias' account the Spartans take advantage of this sensory hiatus, while in Thucydides' account it is the Plataians who benefit. But where the language points to deliberate parallels with Thucydides' treatment of Plataia, the account of watching, counterwatching, and the importance of intervisibility is much closer instead to another Pausanian narrative of exile, the seizure of Plataia in 373 B.C.:

> The Plataians, therefore, looked upon the attitude of the Thebans with suspicion, and maintained strict watch over their city. They did not go daily to the fields at some distance from the city, but, knowing that the Thebans liked to conduct their assemblies with every voter present, and at the same time to prolong their discussions, they waited for their assemblies to be called, and then, even

> those whose farms lay farthest away, looked after their lands at their leisure. But Neokles, who happened to be Boiotarch at Thebes, not being unaware of the Plataian trick, proclaimed that every Theban should attend the assembly armed, and at once proceeded to lead them, not by the direct road from Thebes across the plain, but along the road to Hysiai in the direction of Eleutherai and Attica, where not even a scout had been placed by the Plataians, being due to reach the walls about noon. The Plataians, thinking that the Thebans were holding an assembly, were in the fields and cut off from their gates. With those caught within the city the Thebans made a truce, allowing them to depart before sundown, the men with one garment each, the women with two. (Paus. 9.1.5–7)

Again, as with the stage-managed collection of the dead at Leuktra or the foundation of Thebes and Messene to music, Pausanias' account of the seizure of Plataia in 373 B.C. is built around the senses. The narrative is broadly in accordance with the account given in Diodoros, but, importantly, with the addition of specific information about the visibility of Plataia and Thebes or, more precisely, the lack of intervisibility between the two communities.[36] The Plataians would watch for the Thebans gathering in assembly before farming their lands closest to Thebes at leisure. The Thebans, becoming aware of being monitored, used the invisibility of the Kadmeia and the failure of the Plataians to post scouts to cut off the Plataians from their walls.

Here again, military, political, and social factors are brought together under a visual narrative. At Eira it is the vigilance of the herdsman and the Messenian guard's failure to watch from the walls and more generally his property outside the walls (his house and his wife) that allow the city to be taken; at Plataia in 373 B.C., in the close quarters of Plataia and Thebes, it is the failure of the Plataians to notice themselves being watched while they are outside the walls that leads to the capture of their city and the exile of the population.

Pausanias is clearly borrowing from the historical examples of the two captures of Plataia to inform his narrative of Eira's mythological fall. If Knoepfler's reconstruction of the composition of the *Periegesis* is correct, Pausanias could even have been writing his account of Plataia and Messene side by side. Therefore, as Pausanias stresses the link between the actions of fourth-century Thebes and the foundation of Messene, so might the history of late fifth- and early fourth-century Boiotia inform the narrative style of the *Messenika.*

This notion of exile and return is a significant feature in Pausanias' account of both regions, and the narrative of the capture of Plataia in 373 B.C. ends with a link to the battle of Chaironeia (the last place we reach in book 9) and its effects on Thebes:

> The second capture of Plataia occurred two years before the battle of Leuktra, when Asteios was Archon at Athens. The Thebans destroyed all the city except the sanctuaries, but the method of its capture saved the lives of all the Plataians alike, and on their expulsion they were again received by the Athenians. When Philip after his victory at Chaironeia introduced a garrison into Thebes, one of the means he employed to bring the Thebans low was to restore the Plataians to their homes. (Paus. 9.1.8)

Undermining Theban power by restoring the Plataians to their homes is another instance of the recurring emphasis on the effects of exile and return that pervades the whole of the *Boiotika.* It also accords well with Pausanias' interest in hegemony and control of landscape. It is worth remembering here the structure of book 9, unique in the *Periegesis,* with Pausanias traveling out from and coming back to Thebes on three occasions, which could itself be seen as representative of the patterns of Theban domination that determine the history (in Pausanias' conception) of Boiotia.[37]

In another passage from book 4, the predominance of Boiotia in Pausanias' conception of exile is again reinforced, with displacements suffered by Boiotian communities in the fourth century (Plataia, Orchomenos, and Thebes) providing the majority of his five examples:

> The Messenians returned to the Peloponnese and recovered their own land two hundred and eighty-seven years after the capture of Eira. . . . It was no short time for the Plataians that they were in exile from their country, or for the Delians . . . after being expelled from their island by the Athenians. The Minyans, driven by the Thebans from Orchomenos after the battle of Leuktra, were restored to Boiotia by Philip the son of Amyntas, as were also the Plataians. When Alexander had destroyed the city of the Thebans themselves, Cassander the son of Antipater rebuilt it after a few

> years. The exile of the Plataians seems to have lasted the longest of those mentioned, but even this was not for more than two generations. But the wanderings of the Messenians outside the Peloponnese lasted almost three hundred years, during which it is clear that they did not depart in any way from their local customs, and did not lose their Doric dialect, but even to our day they have retained the purest Doric in Peloponnese. (Paus. 4.27.9–11)

Enchanting the Past

After the narrative of the seizure of Plataia in 373 B.C. at the opening of book 9, the next part of the *Periegesis* considers Plataian cult, and Pausanias lingers longest on the festivals of the Lesser and Greater Daidala (9.3.3–8). The date of the founding of the latter, pan-Boiotian celebration is unclear, but an important aspect of the cult is Pausanias' contention that it directly corresponds with the experience of exile (most immediately that of 373 B.C.) and the restoration of the Plataians, this time permanently, by Philip in 338 B.C.

> The Greater Daidala, which is shared with them by the Boiotians, is a festival held at intervals of fifty-nine years, for that is the period during which, they say, the festival could not be held, as the Plataians were in exile. There are fourteen wooden images ready, having been provided each year at the Lesser Daidala. Lots are cast for them by the Plataians, Koroneians, Thespians, Tanagraians, Chaironeians, Orchomenians, Lebadeians, and Thebans; for at the time when Cassander, the son of Antipater, rebuilt Thebes, the Thebans wished to be reconciled with the Plataians, to share in the common assembly, and to send a sacrifice to the Daidala. (Paus. 9.3.5–6)

Pausanias claims that the Greater Daidala is celebrated every sixtieth year to match the sum of the exile endured by the Plataians, but the total period the Plataians were absent was closer to seventy-five years (427–386/373–338 B.C.). Explanations for this discrepancy are frequently ingenious, and our fragmentary knowledge of the festival means that most are in some way plausible.[38] Whatever the reason, more important than specific calculations of the celebration is that Pausanias' claim that it was linked to the Plataians' exile appears correct, because it was the Plataians' return and reintegration with their neighbors that provided the reason for the creation of this new festival. Pausanias' link of the festival with the experience of exile might indicate that he was choosing to focus on events that pertained to the experiences of exile and return. He goes on to provide further reflection that supports the view of the festival as marking a physical return to a place, describing the final act of the celebration on the peak of Mount Kithairon: "The fire seizes the altar and the victims as well, and consumes them all together. I know of no blaze that is so high, or seen so far as this" (Paus. 9.3.8).

For the reader of the *Periegesis*, the visually driven narrative of the Plataians' exile in 373 B.C. is still fresh when Pausanias describes the climax of the Greater Daidala, and as they were exiled by being watched without their knowledge from Thebes, so their restoration as manifested in this festival makes the commemoration of their exile highly visible. A great conflagration at the peak of Kithairon could be seen from the majority of Boiotia, and it is almost the only place within Plataian territory that would be visible from the Kadmeia. Because the festival was founded as a response to the two periods of exile brought about by conflict with Thebes, the location therefore takes on added significance. The Plataians have woven their experience of exile into their cult, and the phenomena that accompany the festival are also designed to visually reinforce their return and reintegration into the Boiotian landscape. The festival is an unsurprising choice for Pausanias to alight on because he too is involved in weaving patterns of exile and sensory aspects of the process into his account of fourth-century Boiotia.

Indeed, the experience of exile pervades Pausanias' fourth century: the exile and restoration of Plataia and Orchomenos, the destruction of Thebes and its restoration by Cassander, and most of all the career of Epameinondas. According to Pausanias, he refused a suggestion to send all women and children to Athens before the battle of Leuktra, he would have prevented the exile of the Orchomenians had he not been abroad, he is central to the return of the Messenians and the Mantineians, and he brings back Pelopidas from captivity abroad.[39] In a tradition unique to Pausanias, he even frees (apparently contrary to Theban law) those Boiotian refugees he finds in the northern Peloponnese during an early post-Leuktra invasion: "The Thebans had a rule that they should set free for a ransom all their prisoners except such as were Boiotian fugitives; these they punished with death. So when he captured the Sikyonian town of Phoibia, in which were gathered most of the Boiotian fugitives, he assigned to each of those whom he captured in it a new nationality, any that occurred to him, and set them free" (9.15.4).[40]

Epameinondas' clemency is a consistent feature throughout the *Periegesis*, and here he is also presented as breaking the patterns that, in Pausanias' portrait, have plagued Thebes and Boiotia from its earliest mythical past.[41] At the battle of Mantineia, Epameinondas is mortally wounded, but in another explicit nod to the visual (and another tradition unique to Pausanias),[42] he survives long enough to watch the outcome of the battle:

> When Epameinondas was wounded, they carried him still living from the ranks. For a while he kept his hand to the wound in agony, with his gaze fixed on the combatants, the place from which he looked at them being called "Scope" by posterity. But when the combat came to an indecisive end, he took his hand away from the wound and died, being buried on the spot where the armies met. On the grave stands a pillar, and on it is a shield with a dragon in relief. The dragon means that Epameinondas belonged to the race of those called the Spartoi, while there are slabs on the tomb, one old, with a Boiotian inscription, the other dedicated by the Emperor Hadrian, who wrote the inscription on it. Everybody must praise Epameinondas for being the most illustrious Greek general, or at least consider him second to none other. For the Lakedaimonian and the Athenian leaders enjoyed the ancient reputation of their cities, while their soldiers were men of a spirit, but the Thebans, whom Epameinondas raised to the highest position, were a disheartened people, accustomed to obey others. (Paus. 8.11.7–9)

In this passage the pre-eminence of Epameinondas is a result of his relative influence on his otherwise servile home polis. This emphasizes Pausanias' concern with the agency of the polis, and the presentation of Epameinondas in the superlative is consistent throughout the *Periegesis* with his involvement in building the strongest walls, winning the greatest battle, and ending the longest exile. Including the detail of the dragon emblem on the shield allows Pausanias to allude to Epameinondas' descent from the Spartoi, the mythical, autochthonous Thebans who sprang from dragon's teeth sown by Kadmos. The only other mention of the Spartoi in the *Periegesis* is in chapter 5 of book 9. In the same place Pausanias relates the early awareness of the Thebans of the destruction brought on their city because of trusting their government to one man, a passage that could have been written to summarize the inherent fragility of Epameinondas' influence on the Thebans: "After this the Thebans thought it better for several people to govern, rather than to fasten everything to one man" (Paus. 9.5.16).

In Pausanias' account Epameinondas had an almost undiluted positive influence on his home polis while he lived, but the eventual effects of the reliance on his leadership were as calamitous as those of the early leaders of Thebes. Through the dragon on his grave, Epameinondas is linked with the very earliest days of Thebes' existence and the cyclical problems that would again lead to the destruction of the city and the exile of its inhabitants. As elsewhere in the *Periegesis*, autochthony and the identity of a region are bound together, and the recurring experience of a site and the community that occupies it is emphasized.[43]

* * *

The *Periegesis* is undoubtedly a sophisticated piece of literature, but at the same time it contains intelligent historical reflection based on diligent autopsy of landscape. The composition of the books, the choices of subjects, the cross-referencing, and the elegant interweaving of information indicate a high level of control of material and considered organization of the work as a whole. Despite some famous blunders, there are indications that Pausanias' treatment of history was planned in great detail and was structured carefully to allow him to focus on themes that he considered important to specific sites and regions. Fourth-century Boiotia is assured prominence in the *Periegesis* because it is a region inextricably involved in the aspects of the past that Pausanias regards as most important: the vitality and agency of the polis, the achievement of "freedom" for Greeks, and the changes eventually brought about by the ascendency of Macedon.

Pausanias' Boiotia is also a *terre d'exil*, and the fourth-century experiences Pausanias chooses to relate bring this particularly to the fore. Thespiai, Orchomenos, Plataia, and Thebes all have populations who are displaced and later return, and Epameinondas is consistently presented as overcoming this problem, giving new homes to exiled Boiotians as well as being credited as the key agent in the return of the Messenians from their long exile. The Messenians' exile and return is a rich sensory cocktail, of which part of the blend is made from various episodes in Boiotian myth and history. The visually focused capture of Eira is closely linked in its description to the historical exiles of Plataia in 427 B.C. and 373 B.C., and in the construction of Messene, Epameinondas is seen inviting musical performances that allude to the foundation of Thebes and to the war between Argos and Thebes, in which the Messenians also took part. Pausanias considers the walls the most visually impressive in the world, and Epameinondas is shown as similarly aware of the importance of combining military victory and managing sensory impressions in his use of symbols such as the treatment of the Spartan dead at Leuktra. By the end of the century, the Messenians had themselves learned to manipulate perception to their advantage, deceiving their way into Elis by painting Lakonian blazons on their shields, echoing a ruse employed by Epameinondas.[44]

In his interest in the experience of history (both his own and that of the past inhabitants of a region), Pausanias is attuned to phenomenal aspects of experience that are often missing from ancient and modern accounts alike. Although two of his great models, Herodotus and Thucydides, are clearly interested in sensory aspects of history, they do not prioritize it to the extent Pausanias does. This is perhaps a product of the shaping of the narrative of the *Periegesis* around the autopsy of the author and into a spatial structure where a historical event and its physical aspects are more naturally connected. In this reconstruction, what can be seen informs the relation of history, but history also informs what can be seen. Pausanias' geography is at once agent and instrument, invested with a living past that is as immediate in his own experience as in the present of the pasts he seeks to explore. More than any other writer on Boiotia, Pausanias understands the immutable influence of geography on all aspects of human experience, and although his historical acuity can be criticized for its regular intermingling with the distant past, from any perspective the history of fourth-century Boiotia is suffused with the influence of its own imagined antiquity. Pausanias makes his reader aware that the landscape of fourth-century Boiotia is saturated with historic and mythological experience to the extent that almost no event of any magnitude would have taken place without reference to the distant or less distant past.

In further support of his approach, the way in which Pausanias envisions the fourth century in Boiotia accords well with what we know from the best extant contemporary sources. The interest in the control of the visual and the aural to achieve beneficial responses would not have been out of place among the dark semiotics of Aineias Taktikos' *Poliorketika*. The focus on the manipulation of mythological and quasi-historical symbols in the conduct of politics and war is something we see in the presentation of Theban activity in the 370s and 360s B.C. by Xenophon in the *Hellenica*.[45] And the seamless interweaving of the experience of exile, mythological precedent, and contemporary justification and reasoning is nowhere better presented than in Isocrates' *Plataikos*.[46]

Pausanias is clever and thoughtful with his history, and an awareness of his historical predilections and thematic choices throughout the entirety of the ten books is necessary in order to employ his testimony with appropriate critical awareness. But as well as useful pieces of historical information not preserved elsewhere, he offers unique reflections on the experience of this history, often in sensory terms. Pausanias' fourth-century Boiotia is alive with sensory stimuli: sights, sounds, and experiential allusions to the past, which are effective in transporting the reader from the place to the time described. Pausanias combines an intimate reading of the experience of Boiotian history with an awareness of past human geography, and although he was not the most diligent or comprehensive of historians of fourth-century Boiotia, in his efforts to convey the human experience of the past, he should perhaps be considered among the best. His approach, focused on corporeal experience of landscape and event, is perhaps his greatest legacy to historians, and one that can help inform new modes of inquiry into Boiotia and other areas of Greek history.

CHAPTER 7

The Performance of Boiotian Identity at Delphi

MICHAEL SCOTT

In this chapter, I focus on how Boiotia, and in particular its largest polis, Thebes, interacted with Delphi during the fourth century B.C. In doing so, I am heading back toward what is a familiar—if still often debated—historical narrative.[1] But I argue that through a reexamination of the artistic, epigraphic, and archaeological evidence for Boiotian activity within the Apollo sanctuary at Delphi, we can analyze the ways in which Thebes and other Boiotian communities chose to represent and memorialize at Delphi their important roles in this period, as well as the evolving complexity of Boiotian identity that was as a result put on display. Therefore, this chapter uncovers the skill and forcefulness with which, above all, the Thebans manipulated the Delphic monumental landscape. At the same time, it argues that the extent of Theban involvement with Delphi, combined with the physical absence of most other Boiotian communities up to 338 B.C., underlined in a very visible way the particular nature of the Theban-led Boiotian koinon in this period, and that the ways in which different Boiotian individuals inscribed their presence on monuments at Delphi in the period after 338 articulated the complex and constantly evolving nature of the Hellenistic Boiotian Confederacy. Therefore, this chapter demonstrates that Delphi was a crucial location for the construction, display, and communication of the particular and changing nature of Boiotian identity and, as a result, an important locus for the formation of the wider Greek world's perceptions of what made Boiotia different in the fourth century B.C.

Thebes and Delphi in the Aftermath of Leuktra

The sanctuary of Apollo at Delphi in the early part of the fourth century B.C. was basking in both very welcome and very unwelcome forms of attention. It had, since the victory of the Spartans at Aigospotamoi in 405 B.C., been the recipient of several major monumental dedications by generals and kings of the Spartans (Figure 7.1).[2] But at the same time, several different players within the Greek world, like Dionysios of Syracuse and Jason of Pherai, supposedly had designs on annexing the sanctuary, while others interfered with its traditional activities, like the general Iphikrates of Athens, who is reported to have intercepted a ship full of statues destined for the sanctuary around this time.[3] In 373, moreover, the sanctuary was hit by a massive rock slide that caused horrendous devastation to the temple and to the sanctuary, leaving it a building site until the 320s B.C. as the reconstruction work slowly took place.[4]

Apart from the appearance of a Boiotian commander in statue form within the ranks of the Spartan monument to Aigospotamoi erected at Delphi after their victory in 405 B.C., Boiotian interaction with Delphi in the first thirty years of the fourth century was minimal.[5] In the aftermath of 371 B.C., however, and amid the efforts to rebuild the Apollo sanctuary, the Thebans chose to offer at Delphi a monumental dedication (Scott **224**; Jacquemin **461**) in honor of their victory over the Spartans at Leuktra (a treasury "from the spoils of war taken at the battle of Leuktra," Pausanias 10.11.5).[6] The Apollo sanctuary was in disarray; the epigraphic evidence suggests not only that the temple was in all but ruins, but also that parts of the north, south, or (depending on how the inscriptional evidence is read) entire east boundary wall of the sanctuary had collapsed (Figure 7.2).[7] In light of the potential inaccessibility of the temple terrace, which had been a favorite place for the commemoration of military victories since the Persian Wars, it is understandable that the Theban monument was located elsewhere, in the southern half of the sanctuary.[8] Yet its eventual location, in the southwestern corner of the sanctuary, can initially seem an odd and somewhat undistinguished choice for several reasons.

First, the west side of the Apollo sanctuary had traditionally been left rather bare of monumental dedications since the second half of the sixth century B.C., when it was first incorporated into the Apollo sanctuary, because

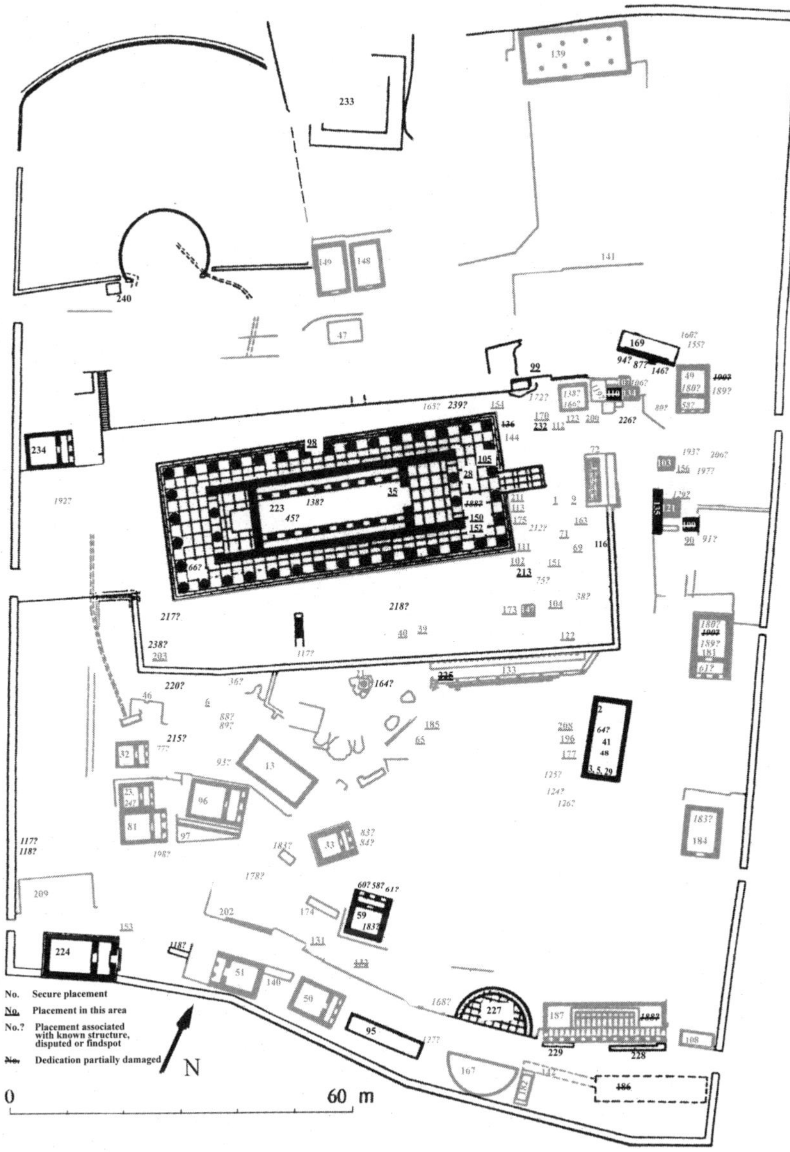

Figure 7.1. Map of the Apollo sanctuary showing new dedications in the period 400–350 B.C. © Michael Scott.

Figure 7.2. The Theban treasury on top of the sanctuary boundary wall in the western corner of the sanctuary. © Michael Scott.

this side of the sanctuary was subject to significant water channeling after heavy rainfall and thus required more careful and expensive construction techniques and materials, and also because the first spate of late sixth-century treasury structures in this area had reduced the potential visibility of any further structures placed in this area (cf. Figure 7.2).[9] Second, a quick glance at any traditional map of the Apollo sanctuary seems to indicate that the main entrance to the sanctuary was at the southeastern corner, and thus the southwestern side, despite the fact that it too had an entrance point, was little more than a back door into the sacred area. Third, the very architecture of the treasury, with its entrance door looking to the southeast rather than the much closer southwestern sanctuary entrance, seems only to reinforce the sense of its marginal location (cf. Figure 7.3).[10]

How are we to understand the Thebans' choice?[11] One way of understanding the location is the resonance it held with previous Boiotian interaction with Delphi. It was in this area, during the second half of the sixth century B.C., after the expansion of the boundaries of the Apollo sanctuary, that a treasury structure had been erected (Scott **43**; Jacquemin **660**), using part of the old

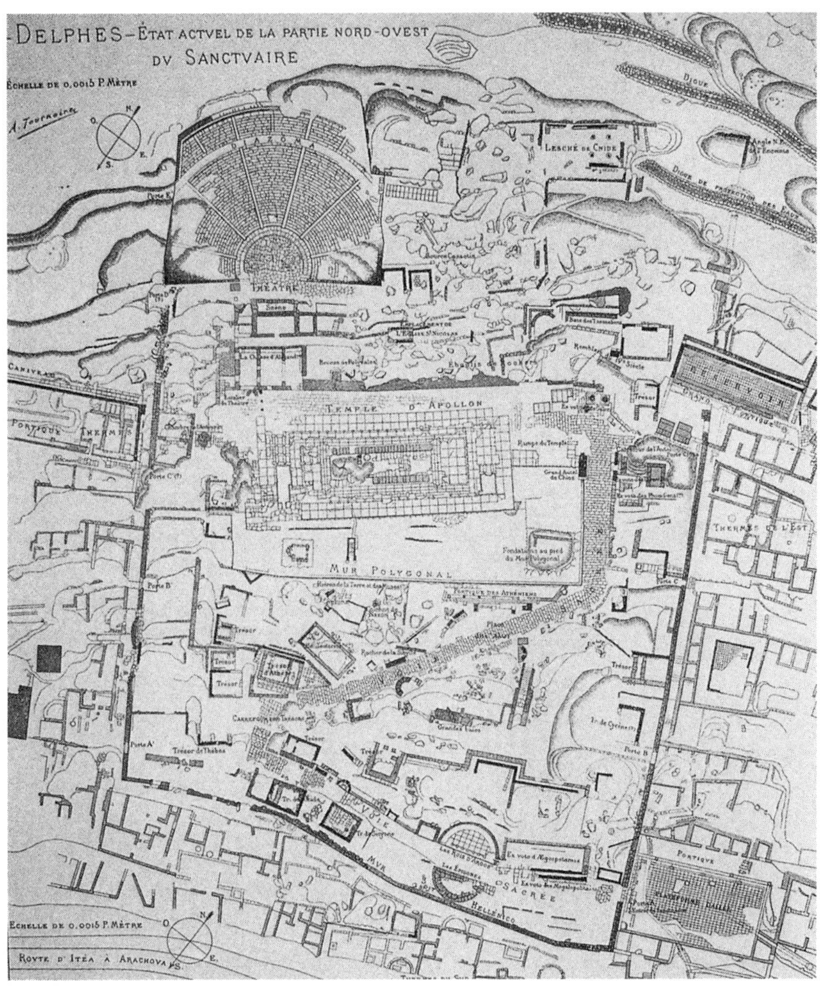

Figure 7.3. Traditional map of the Apollo sanctuary at Delphi after initial excavation, with the sacred way marked in. From *Fouilles de Delphes*, vol. 2 (Atlas).

Apollo sanctuary boundary wall as its foundation.[12] The treasury was destroyed by the end of the fifth century and built over by another "niche" dedication (Scott **209**; Jacquemin **652**).[13] It has been argued that the treasury was erected by an early koinon of Boiotian cities, thanks to a number of names inscribed in the Phokian alphabet on stones laid in the lowest levels of the building and interpreted not as the names of the builders but as the names of those financing and dedicating the monument.[14] Others have argued that such an association of individuals, even if they were Boiotians from a variety of poleis, does not imply the existence of any larger community identity, and still others have argued that the structure should not be attributed to Boiotia at all.[15]

Although the community identity of the dedicators of this treasury remains heavily debated, we are certain that a sense of Boiotian community was on display somewhere within the Apollo sanctuary at Delphi in this period. Dating to the mid- to late sixth century B.C., the earliest surviving epigraphic attestation of the collective regional ethnic *Boiotoi* from outside Boiotia is inscribed around the feet settings of a statuette on a stone base found in the Apollo sanctuary at Delphi.[16] The use of Delphi for such statements of community identity continued throughout the fifth century, in contrast to other sites of Hellenic interaction like Olympia.[17]

Therefore, Delphi, it seems, had a particular role as one of the sanctuaries, if not the only one, in which Boiotians had been making express monumental statements of their developing community identity since the mid-sixth century.[18] Moreover, they had perhaps done so in the very region of the Apollo sanctuary to which the Thebans returned after Leuktra. Given Thebes' reconstitution of the Boiotian Confederacy after 378 and its ever-increasing regional dominance in the aftermath of Leuktra, this return to Delphi—and to this particular location—should perhaps be understood as a very particular attempt to echo the past use of Delphic space for the specific articulation of Boiotian community identity and, therefore, to strengthen Thebes' claims that its hegemony was a return to past tradition (cf. Figure 7.1).[19]

The choice of Delphi and of this particular southwestern location, however, was not, I argue, made simply to chime with previous Boiotian expressions of community identity. This location, in the southwestern corner of the sanctuary, facing the southwestern entrance to the Apollo sanctuary, also offered an opportunity for the Thebans to mirror spatially the major Spartan offerings placed by the southeastern entrance to the Apollo sanctuary after their victory at Aigospotamoi.[20] The Theban offering would have been the first to be seen by visitors entering the sanctuary from the southwest, just as the statue group and the stoa of the Spartans would have been the first to be seen by visitors entering the sanctuary from the southeast (cf. Figure 7.4).[21]

I argue that we are mistaken to think that to achieve this spatial mirroring, the Thebans had to locate themselves in a marginal area. We are given this impression today principally because of the sacred way, the zigzag path through the sanctuary, which begins at its southeastern entrance (cf. Figure 7.3). But we need to remember that this set pathway dates only from the

Figure 7.4. The Theban treasury at the southwest and Spartan dedications at the southeast of the Apollo sanctuary. © Michael Scott.

very final phase of Delphi's history after the conversion of the Roman Empire to Christianity.[22] For the vast majority of its life, the Apollo sanctuary was accessed through a variety of entrances on both east and west sides at different levels on the hillside, enabling free movement from the polis of Delphi (which surrounded the sanctuary) into and out of the sacred area. In addition, there was also a much greater degree of flexibility for moving among the different constructed terraces within the Apollo sanctuary thanks to a number of staircases connecting the different levels, which were built at different points in Delphi's history (cf. Figure 7.1).[23]

Therefore, this southwestern area of the Apollo sanctuary was not the backwater that it can seem from traditional maps. This impression is confirmed by both the archaeological and epigraphic evidence relating to the monumental dedications in this area. The Siphnian treasury, for instance, built in the second half of the sixth century B.C., faced the southwestern entrance of the sanctuary, not toward the southeast (cf. Figure 7.1); and in several inscriptions this region of the Apollo sanctuary is called an *epiphanestaton topon*—a sought-after and highly visible location within the sanctuary.[24]

One of the other reasons for considering this southwestern corner a more marginal location has been the architecture of the Theban treasury itself. In most discussions of this monument, the structure's doorway is understood to have faced toward the southeast, reflecting the prioritization of that entrance and as a result making it look like the treasury itself had turned its back on the nearby southwestern access point (cf. Figures 7.1, 7.2, 7.3, and 7.4).[25] Yet the most recent archaeological analysis, undertaken by Anne Jacquemin and Didier Laroche, demonstrates that the treasury's entrance faced toward the southwest and the entrance immediately beside it (as the Siphnian treasury did nearby), reinforcing the idea that both ways into the sanctuary were equally valid (Figure 7.5).[26] Moreover, the inscriptions that were later carved on the monument are all placed along its north wall (in order to be seen by those coming by from the southeast) or on its front (southwest-facing) side, once again underlining the equal importance of both pathways.[27]

The Thebans, then, should be understood to have chosen a high-profile position in the sanctuary from which they could mirror the rivals over whom they had enjoyed victory in battle. But it is clear that the form of the Theban monument is very different from that of the Spartan statue group and stoa. The Thebans chose to build a treasury. Once again, however, the traditional maps often shown of Delphi are misleading (cf. Figure 7.3). The Theban treasury seems to be just one of a number of treasury structures built at Delphi. But what these maps of the sanctuary as seen in Pausanias' time (second century A.D.) fail to highlight is that the Theban treasury was built approximately one hundred years after the last certain new treasury structures had been dedicated at Delphi (that of the Athenians after Marathon in 490 B.C. [Scott **96**; Jacquemin **86**] and another probably Athenian treasury [Scott **130**; Jacquemin **657**] in the Athena sanctuary c. 470 B.C.).[28] In opting for a treasury, therefore, the Thebans wound back the clock in terms of the style of their dedication and ignored what had become the overwhelmingly traditional format for a victory commemoration: a statue group.[29] It is worth not-

Figure 7.5. CGI reconstruction of what the Theban treasury would have looked like at the approach from the southwest. From fig. 13 in A. Jacquemin and D. Laroche, "Notes sur quatres edifices d'époque classique à Delphes," *BCH* 136–137 (1) (2012–2013): 112.

ing that in so doing, they also deviated substantially from the way in which they commemorated this victory on the battlefield at Leuktra (with a structure displaying Spartan shields) and at home, where, Pausanias informs us (9.16.5), they placed the shields of Spartan officers who fell at Leuktra in the temple of Demeter the Lawgiver at Thebes.[30]

So, why a treasury? In part, the decision to build a treasury may have been both suggested and necessitated by the immediate environment. This was, after all, what the French excavators call "le carrefour des trésors," an area in which the Sikyonians, the Siphnians, possibly the Megarians, the Athenians, and two western Greek dedicators all built treasuries, not to mention the now-destroyed Boiotian treasury from the sixth century (cf. Figures 7.1 and 7.2).[31]

Unlike any other treasury in this area, however, the Theban treasury was built on top of the southern boundary wall of the Apollo sanctuary (cf. Figures 7.2 and 7.5).[32] The archaeological analysis of the treasury shows that part of this boundary wall seems to have been rebuilt and repaired at the same time as the construction of the treasury.[33] Moreover, pieces of the Alkmaionid-era temple of Apollo, ruined in the 373 rock slide, have been located in the foundation of the Theban treasury.[34]

The Thebans thus seem to have taken the opportunity presented by Delphi's ruined state, with major consequences for the nature and impact of their dedication. Not only did their monument stand—unlike almost any other dedication at Delphi—on top of the boundary wall of the sanctuary, thus being more visible to those outside the sanctuary, but also the whole structure was as a result on a high bastion constructed in part out of the reused Apollo temple blocks, which made it much more visible to those inside the sanctuary (cf. Figure 7.4).[35] The Theban monument was also the largest treasury to that date at Delphi (12.29×7.21 meters, and 5.17 meters high).[36] In returning to this form of dedication, the Thebans, it seems, had also outdone all previous versions of it.

But in two other respects, the Theban treasury was also very different from the structures in its immediate surroundings. First, its "window," a small open space in the middle/upper part of its "rear" wall, is unknown in any other treasury at Delphi. Previous analyses, particularly when the treasury was thought to be oriented with its entrance toward the southeast, argued that this window (then looking toward the southwest) was put in to negate the way in which the treasury was "turning its back" on the southwest entrance (cf. Figure 7.6).[37] But I think that such explanations fall short, especially now that the treasury has been reoriented with its entrance to the southwest, on the same side as the window (cf. Figure 7.5). Moreover, in the most recent archaeological analysis, it has been argued that this was not a window per se but a much smaller ventilation opening.[38] It has been suggested that ventilation was needed either perhaps for the objects contained within the treasury or perhaps simply because of the size of the structure (and specifically because of the creation of an internal *prodomos*).[39] Given our paucity of knowledge about the contents of treasuries at Delphi and indeed anywhere else, we cannot resolve the purpose of the opening any further.[40] No other treasury at Delphi, however, has such an architectural feature, and the nearest parallel is with the "oikos" structure of the Andrians on Delos and the portico in the agora of Aigai in Aiolis in Asia Minor.[41] Once again, the Theban offering marked itself out as different.

The second remarkable aspect of the treasury is its lack of decoration. It stood directly opposite the Siphnian treasury, one of the most ornate structures of the Archaic period, and indeed of all periods, at Delphi.[42] It also stood near the Athenian treasury with its exquisitely carved metopes and expensive marble walls.[43] Yet the Theban treasury, despite having a well-developed and

Figure 7.6. The "window" in the rear of the Theban treasury. © Michael Scott.

precise metope/triglyph formation, had no carved metopes or pedimental sculpture.[44] Instead, as the original archaeological reports seek to emphasize, its grandeur comes from architectural details like its three-stepped krepis, its doorway casing, and in particular the precise play of different types of tooling on the local (and very beautiful) Saint-Elie limestone used to construct the building, which gave the material a variety of luminescence.[45] In the final analysis the Theban treasury stood out to visitors to Delphi not only because of its highly visible position and its size but also thanks to its "pureté architecturale," and it should be admired for "rien de plus que les impeccables linéaments architecturaux, rien d'autre à admirer que la justesse des proportions, la qualité de l'exécution et de la matière."[46]

Therefore, although some scholars have argued that in harking back to an era before Spartan dominance in the chosen form of their dedication, the Thebans wished to suggest an affiliation with the last major treasury dedicators of the past, in particular, Athens, such affiliations were, it seems, purposefully denied particularly by the architectural and artistic details of the Theban monument, which classed it as different from (and in many ways superior to) the treasuries around it.[47] More important, the treasury was also different in style from the Spartan statue-group monument for victory at Aigospotamoi, which it spatially opposed. A Boiotian commander was present in that statue group, a testament to a former era of alliance between Boiotia and Sparta. The Boiotian commander was one of a number of representatives of the allies who had fought with the Spartans against the Athenians depicted on the monument (there were twenty-eight allies represented in the back row of statues, with another ten figures of the gods and of Spartans in the front).[48] The Aigospotamoi monument, as a result, was a (Spartan-led) community dedication representing an alliance of Greek states fighting against the tyrant that was Athens.[49] In contrast, the Theban treasury, through its architectural choice of a structure dedicated to its glory alone, dispensed with any sense of alliance: this was a Theban victory and no one else's.

That sense of Theban ownership over the structure (and the victory it celebrated) would only have been reinforced by the nature of the inscriptions that covered the building over the next three centuries.[50] Jacquemin has pointed out that every inscription on the Theban treasury is concerned with the Thebans in one way or another.[51] That is a record not matched by the nearby Athenian treasury (only 90 percent related to Athens) and overwhelming compared with the Siphnian treasury (only 1 percent related to Siphnians), located just behind the Theban dedication. As a result, this building stood out as a zone of unprecedented dedicator control within the Delphic sanctuary.

The Theban treasury constructed in the southwest corner of the Apollo sanctuary at Delphi thus offered a plethora of messages for the many visitors who came to Delphi. On the one hand, this structure, in being placed at Delphi, and in the southwest corner of the Apollo sanctuary, echoed a tradition of the Boiotians using Delphi for displays of community identity. On the other hand, the placement and architectural and artistic styling of the treasury set it apart not only as different from, and superior to, all other treasuries at Delphi but also as much more individually oriented than the Spartan "community"-alliance statue-group dedication to victory at Aigospotamoi. The Theban monument, as a result, offered conflicting senses of both community identity and individual glory, reflecting the very unusual nature of the Boiotian Confederacy and koinon in the period after 378 B.C. as in effect a Theban hegemony.[52] Crucially, that particular and peculiar mix of community and individuality had been made possible thanks to the specific monumental landscape on offer at Delphi (and indeed the specific state of disrepair of the sanctuary after 373), which enabled such emphatic and polyvalent spatial, architectural, and artistic expressions of Theban power and identity.[53] Visitors to Delphi in this period could have been left in no doubt that this new turn in the story of Delphic dedication mirrored a new turn in the history of Greece, and that the Delphic monumental landscape now reflected the realities of a Greek world in which Thebes was the new power to be reckoned with.

Boiotia and Delphi to the Aftermath of the Third Sacred War

There has been fierce debate surrounding the complex relationship among Thebes, Boiotia, and Delphi in the period 371–346 B.C., particularly in regard to explaining the ongoing stasis within the polis of Delphi, the politics in the run-up to the Phokian occupation of the sanctuary, and the Third Sacred War. Scholarly opinions range from seeing Thebes as the principal instigator of conflict to seeing Thebes as being courted by Delphi for support as part of the bigger struggle between Athenians and Thessalians for dominance over the sanctuary.[54]

In the Theban/Boiotian archaeological and epigraphic footprint on the sanctuary at Delphi in this period, an increasing degree of support for and admiration of Thebes is noticeable from both the polis of Delphi and other major Greek poleis constructing monuments in the Apollo sanctuary. The polis of Delphi granted an unusually fulsome declaration of *promanteia* to Thebes, inscribed on a stele set up near the treasury and often thought to have been erected just after the treasury's completion.[55] And during the slow rebuild of the sanctuary, which stretched across fifty years after 373 B.C., the Argives demonstrated their (much-changed) stance toward Thebes with a semicircular statue group (Scott **227**; Jacquemin **69**) mirroring a similar earlier dedication of theirs (Scott **167**; Jacquemin **70**) in the southeastern corner of the sanctuary after they had aided Epaminondas in reestablishing Messenian independence at Spartan expense (cf. Figure 7.1). Their first semicircular offering had taken the theme of the seven against Thebes, but now their theme was the Argive kings alongside Herakles, the hero born in Thebes.[56] The monument, as a result, celebrated not only their joint success with Thebes but also their blood alliance with the city. At the same time, these two Argive dedications, opposite each other, offered a visible narrative of changing allegiance over time and the emergence of Thebes as a dominant power.[57]

The Thessalians too offered a statue in honor of Pelopidas after 369 B.C., the first honorific statue to an individual from their community in evidence at Delphi (Scott **226**; Jacquemin **465**).[58] The fact that Pelopidas was the first recipient of this new trend of dedication at Delphi (and that we think that this statue was carved by Lysippus) not only underlines his importance as a figure in fourth-century Greece but would also have ensured that his statue stood out at Delphi and, as a result, continued to reinforce the message of Theban power and authority within Greece at this time. In addition, a Spartan, Landridas, who has been argued to have fought on the Theban side at Leuktra, made a dedication of unknown form on top of a column (Scott **239**; Jacquemin **328**) in the sanctuary.[59] In turn, the Arcadians set up a statue group (Scott **228**; Jacquemin **66**) after 369 B.C., which stood in front of the Spartan stoa at the southeast entrance to the Apollo sanctuary and claimed in its dedicatory inscription to celebrate a victory over the Spartans, often associated with Leuktra (cf. Figure 7.1).[60]

Admiration for and alliance with Thebes stand out in the monumental record at Delphi in this period, as we would expect.[61] But it is the marked absence of monumental dedications by other Boiotian poleis that is most striking (all the more so given their geographical proximity to the sanctuary). Despite the existence of a Boiotian koinon after 378, the reality on the ground at Delphi was that Thebes was the only polis that mattered. This Delphic impression corresponds directly with the reality of the Theban hegemony over the Boiotian koinon and, indeed, the destructive way in which Thebes exerted its power over other Boiotian poleis.

In fact, the only non-Theban Boiotian monumental dedication in this period came from an individual: the courtesan Phryne from Thespiai (Scott **232**; Jacquemin **464**). The inscription, according to Athenaeus, made this clear: "Phryne, daughter of Epikles, of Thespiai."[62] This dedication would have stood out to visitors at Delphi for a number of reasons. It was, according to Pausanias, the only example—apart from that of the philosopher Gorgias (Scott **213**; Jacquemin **334**) dedicated earlier in the century—of the dedication of a statue of oneself in one's own honor.[63] Gorgias' statue stood by the pronaos of the temple, as did Phryne's, and both of them stood on columns and were *epikrusoi*—gold encrusted (cf. Figure 7.1).[64] As if this were not enough, Phryne's statue was also, of course, that of a woman. Her femininity would have been emphasized to visitors thanks to her direct surroundings on the temple terrace, amid statues of kings and generals.[65] In fact, Keesling argues that Phryne's statue was the only female portrait statue to stand alone (i.e., not part of a family group) at Delphi before the Roman period, as attested by the literary and epigraphic sources.[66]

Therefore, Phryne's statue stood out strongly in terms of materials, its subject matter (a woman), and its location (as a woman, a courtesan, among kings and generals). And because of the way in which this statue would have caught visitors' attention, Phryne's statue would also—as that of an individual Thespian, specifically a female Thespian, and even more specifically a courtesan—have served only to reinforce the absence of monumental dedications by other Boiotian poleis from the sanctuary at this time and, more generally, their beleaguered state as dependencies of Thebes.[67]

If we widen our focus from monumental dedications to attested interaction with the sanctuary at Delphi in any capacity, Phryne was not the only Boiotian individual to have a role in the sanctuary at this time. But once again the record is pointed: out of all the Boiotian communities, only individuals from Thebes and Thespiai are attested as epigraphically interacting with Delphi in the period down to the end of the Third Sacred War, suggesting perhaps that among all the Boiotian poleis, it was Thespiai that recovered more quickly from the Theban blows it had been dealt.[68] In 363 B.C., for example, private individuals from Thebes and Thespiai each gave a drachma toward the rebuilding of the temple.[69] In 350 and 342, respectively, a Theban and a Thespian were the focus of proxeny decrees.[70] In 340 and 339 a Theban and a Thespian served as *hieromnemones* at Delphi, and several Thebans served as *naopes* and in other administrative capacities within the sanctuary between 346 and 341 B.C.[71]

In all cases, the epigraphic record offers only their city affiliation.[72] Only three instances of individuals described as "Boiotians" are recorded in this period, all of whom seem to have been workmen working on the reconstruction in 344–343 B.C. (they are named in the inscriptions as *ergonai*). Moreover, given that none of them are inscribed with patronymics, it has been argued these individuals were not full citizens.[73] Therefore, it is interesting to note that only Thebans and Thespians seem to have left a permanent mark on Delphi in this period, and that these citizens seem to have done so exclusively as members of their own city and not of any wider Boiotian community. Instead, the Boiotian identifier seems to have been reserved for the lowest rungs of Boiotian society.

None of the monumental dedications discussed so far seem to have suffered in the Phokian ravishing of the sanctuary during the final years of the Third Sacred War when the Phokians sought to pay for troops.[74] On the one hand, this may well have been because of the materials from which they were constructed (the marble Theban treasury was not a structure that could be turned into cash quickly). On the other hand, the fact that the gold-encrusted statue of Phryne was spared (we presume its survival given that it was seen by Pausanias) is remarkable. Perhaps the honorific (some argue religious) nature of the monument saved it; the other gold-encrusted honorific statue of this period, that of Gorgias, was also left unscathed.[75] In contrast, however, in the aftermath of the Phokian expulsion, the Amphiktiony, according to the inscriptional evidence, seems to have taken the unique decision to expel two Phokian statue dedications (those honoring the generals Philomelos and Onomarchos, who had led the occupation of the sanctuary) from the sanctuary.[76]

What was the Theban and wider Boiotian response to the Third Sacred War and Phokian occupation of the sanctuary in the years after 346 B.C.? On the one hand, as was noted earlier, Diodoros (17.10.5) speaks of a "naos" built from the spoils of the conflict of Phokis, which some have taken to refer to the Theban treasury and some to a second Theban treasury somewhere in the sanctuary, which remains archaeologically and epigraphically unidentified. More definitive, however, is the archaeological evidence for two monuments, one offered by Thebes and one thought to be by the Boiotians as a group, offered in the years immediately after 346 B.C. and the end of the Third Sacred War. The first, by Thebes, was a statue of Herakles (Scott **252**; Jacquemin **460**), placed neither near the Theban treasury nor on the temple terrace near the statue of Phryne but below the temple terrace in an open area known in the French excavation reports as the "aire" (cf. Figure 7.7).[77] This aire space, not technically identified as such in any surviving inscriptions, seems to have been considered as special within the Apollo sanctuary: it was the only area in the sanctuary to be kept almost empty of dedications throughout Delphi's history and also the area in which many of Delphi's sacred festivals began or invested considerable time.[78]

It was also around this sacred aire just below the temple terrace that the Phokians were said not only to have set up the statue dedications of their generals that had now been removed but also to have dedicated back in the fifth century B.C. a series of statues that still remained in the sanctuary (Scott **90**; Jacquemin **409**).[79] It is not certain just how close this earlier Phokian dedication was to the new Theban Herakles, and thus just how direct the sense of confrontation might have been. But without doubt the move away from the Theban treasury and the traditional area of Boiotian dedication in the southwest corner of the sanctuary and toward the "aire" is most easily explained by a desire to demonstrate victory over Phokis in a region previously associated

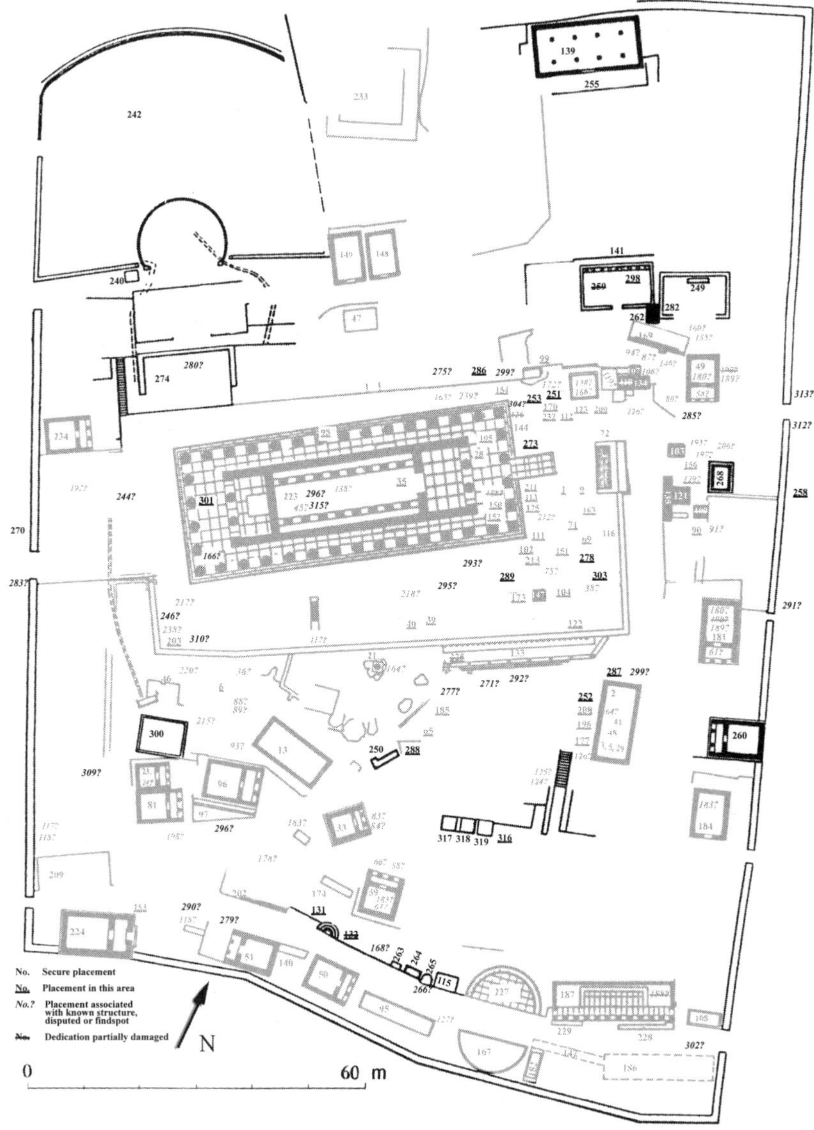

Figure 7.7. Map of the Apollo sanctuary with new dedications in the period 350–300 B.C. © Michael Scott.

with Phokian dedications.[80] Equally, the choice of Herakles is best understood not only as an appropriate Theban symbol but also as one with particular Delphic resonance: Herakles had appeared on a number of monumental dedications since the sixth century B.C. at Delphi (e.g., the Argive semicircular monument at the southeast entrance, the pedimental sculpture of the Siphnian treasury near the Theban one, and the metopes of the Athenian treasury) and was tied through myth to the sanctuary in a number of ways, not least the story in which Herakles tried to steal Apollo's oracular tripod.[81]

Likewise, soon after 346 B.C. another dedication was placed in the area around the aire (Scott **250**; Jacquemin **99**). The surviving dedicatory inscription (*FD* III 3 77) is extremely fragmentary and crucially is missing key information: the name of the dedicator. It is, however, most often reconstructed *Boiotoi*, principally because of the large collection of later Boiotian inscriptions also inscribed on this monument (and the absence of any inscriptions related to any other ethnic or non-Boiotian polis).[82] In contrast, what does survive in the inscription is the way in which those the dedicators triumphed over were labeled (in the final powerful word of the inscription): *as*]*ebeisantas*—the "unholy ones"—a fitting name for those guilty of melting down the sanctuary's dedications.

That neither Plutarch nor Pausanias mentions this monument leads scholars to assume that its statues were perhaps removed by Sulla or Nero.[83] Yet it offers us a fascinating picture not only of the way in which this area of the sanctuary worked, but also of the way in which members of the Boiotian community sought to portray themselves over the course of the fourth and third centuries B.C.

All the inscriptions, including its dedicatory inscription, do not face the aire but are rather to be found on the north side of the monument (cf. Figures 7.7 and 7.8).[84] At the same time, the lowest levels of the monument on the north side are only roughly worked, indicating that they were hidden from view, whereas on the south side much more of the material has been finely worked.[85] Once again, we have to imagine here that the sacred way was not the main route through the aire, as it is today, but rather that there was a pathway to the north of the monument that was a main thoroughfare, and that there was a difference in level of almost one meter between the north and south sides of the monument, making it once again an extremely visible raised bastion of a dedication for those approaching from the south (cf. Figure 7.8).

This statue group thus once again seems to have been located and constructed so as to take advantage not only of the steep natural geography of

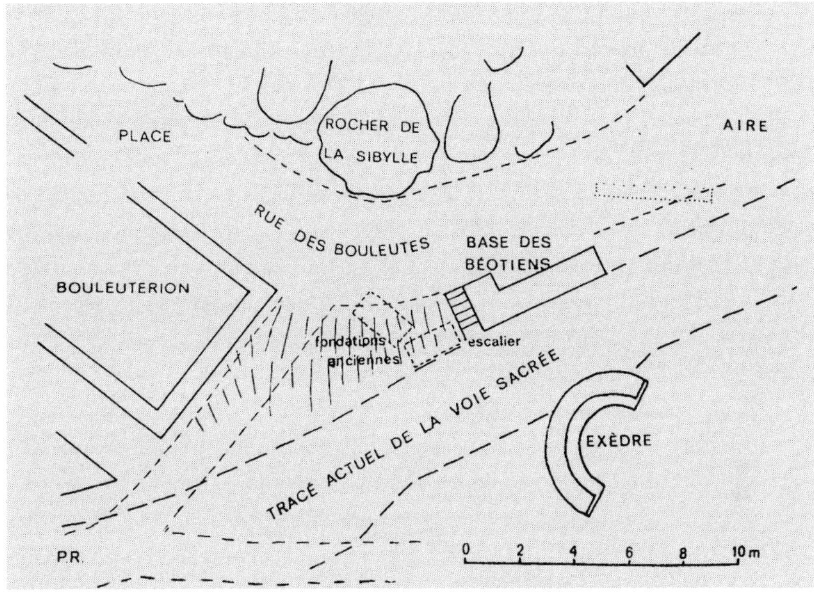

Figure 7.8. Detail drawing of the Boiotian base monument and the aire. From fig. 8 in P. Roesch, "La base des Béotiens à Delphes," *CRAI* 1984: 188.

the site and the way in which visitors moved around it, but also of the resonances it could have with those whose defeat it commemorated (the Phokians and their still-present and now-absent dedications in this area). The dedicatory inscription's choice of language for the Phokians as the "unholy ones" would surely also have resonated with the particularly spiritual nature of this part of the sanctuary as the epicenter of many Delphic festivals. More widely, the style of the monument seems to have echoed that of the Arkadian Confederacy statue-group dedication by the southeastern entrance to the sanctuary (cf. Figure 7.7).[86] That monument had, in commemoration of victory over Sparta, announced and articulated the formation of a new community identity in the Peloponnese (just as we saw earlier that the Spartan monument to victory at Aigospotamoi had also tried, through a statue group, to display a sense of Greek alliance against Athens).[87] In copying the style of the Arkadian dedication, as well as in the use of the collective *Boiotoi* in the dedicatory inscription (if this reconstruction is correct), the Boiotians may have been attempting to underline the similarity of their monument's purpose through similarity in artistic style: the public display of a new sense of ethnic collective identity.

The use of such a community-focused style of monument, along with the possible use of *Boiotoi* in the dedicatory inscription, marks a watershed in the nature of the Boiotian koinon on display at Delphi. Since the erection of the Theban treasury after Leuktra, any sense of Boiotian community had been resolutely centered on Theban power and hegemony. The lack of Boiotian engagement with Delphi had been pitifully underlined by the opulence of the one monumental dedication that was there: that of the Thespian courtesan Phryne. And even at the level of individual interaction with the sanctuary, only those from Thebes and Thespiai had left their mark. But all that now began to change in the aftermath of the dedication of this monument as the nature of the Boiotian koinon itself changed drastically in the wake of Philip's victory at Chaironeia.[88] That change is noticeable not simply in terms of monumental dedications within the Apollo sanctuary. In the period 338–335 B.C., for example, a much wider range of individuals from different Boiotian poleis are publicly recorded at Delphi serving as *hieromnemones*, *naopes*, and treasurers: those from Orchomenos, Tanagra, Plataia, and Koroneia (in contrast, Thebans are absent from these offices between 335 and 288 B.C., not surprisingly, perhaps, given the fate that befell their city at the hands of Alexander in 335 B.C.).[89] And it is also after 338 B.C. that the terms *Boiotios*, *Boiotos*, and *Boiotoi* are recorded in the surviving inscriptions as a key part of the way in which individual Boiotians identified themselves (not only at Delphi but across the Greek world).[90]

The first texts to be inscribed on the Boiotian statue group at Delphi after its initial dedicatory inscription were placed there probably between 313 and 300 B.C.[91] These inscriptions are proxeny decrees inscribed for individuals from Tanagra, Thebes, Thespiai, Koroneia, and Chaironeia. For all except those from Thebes, the way in which they identified themselves now prioritized their Boiotian identity first, followed by that of their individual city. The Thebans, however, in particular periods, remained resolutely Theban only. This can be attributed not only to their status as refugees from their destroyed city until around 316 B.C. but also to their reoccurring exclusion from and inclusion in membership in the post-Chaironeian Hellenistic Boiotian Confederacy (particularly during the periods 335–309/308 and 292–288 B.C.).[92] Therefore, viewers of the monument, and particularly those who took time to read its inscriptions (which were grouped on the monument in chronological batches, making the change over time easier to perceive), would have been presented with a very clear picture of the oscillating inclusivity and exclusivity, not to mention the overtly political nature, of Boiotian identity.[93]

This distinction between Thebans as Thebans and citizens of other cities as Boiotians not only is found on the Boiotian statue-group dedication but also can be paralleled by proxeny decrees inscribed elsewhere in the sanctuary during this period and by the full range of inscriptions carved on the Theban treasury.[94] Moreover, that separation, at times acute, apparent in the inscriptions between the approach of Thebans and those from other Boiotian cities would only have been reinforced through the presence of specifically "Theban" and "Boiotian" monumental dedications within the Apollo sanctuary and more specifically within the aire itself: a Theban monument to victory over the Phokians (the Herakles statue) near a monument of the Boiotians celebrating the same at Delphi.

That already complex ascription of identity at Delphi, however, depended also on the role one performed in the sanctuary. Despite the increasing use of *Boiotioi* for monumental dedications, honorary decrees, expressions of religious worship, and decrees of proxeny, records of service as a receiver of the *theoroi* (the messengers sent out to announce the Delphic games), as well as honors granted in thanks for service as *hieromnemones* and *naopes*, continued to be recorded only with reference to the individual's specific city.[95] It seems that at Delphi, what kind of Boiotian identity one put forward, or at least had recorded, depended as much on the way in which one was involved with the sanctuary as it did on one's sense of identity and current membership in a wider community.[96]

* * *

What I hope that this reexamination of the archaeological and epigraphic footprint of Boiotian interaction with Delphi during this complex period has shown is threefold. First, the monumental Theban celebration of their victory at Leuktra and their leadership (indeed tyranny) over a new emerging Boiotian koinon, within the confines of the Apollo sanctuary at Delphi, was carefully situated, as well as architecturally and artistically designed, both to create a link with past uses of Delphi by the Boiotians for expressions of community identity and, at the same time, to stress the fact that Thebes, its victory, and its leadership were substantially different from, and superior to, anything and everyone else.

Second, the absence of monumental dedications by every other Boiotian polis at Delphi down to the end of the Third Sacred War, reinforced by the presence of a strikingly noticeable dedication by the Thespian courtesan Phryne, coupled with the erection of monuments underlining the glory and power of Thebes, served only to articulate even more strongly the unusual nature of the Boiotian koinon in this period as a koinon in name only and in reality a Theban hegemony.

Third, the way in which the koinon evolved to include a wider range of community involvement, coupled with the loss of leadership by Thebes, particularly in the aftermath of the Third Sacred War and the battle of Chaironeia, was made painstakingly clear at Delphi both architecturally and epigraphically through the erection of Boiotian community monuments and the appearance of Boiotians from a variety of poleis taking up roles of importance in Delphic business. In turn, the complex and frequently changing nature of Boiotian community identity, not just in the remainder of the fourth century but also over the next two centuries, was equally on display at Delphi through the way in which individuals from different Boiotian poleis (particularly Thebes) chose to identify themselves in relation to their wider community.[97] How they did so at Delphi was not simply dependent on their individual attitudes toward the wider Boiotian community or on the status of their respective poleis as official members of the koinon, but also on the role these individuals played in Delphic business.

The Boiotian koinon and its individual members were by no means the only ones to use Delphi in this way for the declaration of changing identities and positions of power in Greece. What is special about the relationship between Boiotia and Delphi, above all in the fourth century B.C., is the way in which the specific opportunities presented by the monumental and inscriptional landscape at Delphi made possible the articulation of the particularly complex and layered sense of Boiotian identity. It has often been commented that the Boiotians, geographically at a crossroads as they were between the ethne of northern Greece and the poleis of southern Greece, had a singularly complex sense of identity as members of poleis, of ethne, and of a koinon (which itself often changed in nature and purpose).[98] Their subtle, layered, and changing sense of identity required an equally subtle, layered, and evolving international landscape in which to be satisfactorily represented and articulated.[99] It is no wonder that Delphi was not only *the* Hellenic sanctuary in which the Boiotians chose to invest so much time but also the one in which they guarded more jealously than any other dedicator the subsequent use of their monuments as notice boards for inscriptions for centuries to come. As a result, it is without doubt in large part through Boiotian interaction with, and display at, Delphi that the perception among the communities of the wider Greek world of the particular and complex nature of Boiotian identity would have been formulated.

CHAPTER 8

The Epigraphic Habit(s) in Fourth-Century Boiotia

NIKOLAOS PAPAZARKADAS

The collocation "epigraphic habit" is more often than not associated with the two most important polities of classical antiquity: Athens and the Roman Empire. The term was first introduced by MacMullen in 1982 in a now-celebrated article, "The Epigraphic Habit in the Roman Empire."[1] Charles Hedrick, Jr., became the first scholar to apply the concept to a purely Greek milieu in his classic *Hesperia* article "Democracy and the Athenian Epigraphical Habit."[2] In his treatment Hedrick questioned some of the axioms credited by earlier historians, primarily that the relationship between Athens' democratic constitution and its habit of erecting inscriptions was a straightforward case of cause and effect. Hedrick did not deny that a link between the two existed, but he attempted to show that democratic ideology could be discerned less in the sheer number of Athenian inscribed documents and more in the so-called formulas of disclosure. Hedrick's article initiated a scholarly debate that has not ceased to this day: in 2009 James Sickinger published a direct response to Hedrick's article in which he undermined even further the link between the erection of inscriptions and democracy, although he stopped short of dismissing it altogether.[3] In the same 2009 volume that contained Sickinger's essay, Robin Osborne took up for the first time, as far as I know, an investigation of the epigraphic habit in a Greek city-state other than Athens.[4] Taking Thasos as his case study, he forcefully argued that the epigraphic output of the island polity was very much influenced by its geographical position and its external economic activity. Osborne thus demonstrated that different factors might have been at play in different poleis in regard to their propensity to set up monumental inscriptions.

In this chapter I too plan to avoid Athenocentrism and perform a similar exercise by looking at three political entities located in, or closely associated with, Boiotia: Thespiai, Oropos, and Thebes. My choices have largely been determined by considerations of evidence and convenience. Oropos is well served by Petrakos' magisterial corpus of Oropian inscriptions (hereafter referred to as *I.Oropos*),[5] and Thespiai by the electronic corpus of inscriptions first launched in Lyon in 2007 (hereafter *I.Thespiai*).[6] As for Thebes, it is a city that in the past decade or so has produced extraordinary epigraphic evidence that calls for some reflection. A by-product of this choice is that the geographical focus of my investigation ends up being southern Boiotia. As a result, we lose from the picture northern Boiotia, where Lokrian and Phokian connections could potentially give a considerably different impression of the topic investigated in this chapter. However, the fact that the region under consideration, bar Tanagra, is a homogeneous zone stretching from the Euboian Gulf in the east to Mt. Helikon in the west should preempt some of the shortcomings of geographically dislocated historical analysis.

In his aforementioned article on the epigraphy of Thasos, Robin Osborne made an apt methodological observation: although MacMullen's epigraphic habit had encompassed both public and private writing, in the course of time the scope of the debate regarding Greece had narrowed and had ended up referring almost exclusively to the frequency with which public inscriptions were erected. I would go even further and add that scholars have used the umbrella term "epigraphic habit" to pose a series of interrelated but by no means identical questions. For instance, what types of inscriptions were erected at any given time and in what numbers? How many people looked at them, and how many were able to read and comprehend them? In turn, what does epigraphy teach us about ancient literacy or literacies (a notorious problem)? Is there a correlation between public and private inscriptions? And last but not least, is there a correlation between constitutional forms and public writing? The reader should keep these questions in mind because they implicitly or explicitly inform my discussion, but he or she should also remember that the extant evidence cannot always be made to bear on these specific queries.

I start with Thespiai, which in 371 was sacked and depopulated by Thebes.[7] It is not quite clear exactly when Thespiai was rebuilt and resettled, but the epigraphic output of the third century shows a thriving polis. Yet much of the epigraphic dearth of the fourth century should surely be ascribed to the dramatic Theban intervention of 371.[8] In what follows, I have made use of the electronic corpus of Thespian inscriptions, although it has to be said that most of the dates given there and adopted here are provisional, and that they very often cover a wide span, such as mid-fourth to mid-third century.

Of a total of thirty-seven Thespian decrees, only one or possibly two can be dated at the earliest to the late fourth century. Here absence of evidence may be attributable to the discontinuation of the Thespian state apparatus after 371. Yet two inventories, the fragmentary *I.Thespiai* 39 and the complete *I.Thespiai* 38, make it clear that early fourth-century Thespiai had acquired a taste for creating lists of a type usually associated with Athens. Both inscriptions date to the first quarter of the fourth century, and both have featured heavily in discussions of Boiotian epichoric scripts.[9] The complete example gives a record of the "sacred property of the Thespians" (hιερὰ χρέματα Θεσσπιέων) in the archonship of Diopeithes. This property included metal vessels, pieces of furniture, and sundry objects and has been identified as the equipment of a formal dining hall. The first editors associated the list with the King's Peace and the dissolution of Thespiai, primarily because the inventoried objects appear to have been stored in three different locations: Chorsiai, Siphai, and Kreusis.[10] Note, however, that the name of the archon Diopeithes has been inscribed over a previously erased name, Onchesstichos. This might be taken to suggest a process of handing over authority, in which case the motivation for the inscribing could have been purely administrative rather than political.

Going through the fascicles of *Les Inscriptions de Thespies*, one is struck by the variety and number of Thespian inscriptions that cannot be used for the purposes of this discussion. None of the famous Thespian leases (*I.Thespiai* 44–57) predate the third century, and the same is true of the equally numerous military catalogs and lists of victors. Thankfully, we can do slightly better with dedications. I have been able to count 29 dedicatory inscriptions dating to the fourth century, although for half of them the editors do not exclude a date in the early third century. Here again, their number may be attributable to numerous factors, including cultic popularity.[11] Fascicle VII contains about 115 or so honorific inscriptions, of which only *I.Thespiai* 341 is firmly placed in the fourth century, whereas four others (*I.Thespiai* 342, 343, 344, 348) may be late fourth- to early third-century texts. I will add three fourth-century sculpture signatures,[12] the graffito *I.Thespiai* 463 (a dedication to an unidentifiable divinity), and finally a fourth-century tile with the collective ethnic Θεσπιέων (*I.Thespiai* 467). Of course, new discoveries could always alter the picture: the ongoing Thespiai survey project recently brought to light a dedication or an honorific herm set up by local tax farmers called *pentekostologoi*. The editors of the text reasonably detected Athenian institutional influence.[13]

So far, one is left rather unimpressed by the epigraphic production of fourth-century Thespiai. It is only when we move to the gloomy sphere of the epigraphy of death that we see, at last, some epigraphic vigor. There are 103 epitaphs in the epichoric script that have been provisionally dated to the late fifth or early fourth centuries, and another 217 fourth-century funerary inscriptions in Ionic script. The vast majority of these epitaphs are of the simplest possible form: single names in the nominative, no patronyms or patronymic adjectives, and no further designations. This austerity of Boiotian sepulchral inscriptions has long been observed[14] and constitutes a kind of local peculiarity. It has often been seen as a manifestation of conservatism, without further explication. I am not quite sure what is meant by that, although one could claim that these epitaphs seem to emphasize the individual conceived as devoid of any familial or societal affiliations. I also wonder whether it is because of this minimalistic fashion rather than any latent xenophobia that Thespiai has produced only two fourth-century epitaphs stating the foreign ethnic origin of the deceased (*I.Thespiai* 999, 1000). There is one single metrical epitaph that appears to date to the mid-fourth century (*I.Thespiai* 1244); otherwise, funerary epigrams are Hellenistic or Roman Imperial.

One fourth-century funerary inscription merits further consideration: *I.Thespiai* 486 is a fragmentary gray pedimental stele recording men who died in a war: [ἐν τοῖ] πολέμοι ἀ[πέθανον] (Figure 8.1). But which war? The Corinthian War of the 390s has often been suggested.[15] At first glance, this stele attests to a type of document we tend to associate with Athens, namely, casualty lists. Add to this that whereas the names of the left column are in the epichoric script, those of the right column are inscribed in the "alphabet attique," to use the French terminology of the corpus, and that the Thespians fought along with the Athenians in the Corinthian War, and a neat picture emerges: Athenian epigraphic practices were being adopted by willing allies, the heroic Thespians in this case.

However, the actual story proves to be more complicated. Moving back to the fifth century, we find Thespiai producing one of the best examples of casualty lists outside Attica, namely, *IG* VII 1888 (=*I.Thespiai* 485). Nine stelai, eight of them complete, discovered in the late nineteenth century, are widely thought to have been part of a *polyandrion* commemorating the dead hoplites of the battle of Delion in 424. Thus the fourth-century Thespian

Figure 8.1. *I. Thespiai* 486. Museum of Thebes, courtesy of the Ephorate of Boiotia. Photograph by Y. Kalliontzis.

casualty list turns out to have a local predecessor. In a sense, this does not contradict the theory of "Athenian influence," for, as one would have expected, the Thespian monument for Delion appears to imitate Athenian prototypes with its stoichedon script and general form. It is a good reminder, however, of the limitations of the chronological analysis undertaken here—it would be foolish indeed to believe that all our questions can be answered by fourth-century evidence only—and of deficiencies of simplistic models that see influences, epigraphic influences in our case, only where there is political and constitutional congruity. Thespiai in 424 B.C. was neither pro-Athenian—far from it: the men recorded in *IG* VII 1888 actually fell fighting against Athenians—nor democratic.[16]

Irrespective of casualty lists, Thespian epitaphs appear to be anything but spectacular. Even those slightly acquainted with epigraphy know well that epitaphs constitute the single largest category of ancient inscriptions. Writing was used as a last desperate resource for the preservation of one's memory in the face of the grim inevitability of death.

Yet this almost banal truth is put to the test when we move to Oropos. Remarkably, out of 213 Oropian funerary inscriptions recorded in Petrakos' corpus, only 6 can be dated to the fourth century B.C.[17] This tiny number violates much of what we know about Greek epigraphic practices and calls for an explanation. One possibility is, of course, that our epigraphic picture is distorted by the archaeologists' preoccupation with the famous shrine of Amphiaraos. This is probably true, although even archaeological bias cannot explain away the almost entire absence of pre-Hellenistic funerary inscriptions. I suspect that a more sinister factor is at play here.

Inconveniently wedged between Attica and Boiotia proper, Oropos was throughout the fourth century fiercely contested by Thebes and Athens, which held sway in the region at different periods. Thebes' presence has left few traces on the ground; Athens is more prominent in the archaeological record, but we do not know what happened to the local population when the Athenians took over. Were they expelled or allowed to live as mere farmers of their erstwhile properties? It is hard to say, although the case of Samos, whose entire population was expelled by the Athenians in the 360s,[18] does not inspire confidence in Athenian magnanimity.

A common way of establishing property rights in antiquity was by means of funerary monuments.[19] It is therefore a logical assumption that such monuments would have been overturned, if not outright destroyed, in the course of continuous regime changes. It is in this context, I contend, that we should

Figure 8.2. *I.Oropos* 359. Courtesy of the Archaeological Society at Athens.

be viewing Oropian land consecrations. I have argued elsewhere that not only Amphiaraos but also Athena Polias was endowed with Oropian land.[20] But sacred lands and tombs make for an explosive mix: death brings about miasma, pollution. In 426/425 B.C., on the occasion of the purification of Delos, the Athenians notoriously removed all the graves from the island and went on to celebrate in splendid fashion the penteteric festival of the Delia.[21] Did the Athenian administrators of Oropos in the 330s take similar drastic action before celebrating the equally splendid penteteric festival of the Amphiareia? The dearth of Oropian funerary monuments may well substantiate this hypothesis.

After the Lamian War the roles of villain and victim were reversed. That *damnatio memoriae* was current in fourth-century Oropos has long been known. Again the evidence is epigraphic and allows me to introduce another aspect of my topic. Several Oropian inscriptions show traces of erasure and sometimes reinscription.[22] The victims in almost all cases are Athenian demotics. A striking example is the dedication of the wealthy Athenian Meidias, of Demosthenic *Against Meidias* fame, who had his demotic Ἀναγυράσιος obliterated.[23] Such demotics are sometimes replaced by the ethnic Ἀθηναῖος (Figure 8.2),[24] a practice that automatically turns the individuals in question into foreigners.[25] In this case we can say that the continuation of the Oropian epigraphic habit was secured via minimal corrections.

However, Oropos' epigraphic material is characterized not only by the region's variegated fortunes but also by the prominent sanctuary of Amphiaraos. The latter could even allow us to speak of a conspicuous religious epigraphic habit. I start with the umbrella term *leges sacrae* (sacred laws), which in Oropia is represented by at least four examples. By its reference to an entrance fee assessed in Boiotian drachmas, the earliest of these texts almost certainly dates to the period of the Boiotian occupation of Oropia from 402 to 387.[26] Two fragmentary examples add little to this list,[27] but most Greek historians are familiar with Rhodes and Osborne, *GHI* no. 27 (*I.Oropos* 277; Figure 8.3). This sacred regulation is widely thought to date to the decade of independence that Oropos briefly enjoyed after the King's Peace and the dissolution of the Boiotian koinon.[28] Yet in this local text we encounter a phrase that takes us back to the realm of Athenian praxis: according to the drafter of the sacred law, upon paying his or her fee, every pilgrim performing incubation was to have his or her name and ethnic written on a wooden tablet (πέτευρος) σκοπεῖν τοῖ βολομένοι, "for anyone who wishes to examine/inspect."[29] This formulaic phrase, we have known well since Wilhelm,[30] is emblematic of Athenian notions of wide accessibility to public information. Here

Figure 8.3. *I.Oropos* 277. Courtesy of the Archaeological Society at Athens.

we have the only Classical attestation of the phrase outside Athens, significantly in a text not issued by Athenian authorities. This, I contend, is a good example of administrative mimicry as a means by which the epigraphic habit was disseminated. Be that as it may, other peculiarities of *I.Oropos* 277, such as the use of empty spaces (*vacats*) and triple dots as punctuation marks, also allude to Athenian influences.[31]

Still in the religious domain, one should heed the large list of victors at the Great Amphiareia, *I.Oropos* 520 (Figure 8.4), which current orthodoxy places in a period of Athenian occupation of Oropos, most probably in the Lykourgan epoch.[32] Here again, Athenian inspiration should be conjectured, although a more imaginative approach would be to think of the influence that the Oropian list itself exercised on the future epigraphic output of Boiotia. Festival victory lists are a staple of Boiotian epigraphy in the Hellenistic and Roman Imperial periods, and I dare suggest that the inception of the tradition should be sought in Oropos.[33]

A much larger epigraphic dossier is offered by Oropian dedications, including ephebic documents.[34] We also find boundary stones, some in the local dialect, including an example that seems suspiciously Boiotian (Figure 8.5);[35] some others, however, demonstrate strong Athenian influences (here the preservation of the aspirate in the word *horos*).[36] Such influences were accentuated once the Athenians returned in 371, as evinced in the *syngraphai*, the contract, for the repair of the spring of Amphiaraos and his baths (*I.Oropos* 290). The proposer of this document is an Athenian; the process—a letting (μίσθωσις)—is supervised by the Athenian council. The inscribing of the contract on a stone stele and its erection in the shrine of Amphiaraos all resonate with typical Athenian processes. The numbers of this type of inscription increased after Athens returned to Oropos in 335, with three further technical contracts.[37] Inventory lists, another Athenian specialty, are also well represented in this period.[38]

What about decrees? After all, as public texts par excellence, decrees constitute a class of material long favored by students of the epigraphic habit. Oropos has produced the largest number of federal decrees of all Boiotian cities, twenty-three, all of them Hellenistic.[39] There is little to marvel at here, since the Amphiareion was, along with the Itonion, a major shrine of the Boiotian koinon and a prominent site for the display of their documents. Oropos has also produced more proxeny decrees than any other Boiotian city, a staggering 196 proxenies;[40] interestingly, the prominence of the Amphiareion resulted in the shrine attracting city decrees out of their natural habitat, that is,

Figure 8.4. *I.Oropos* 520. Courtesy of the Archaeological Society at Athens.

Figure 8.5. *I.Oropos* 281. Courtesy of the Archaeological Society at Athens.

the city of Oropos itself. But what is the picture we get when we focus on the fourth century?

In contrast to the epigraphic dearth of Thespian civic administration, fourth-century Oropian decrees constitute a sizable sample, even though they are dwarfed by the vast number of city and koinon decrees of the third, second, and first centuries. Thanks to Denis Knoepfler's scrupulous work, it is now widely recognized that Oropos enjoyed a spell of independence from the battle of Chaironeia down to 335;[41] three honorific decrees (*I.Oropos* 1–3), of which two are proxenies for members of the Macedonian elite,[42] may be taken to prove that the Oropians were willing to adopt the epigraphic trends of Athens and to duly adapt them to their own needs. Yet there is also something intentionally anti-Athenian here: note the mixed Oropian dialectal forms, infinitive εἶν and genitive οἰκίης, but also the use of the aorist ἔλεξε instead of

Attic εἶπε, or ἐκκλησίῃ instead of the Attic δῆμος.[43] Interestingly, once Oropos was liberated anew from the Athenian yoke, it produced four further honorific decrees (*I.Oropos* 4–7), which stood much closer to Athenian templates. Should we assume then that Lykourgan Athens' systematic attempt to annex Oropos had started paying dividends?[44] Perhaps we should.

The preceding analysis leaves no doubt that the crucial determining factor behind Oropos' flourishing as a producer of public (and private) inscriptions was Athens' involvement in Oropian affairs in the fourth century. In Oropos the epigraphic habit was imported from outside—one might even claim that it was violently imposed—but it was readily adopted and had a long-lasting legacy. In anthropological terms, I think that we should speak of an original stage of forced diffusion followed by a milder process of direct diffusion, both into and out of Oropia, toward the end of the fourth century.

I finally move to Thebes, the area that inspired the topic of this chapter in the first place. Some of the difficulties in analyzing the epigraphic output of this city were duly sketched by Guy Vottéro more than a decade ago. Of the 958 Theban inscriptions that Vottéro was able to adduce in 2001, only 48, or 5 percent, fell within his category of "textes civiques."[45] Unfortunately, his chronological system does not correspond to the chronological scope of this volume, although his database can be used with the necessary precautions to serve the aims of this chapter. Using Vottéro's material, I have been able to count 168 inscriptions that could belong to the fourth century B.C., that is, 17.5 percent of the total. For most of them, however, the date given is either fifth/fourth or fourth/third centuries B.C. In actuality, this means that the real number of fourth-century Theban inscriptions is considerably lower than 168, or at least this was the case in 2001. Therefore, a proportion around 10 percent is probably closer to reality. The tally is not particularly impressive, and given the statistical uncertainties highlighted here, it is not particularly helpful either. It may be more productive to leave aside shaky statistics and attempt a qualitative analysis.

In 2008 Vassilis Aravantinos, then director of the Museum of Thebes, invited me to join him in publishing an inscription he had discovered at a rescue excavation in 2006. The inscription turned out to be the earliest extant treaty of Thebes, a treaty with the Euboian city of Histiaia.[46] One of the most striking features of the new document is its script: with its "red" chi (Ψ), tailed rho (R), and L-shaped lambda, the treaty was unmistakably written in the epichoric script of Boiotia. This seemed to have chronological implications incongruent with another striking feature of the inscription, for surely the term *hagemonia* (hαγεμονία) in line 2 led one to think of the celebrated post-Leuktra Theban hegemony. Eventually, however, Aravantinos and I, although we took a flexible and open-minded position, expressed our preference for the year 377/376 B.C., when, according to Xenophon, the Thebans captured Histiaia's citadel and made the city revolt against Sparta. In electronic exchanges, several Boiotian experts have expressed their sympathy for that date,[47] and consequently we feel increasingly confident that the new treaty offers one of the best anchors for early fourth-century Boiotian epigraphy.

In any case, the new stele is a good reminder that there is much that awaits discovery in the field of Theban epigraphy. The salient point is not that Thebes was willing to enter bilateral agreements with other poleis—that we could have guessed from our literary sources. Rather, the point is that Thebes was prepared to record them on stone and publicize them. Unfortunately, in its current state of preservation, the stele does not contain a publication clause, and the stone has no good archaeological context. Thus Aravantinos and I were forced to indulge in some speculation. Primarily by analogy to non-Theban cases, and owing to topographical considerations, we hypothesized that the stele might have stood in the shrine of Herakles, the religious core of Theban military power. We also noticed a strange feature of the stele: it has *anathyrosis* on both lateral sides. This feature self-evidently suggests that ours was not a freestanding stele. In our analysis we briefly pointed out that a wall made of contiguous inscribed stelai was known from another Boiotian city-state, Lebadeia. The stelai in question contained the contract for the construction of the temple of Zeus Basileus. The "epigraphic wall" from Lebadeia could therefore suggest a local trend. However, the temple and the stelai probably date to the third century B.C.; that is, they are much later than the Theban treaty. The Lebadeian example cannot be a predecessor.[48]

It is conceivable that inspiration had come from *polyandria*; I have already mentioned the Thespian monument for the dead of Delion, itself influenced by Attic prototypes. One is reminded of Nathan Arrington's reconstruction of a notorious monument, *IG* I³ 1163, which, in the aftermath of increasing scholarly rehabilitation of Mattingly's chronologies, Arrington has now associated anew with the battle of Delion.[49] Yet although I tend to agree that the blueprint for the Theban treaty was Attic, I suspect that we should be looking somewhere else in Athens. I am thinking primarily of that emblematic monument of late fifth and early fourth-century Athens, the sacrificial calendar. In his thorough treatment of the monument, Stephen Lambert, while following Sterling Dow's 1961 reconstruction in its essentials,[50] argued in strong terms that the monument should be described as "a stele-series" rather than as a wall.[51] The law codification and therefore the erection of the inscribed monument were major political events in late fifth-century Athens and were fiercely debated, as we know from Lysias' thirtieth oration, *Against Nicomachus*. And the Thebans? We have to remember that in the late 380s members of the so-called Theban democratic party had sought refuge in Athens. They would have had plenty of opportunities to gaze at the inscribed law code, and they would surely have been informed of the surrounding controversy that went on throughout the constitutional upheavals of Athens in the last decade of the fifth century B.C. According to Plutarch, while Pelopidas and his followers were preparing for their return to Thebes, they drew inspiration from the triumphant return of the Athenian democrats under Thrasyboulos in 403.[52] It is not inconceivable that such inspiration expanded to encompass the Athenian democrats' actions after their defeat of the Thirty, including the alphabetic reform of Archinos.[53] This observation allows me to move to my next topic.

Patterns of morphological mimicry may be one way in which the new Theban treaty with Histiaia matters. The other issue at stake is the introduction of the Ionic alphabet in Boiotia. In 1966 Taillardat and Roesch expressed what became the orthodox view for a whole generation, namely, that the Boiotians adopted the Ionic alphabet in the 390s, around the time of the Corinthian War. In 1992 Denis Knoepfler put forward another theory and suggested that the liberation of Thebes and the expulsion of the Spartan troops from the Kadmeia in 379 offered a better historical context for the adoption of the Ionic script.[54] Not much later, Vottéro modified this picture; he argued that the reform began in Thebes around 379–376, and after a period of experimentation throughout Boiotia, the Ionic script was finally adopted by the Orchomenians in 370. Vottéro's theory sounds cogent, but the new treaty, if rightly dated, offers a subtler picture; it shows that at least in Thebes—and here we should be careful not to assume automatic and simultaneous application of the Theban model to the entire Boiotian region—the epichoric alphabet was still being used in official documents as late as 377/376, which becomes a fairly secure *terminus post quem* for the introduction of the Ionic script.

What triggered the alphabetic reform, and how was it implemented throughout Boiotia? In another milieu the debate is familiar. As already mentioned, in 403/402 B.C., after the overthrow of the Thirty, the Athenian politician Archinos passed a decree that legislated the official adoption of the Ionic alphabet by the state. That was the archontic year of Euclides, whose name has entered epigraphic jargon: we all speak of pre-Euclidean and post-Euclidean

Attic inscriptions. Recent work has demonstrated that Archinos' alphabetic reform was not as dramatic as previously assumed, and that the Ionic alphabet had been in use in Attica with increasing frequency from the 440s onward, especially in private and in nonstate documents.[55] Thus the Athenians of the late fifth century simply made official a preexisting trend, and one that was of practical importance, for the Ionic script differentiated between short and long vowels and even had specific letters to indicate double consonants. Its use facilitated writing and reading—in other words, it facilitated literacy. Without intending to make sweeping generalizations, I believe that the epigraphic explosion in fourth-century Athens was aided to some extent by the adoption of the new script.

It would be easy to argue that the Ionic alphabet had a similar appeal in the case of Boiotia, and it almost certainly did. Nevertheless, there is also a substantial difference between Athens and Boiotia. Athens was culturally Ionian, and it was the center of a power structure that was predominantly, albeit not exclusively, Ionian. This obviously does not apply to Thebes and Boiotia. Nino Luraghi has strongly argued that scripts should not be dissociated from dialects—a rather obvious point—and that epichoric scripts functioned as markers of ethnic identity and as political demarcators.[56] In this light, the Thebans' and the Boiotians' decision to shift from their local alphabet to the Ionic script at some point in the 370s becomes perplexing. One could have recourse yet again to the mantra of Athenian influence. If the pro-Athenian Theban liberators returned to their hometown as new converts to democracy, as is usually assumed, it is not unthinkable that they would have carried with them aspects of the alphabetic reform discourse. This ingenious theory was first proposed by Vottéro and later adopted by Luraghi.[57]

Here is the place to bring up another Theban document that has featured heavily in the debate on the Thebans' adoption of the Ionic alphabet, namely, *IG* VII 2427 (Figure 8.6). This fragmentary list of names and patronyms or patronymic adjectives is written primarily in the epichoric alphabet but also shows extensive contamination from the Ionic alphabet.[58] A very extraordinary feature of the text is the first, albeit sporadic, use of patronyms in lieu of the typically Boiotian patronymic adjectives. Vottéro brilliantly ascribed this to the establishment of a democratic system in Thebes after 379, and he consequently proposed to place *IG* VII 2427 chronologically in the 370s. By itself, the use of patronyms is indeed important. However, I suspect that the phenomenon is attendant on something bigger, and what is more, something that has a bearing on the topic of this chapter, for surely the important

Figure 8.6. Thebes: *IG* VII 2427. Museum of Thebes, courtesy of the Ephorate of Boiotia. Photograph by Y. Kalliontzis.

element here is the decision to set up lists of citizens. We do not know of any such Theban texts in the preceding period. We do not even know the identity of the Thebans recorded in *IG* VII 2427. Are they hoplites or members of a religious association, as hesitantly suggested by Vottéro? It is hard to say, but other possibilities cannot be excluded. In Athens such lists record councilors, cleruchs, ephebes, etc.[59] Be that as it may, setting up lists was very much an Athenian epigraphic habit.[60] Thus what at first glance was meant to be merely the investigation of an early use of the Ionic alphabet in a specific Theban inscription turns out to tell us something new about the epigraphic habit in early fourth-century Thebes.

Returning to the question of the introduction of the Ionic alphabet, I may put forward a more complex political agenda. It is clear that upon their liberation from Sparta the Thebans, first timidly and later aggressively, were trying to reestablish a Boiotian koinon with themselves as the undisputed leaders. Are we then entitled to assume that abandoning the Boiotian script was part of this Theban policy? At first glance, this attractive interpretation runs into a serious obstacle: one would have expected the exact opposite, namely, the active promotion of the Boiotian script as a way of enhancing Boiotian identity. After all, with the exception of Oropos, every single member of the koinon, willing or compelled, was using the Boiotian script down to that time. But one wonders whether this was precisely the problem, and whether Thebes wished to break with old norms by promoting innovation in the form of an alphabetic reform.

There is another more compelling interpretation, though, and this gives me the opportunity to introduce another inscription, a statue base, published in 2006. This Theban dedication to Zeus Saotes is preceded by an epigram and is signed by none other than the famous sculptor Lysippus. It is worth noting that the inscriptions, which were cut in the Ionic script, were in all likelihood carved by the same man who inscribed the treaty with Histiaia in the epichoric alphabet.[61] Denis Knoepfler has tentatively identified the dedicant Hippias as the homonymous Theban boiotarch of the early 360s. More challengingly, in *BE* (2009) he identified the honoree as Pelopidas himself. Whether or not this is the case, the honoree was almost certainly a Theban general who had, according to the epigram, increased the glory of fearless Thebes when it chose him as its war leader and thus prevailed over the rest of Hellas (Ἑλλά[δος ἄλλης]). The reference to Hellas is striking and can be matched by other epigraphic and especially literary sources that make it clear that after Leuktra Thebes was increasingly promoting itself as a Panhellenic power.[62] Against this background, the introduction of the Ionic script in Boiotia can be seen as yet another Theban ploy for the advancement and solidification of its newly invented Panhellenic identity. The form of the message now mattered as much as the message itself. And the form had to be in the internationally intelligible Ionic alphabet.

Of course, for all their variability, these theories presuppose that the reform was a central and probably legally binding decision that was imposed by Thebes on the periphery of the koinon. In principle, one should not discount the possibility that the alphabetic reform was simply a slow process of acculturation that encompassed all the poleis of Boiotia at approximately the same time.[63] I have already mentioned the casualty list *I.Thespiai* 486, which might belong to the 370s and which could be taken to imply alphabetic developments in Thespiai that run parallel to, but independent from, those in Thebes. On the other hand, Mackil has lucidly demonstrated that after the liberation of Thebes in 379 federal institutions were primarily promoted by Thebes through coercion.[64] In this light, it seems historically more plausible to assume that the adoption of the Ionic alphabet by the members of the Boiotian koinon was actually imposed by Thebes in its effort to establish and advance new institutions promoting federal cohesion. Even in the unlikely event that Thebes was not the instigator of the reform, it was certainly an enthusiastic espouser. In 2014 I had the opportunity to publish two late Archaic epigrams, one funerary, the other dedicatory. In both cases the original texts, carved in the epichoric script, were later reinscribed in Ionic letters (*metagrammatismos*).[65] This retrospective application of the alphabetic reform would appear to suggest that, at least in Thebes, the issue of the script mattered.

With this, we have reached the post-Leuktra period, during which Thebes temporarily developed hegemonic structures.[66] The 360s, we now understand, saw an epigraphic mini revolution in Thebes with the production of a series of decrees passed in the name of the Boiotian koinon.[67] In 2003, in their authoritative collection *Greek Historical Inscriptions*, Rhodes and Osborne could mention three decrees falling within this category, with proxenies awarded to a Macedonian (*SEG* XXXIV 355), a Byzantian (*IG* VII 2408; Figure 8.7), and a Carthaginian (*IG* VII 2407 = Rhodes and Osborne, *GHI* no. 43). Other scholars were willing to include a further example, which had been restored to honor a Rhodian.[68] The publication of two new proxeny decrees in 2008 and 2010 has increased this assemblage. The first decree, stored in the Museum of Fine Arts in Boston, records a proxeny for a Lakonian individual called Timeas, whose father, Cheirikrates, had been a naval commander of Sparta in the early fourth century.[69] The second decree records

Figure 8.7. Thebes: *IG* VII 2408. Museum of Thebes, courtesy of the Ephorate of Boiotia. Photograph by Y. Kalliontzis.

a double proxeny for two individuals, either from Olynthos or from Corinth.[70] According to a popular interpretation, not endorsed by Rhodes and Osborne, this series of the 360s was connected with Thebes' ambitions to build a fleet and establish itself as a naval power. The two recent examples, especially the Boston decree with the emphatic naval iconography of the accompanying relief and the naval connections of the honoree, add more credibility to this theory.

In terms of diction, the decrees show remarkable uniformity. Here again, it would be easy to make a claim for Athenian influence. In the new koinon the power no longer lay with the oligarchical councils, the *boulai*, but with the assembly: ἔδοξεν τοῖ δάμοι. Yet the uniformity includes traits that are patently not Athenian. Almost all these decrees record the grant of ἔπιπασις and ἐνωνά, the right to purchase and own land and a house. The Attic term ἔγκτησις is found only once. Nor are these decrees especially democratic. Prosopographical analysis has shown that the boiotarchs recorded in these decrees all came from Thebes. Last but not least, I point out the conspicuous absence of any formulas of disclosure. Such formulas, often considered to denote democratic principles, are by and large absent from Theban and Boiotian legislative acts. My guess is that the decrees of the 360s, and probably the treaty of the 370s, do show Attic influences, but of a different type: far from being motivated by democratic considerations, they probably performed a propagandistic function. Not very differently from imperialistic Athens, hegemonic Thebes advertised its willingness to honor foreigners who helped considerably with the expansion of its power.

There are certain aspects of the topic that I have touched on only in passing, and others that I simply passed over in silence. The numerous graffiti from the Theban Kabeirion, for instance, tell a totally different story.[71] The recently discovered Archaic dipinti and graffiti from the Theban Herakleion suggest that the Kabeirion material was not unique, and that a certain degree of limited literacy, at least one manifest in modest private dedications, materialized in the realm of private epigraphy.[72] In the case of fourth-century Thebes, I have argued for strong Athenian influences that were cultural in character rather than constitutional, although I stress that these two aspects are by no means mutually exclusive. I repeat that the temptation to automatically ascribe everything to the democratic transformation of the Theban constitution should be resisted.[73] Epigraphic finds reported in 2014 include four bronze tablets, part of an archive, dating to around 500.[74] Those and a fifth-century bronze honorific decree, all from Thebes, should suffice to show that the notoriously oligarchic Thebes of the sixth and fifth centuries was at ease with producing documents.[75] Democratic, or at least pseudodemocratic, Thebes after Leuktra did not invent epigraphic literacy ex nihilo.[76]

Study of epigraphic material from Thespiai and Oropos also shows a variety of epigraphic practices with several subpatterns. These cities too were probably influenced by Athens, but via different trajectories. For Oropos, Athenian epigraphic contamination was often the aftermath of bitter political developments on the ground. Paradoxically, these bad seeds led to Oropos' epigraphic blossoming in the Hellenistic period. The case of Thespiai is less straightforward. Attic influences in the case of the casualty lists do not necessarily reflect direct Attic political influence, constitutional or otherwise. It is not impossible that much of Thespiai's epigraphic culture came about in direct opposition to Thebes or as the repercussion of open hostility from Thebes.

The epigraphic variety shown in the practices of these three contemporary polities of south Boiotia compels us to accept that it may be better to speak of epigraphic *habits*, not an epigraphic habit. In that respect, one even wonders how useful the whole "fourth-century" concept is when it is used unqualifiedly. Some of the epigraphic habits analyzed in this chapter originated in the fifth century and, transformed, survived well into the Hellenistic period. This is not to deny, however, that the fourth century saw many novelties. The liberation of Thebes in 379, in particular, ushered in major changes that affected the epigraphic outlook of Boiotia. On the other end, Thebes' epigraphic proliferation was abruptly arrested in 335 as a result of the destruction of the city by Alexander. Some of the most interesting epigraphic developments had already taken place within this very period, Boiotia's "short fourth century."[77] However, I do not wish to push this concept too far or too uncritically. The 330s marked a watershed in the history of Boiotia, but different Boiotian regions were affected in different ways, and the same applies to their respective epigraphic productions, as we have seen. After all, it did not take long for Thebes to become epigraphically active again after its refoundation by Cassander in 316/315.[78] Yet one gets the impression that the epigraphic habits of Thebes, Thespiai, and Oropos in the last quarter of the fourth century prefigure the respective habits of Boiotia's long third century.[79] But this is a topic for another discussion.

Appendix: A Chronological Reappraisal of the Theban Monument for Leuktra (*IG* VII 2462 = Rhodes and Osborne, *GHI* 30)

There are few Theban inscriptions better known or more debated than *IG* VII 2462 (Figure 8.8). The inscription has been associated with the battle of Leuktra ever since its 1877 editio princeps by Koumanoudes: "It is obvious that the epigram refers to the famous battle of Leuktra (371 B.C.)," firmly stated the great Greek epigraphist.[80]

The academic community responded enthusiastically to the new find, and the years following Koumanoudes' edition saw a spite of pertinent publications. The specific question of the script and its date was raised already in 1878.

Figure 8.8. Thebes: *IG* VII 2462. Museum of Thebes, courtesy of the Ephorate of Boiotia.

The important *BCH* article of Egger was preceded by a brief anonymous note that included a majuscule transcription of the inscription in "caractères épigraphiques." The composer of the note affirmed that the lettering indicated "une bonne époque" and concluded that it was very possible that the dedication had been inscribed only a few years after the battle of Leuktra.[81]

Yet writing in the same year as Egger, Kaibel adumbrated sundry reasons—inelegant narrative, obscure diction, inconsistent dialectal forms—for which he thought that the inscription postdated the fourth century B.C.[82] However, Kaibel's protestations were overlooked or simply dismissed. Thus Dittenberger, the editor of *Inscriptiones Graecae* VII, upon making use of a squeeze sent to him by Lolling, compared the lettering of *IG* VII 2462 with that of *IG* VII 2418, the contributions for the Third Sacred War (c. 354–352 B.C.), found the epigram to be slightly older, and rejected Kaibel's dating.[83] Similarly, Hansen dismissed Kaibel's chronological verdict as ill judged.[84]

In any case, Kaibel found no followers, and ever since 1878 scholars have reiterated their belief that *IG* VII 2462 is one of the best-dated Boiotian inscriptions. Thus Tod could unhesitatingly state, "The monument appears, to judge by the script, to have been erected immediately, or at least shortly, after the victory."[85] For Fraser and Rönne, "The criterion for establishing the absolute date of the introduction of the Ionic script in Boiotia is provided by . . . (b) the epigram commemorating the battle of Leuktra, 371 B.C. (*IG*, VII, 2462)."[86] Their statement was duly picked up by Pritchett: "P. M. Fraser and T. Rönne . . . had earlier cautioned that the only two securely dated Boiotian inscriptions of the period were *IG* VII.1888, the casualty-list for Delion, and *IG* VII.2462, the epigram commemorating the battle of Leuktra."[87] In his discussion of the impact of Leuktra on contemporary literature, Shrimpton declared, "The reaction of certain Thebans to the glory won by Epaminondas at the battle of Leuktra was captured in stone shortly after the event. The inscription survives."[88] Likewise, in his thorough treatment of the monument's form Tuplin unequivocally stated, "We should therefore proceed on the assumption that the text, whose lettering is consistent with a date within the Theban hegemony, is an epitaph."[89] Similar was Vottéro's belief in *IG* VII 2462 as a *terminus ante quem* for the introduction of the Ionic alphabet.[90] Keeping in line with this tradition, in the most recent authoritative republication of the text, Rhodes and Osborne placed *IG* VII 2462 in the year 371 B.C.[91] In sum, whereas scholars have long debated the type—funerary or dedicatory—of the monument and the exact meaning of the epigram, especially when read against the literary tradition, with the exception of the early divergence of

Kaibel, there has been an almost total consensus on the date of the inscription. Unfortunately, understandable though it is, such faith is ill based and has to be abandoned.

The state of preservation of *IG* VII 2462 is excellent, and its lettering is easy to study. By itself the lettering is rather careless, as can be seen in the different sizes of omicron in lines 1, 2, and 3. Epsilon has an extremely short central horizontal. The central bar of alpha is even slightly curved. But arguably the most salient feature of the lettering of *IG* VII 2462 is the distinctive serifs in which strokes end. This is very clear in the case of epsilon, sigma, and even iota. In fact, there is hardly any terminal letter stroke without a serif. Such serifs cannot be paralleled in early or mid-fourth-century B.C. inscriptions. Now that we have some well-dated documents of the period of the Theban hegemony,[92] we can see that, contrary to what has been repeatedly affirmed, the lettering of *IG* VII 2462 can under no circumstances be that early.

It is rather odd that Dittenberger assessed the lettering of *IG* VII 2462 as earlier than that of *IG* VII 2418. The letters of *IG* VII 2418 are neat and show no traces of apices, as one would naturally expect from a mid-fourth-century B.C. inscription. We should instead compare the lettering of the Leuktra monument to that of *IG* VII 3206, an Orchomenian dedication traditionally dated to 329 B.C. In a concise paleographical analysis, Fossey described with great precision the pronounced serifs of *IG* VII 3206 and aptly pointed out its significance as "a clear example of how an important document at the beginning of the last third of the 4th century would have been written; . . . an example of the stage of development of the alphabet at the very beginning of the Hellenistic period."[93] Juxtaposition of photographs of *IG* VII 2462 and 3206 will suffice to show that the two inscriptions roughly belong to the same epigraphic tradition. Arguably more appropriate and fruitful is a comparison of *IG* VII 2462 with the inscription recording the monetary contributions for the refoundation of Thebes, a document that definitely postdates 315 B.C. and most probably belongs in the closing years of the fourth century. Such a comparison shows that *IG* VII 2462 is contemporary with, if not slightly later than, the contributions record.[94] Its letter forms are right at home in the period of the Diadochi.

There is only one plausible interpretation for this discrepancy between the historical context of the epigram under examination and its late-looking lettering: the monument for Leuktra that has come down to us was inscribed after the refoundation of Thebes by Cassander in 315 B.C.[95] It might have replaced an earlier monument that had been damaged by the troops of Alexander.

The famous inscribed dedication celebrating Athens' double victory over the Boiotians and the Chalkidians, first erected in 506 and presumably replaced around 457 B.C., several years after the first monument had been destroyed by the Persians, offers a good parallel.[96] Even more relevant, albeit less known, is the case of the monument in honor of the famous Theban musician Pronomos, which along with its accompanying epigram was rescued and restored after it had been damaged by the troops of Alexander the Great in 335.[97] I will leave it to others to gauge the possible implications of my chronological proposal for the form and type of the monument. Here I wish only to note that my theory might help explain a long-observed anomaly: of the three men recorded on the top of the front side, Ξενοκράτης, Θεόπομπος, and Μνασίλαος, only the first features in the epigram.[98] But first and foremost, I will repeat my conviction that *IG* VII 2462 was inscribed toward the end of the fourth century B.C. or even early in the third century B.C. It therefore has no bearing on the discussion about the introduction of the Ionic script to Thebes and Boiotia.

CHAPTER 9

A New Boiotia?

Exiles, Landscapes, and Kings

SAMUEL D. GARTLAND

In 335 B.C. an attempted eviction of the Macedonian garrison situated on the Kadmeia provoked Alexander III to destroy Thebes. The annihilation of one of the most ancient and symbolically important Greek communities decisively brought to a close a significant chapter in the history of central Greece. But as Thebes was being razed, several other major poleis in the region were in the process of being reestablished after decades of formal nonexistence. In this chapter the way in which the Boiotian landscape was reconstructed between the 330s B.C. and the refoundation of Thebes in 316 B.C. will be explored with a particular focus on the physical and human re-formation of the communities, as well as the continuing importance of the relationship between Macedon and Boiotia for both regions.

A catalyst for the inquiry is that the study of Boiotia in the fourth century has been grossly weighted toward the period before 338 B.C., reifying the historiographical inferiority of the later part of the century. Although Boiotian antiquity is never preserved in as much detail as in the first two-thirds of the fourth century, the predominance is not irresistible, and there have been significant improvements in the material evidence from the later fourth century since the turn of the millennium. Although the sources still do not permit a detailed narrative, they make intelligible some elements in the process of change brought about in the region after the establishment of Macedonian power. The relationship between Macedon and Boiotia, central to the period before 335 B.C., is also far richer and more complicated in the period after the destruction of Thebes than has usually been understood.

Four out of the five large poleis in Boiotia were absent from the landscape for long periods in the fourth century. Orchomenos, Thespiai, and Plataia had ceased to exist for several decades before 338 B.C., and Thebes was absent from Boiotia from 335 to 316 B.C. between its destruction by Alexander III and its restoration by Cassander. Despite this turbulence, the communities are regularly treated in modern studies as if they suffered only minor interruptions and were more or less consistent in their behavior, engaging in patterns of discourse similar in character to those that had been traditional in the region. Yet if these poleis are instead considered to some extent new foundations (among the first of the Hellenistic period), the period takes on a radical aspect, an exogenous reconstitution of an entire region. A better understanding of this period can help illuminate longer-term trends in Boiotian history, as well as the dynamic historical changes of the early Hellenistic period and their effects at polis level.

Exiles

The resilience of ancient Greek communities is not in doubt; indeed, versatility in response to stressors is in many respects a defining characteristic of a successful polis. Poleis could be moved, and populations could be resettled or successfully return to the same site after exile. Some of the causes and responses of these movements have been studied.[1] But when a significant number of members are lost, or when a group is in exile for an extended period, how do we assess the community that attempts to reestablish itself? The later part of the fourth century in Boiotia offers several good examples with which to begin a response.

The most famous and best-recorded polis destruction and population movement of the fourth century in Boiotia was the Macedonian obliteration of Thebes in October 335 B.C., but it is not clear what happened to the Thebans after the destruction of their city. Some escaped, most notably to Athens and Akraiphiai,[2] but Diodoros reports on those that did not get away: "Over six thousand Thebans were killed, more than thirty thousand captured, and the amount of property taken was incredible . . . and by selling off the prisoners he [Alexander] raised four hundred and forty talents of silver" (Diod. 17.14.1–4). Six thousand killed is a credible figure in the context of the descriptions of indiscriminate slaughter of combatants and noncombatants in our sources.[3] Arrian consistently claims the process as an *andrapodismos*, and the punishment would have been an understandable desire of other Boiotians as a fate for a community that had overseen the same punishment on at least three occasions (Plataia in 427 B.C.; Orchomenos in 364 B.C. and again in 345 B.C. along with Koroneia).[4] However, the fate of the "thirty thousand enslaved" is less clear. Any use of a "myriad" or its multiples is suspicious, although 36,000 as an approximate figure for the Theban population in 335 B.C. is in line with the best modern estimates.[5] Diodoros states that the prisoners were sold off, but this does not help us understand the more important issue of to whom or where these captives then belonged. There is nothing in our sources or in Boiotian history to suggest that Thebans would have been allowed to stay in Boiotia in any numbers,[6] and the apparent rapidity of events surrounding the denouement of Thebes suggests that the sale of people and property was carried out in some haste, and therefore that the immediate market would have been those in the vicinity.[7] The Macedonians probably took Theban women and children as spoils, and Hyperides bought (or ransomed) a Theban, Phila, for twenty *minae* before keeping her in Eleusis as his mistress.[8] Alexander III also dedicated booty taken from Thebes on his Asian expedition.[9]

The destruction of a large and famous community is naturally attractive to historians, but the attention of our sources leaves Thebes as quickly as Alexander himself did. We hear about only a handful of the many thousands of surviving Thebans, and nothing direct or conclusive about the site of the city until its refoundation in 316 B.C. The lacunae in our evidence here illustrate the difficulty in reconstructing what happened to communities when they were exiled, and they require us to consider the fate of the other exiled Boiotians. The Plataians are the most famous of the exiled Boiotian groups, but their experience of exile is unusual not just for the abrupt change in fortune that ushered in their reentrance to Boiotia after 338 B.C., but also because they held citizenship of another polis outside their home region. The number who fled to Athens is not known, but the relatively small numbers of Plataians killed in either of their two exiles makes possible a fairly comprehensive citizen body in Attica, perhaps around 5,000 individuals, although many might have settled elsewhere during their long absence from Boiotia.[10]

If their exiles are considered in total, the Plataians had been present in Boiotia for a maximum of thirteen years out of the previous ninety (386–373 B.C.), long enough for several generations to develop into a very different group from that which had left the region in the early years of the

Peloponnesian War. Although Athenians prided themselves on their reception of exiles and suppliants, long-term residency in Attica and citizenship of Athens was highly unusual. Some of the problems of this arrangement, the marriage of Plataians, and the cohesiveness of the group (especially the effects of poverty) are articulated in our Athenian sources. The Plataians returned to Athens after their second exile in 373 B.C., and through Isocrates (presumably reflecting the Plataians' own rhetoric) we get a picture of the group shortly afterward:

> We see our own parents unworthily cared for in their old age, and our children, instead of being educated as we had hoped when we had them, often because of petty debts reduced to slavery, others working for hire, and the rest procuring their daily livelihood as best each one can, in a manner that accords with neither the deeds of their ancestors, nor their own youth, nor our own self-respect. But our greatest anguish of all is when one sees separated from each other, not only citizens from citizens, but also wives from husbands, daughters from mothers, and every tie of kinship severed; and this has befallen many of our fellow-citizens because of poverty. For the destruction of our communal life has compelled each of us to cherish hopes for himself alone. (Isoc. *Plat.* 48–49, trans. Norlin, adapted)

Allowing for understandable exaggeration, we have a consistent portrayal of a group broken apart physically and socially, and identifying who was and who was not "Plataian" became more difficult the longer the Plataians were in exile. Whereas in the Plataians' first exile in Athens, Lysias could make inquiries to Euthykritos, "the oldest citizen of Plataea and whom I supposed to be best informed," later inquiries recorded in Apollodoros witness the difficulties that could attend discerning true "Plataians." All three sources attest the mistrust and fear that could accompany being "Plataian" within Athens.[11]

The difficulties of maintaining community might have had lasting effects, according to one suggestive testimony provided by Herakleides Kritikos: "The citizens have nothing to say except they are colonists [ἄποικοι] of the Athenians and that the battle between the Greeks and the Persians took place in their territory. They are Athenian Boiotians ['Αθηναῖοι Βοιωτοί]" (Her. Krit. *BNJ* 369A F.1.11). Herakleides' portrait of Boiotia is selective and capricious, but because he was a *periegete* writing in the third century B.C., this description might provide a way to glean some sense of Plataian identity after the upheavals of the fourth century. The claim that the Plataians were colonists of the Athenians is striking and similar to the self-description of the inhabitants of Oropos reported by Herakleides.[12] The important difference is the explicit claim that the Plataians were colonists (ἄποικοι) of the Athenians, which problematizes the orthodox acceptance of a relatively uncomplicated repatriation of Plataians after 338 B.C. and, if it is correct, has implications for our understanding of Hellenistic Boiotia.

Plataia

The Plataians had endured long exile because of Thebes, their urban center had been destroyed, and their landscape had been governed according to Theban interests for the large majority of the previous century. The scale of this reorganization of the Plataian landscape is unclear, but the survey work undertaken at the site suggests that the polis was essentially a new foundation after 338 B.C. Where previous fortification of the city had focused on the acropolis, this now became only a small part of the large enceinte that encompassed some eighty-five hectares and included one of the largest agoras in the Greek world. There was enough space to house between 7,500 and 9,000 inhabitants within the walls, a number that, if realized, would have represented a significant increase of the population figure from the 430s B.C.[13] The new city had walls with a perimeter of four kilometers and at least six gates and forty towers. The impressive size of the new urban center indicates a community confident of enjoying a more prosperous future than its fifth-century predecessor. The destruction of Thebes and the concomitant redistribution of land, only three years after the battle of Chaironeia, is likely to have changed the scale of the project considerably and might have been behind the anticipated rise in population.

The unusual relationship between Athens and the Plataians had inherent ambiguities that were used by some impostors as a gateway to Athenian citizenship. This could possibly have worked in reverse when Plataians were allowed to return to Boiotia in 386 B.C., but particularly after 338 B.C. When the new community was being founded, an influx of Athenians would have been natural and probably necessary to provide the skills to build the new city and the numbers to fill it. The superior fertility of Boiotian soil was recognized and envied in Attica, and relocation must have been an attractive proposition for many, especially those based in the northwestern extremities of the region, such as the Skourta Plain.[14] The destruction of Thebes would only have further incentivized Athenian settlement north of Kithairon, providing even more land and greater security. The Plataian portrait provided by Herakleides might in these circumstances fit a logical outcome of this situation: a community that regained a sense of regional belonging but remained proud of its (re)foundation by a group wanting to preserve the memory of its Athenian provenance.[15]

Reestablishing a polis that had not existed for several decades must have encountered numerous difficulties. The process of allotting land is likely to have been at the heart of resettlement, but any conflict over ownership after the final thirty-five years of exile would have been quickly eased by the liberation of Theban territory after 335 B.C. that could be parceled up and owned or used by those nearby. The surviving accounts seem to agree on a widespread redistribution of land previously under Theban control, as well as the *astu* itself, although whether this process was all supervised by Macedonians is not clear; a land grab is implied in the surviving accounts.[16] However the breakup of Theban territory took place, the Plataians would have been in a natural position to benefit because they had a long contiguous border with Thebes and could simply extend their holdings over the Asopos. There was an apposite precedent for such expansion. Thucydides (3.68) reports that in 427 B.C. the land of Plataia had been divided into allotments and given for a year to Megarian exiles and pro-Theban Plataians before being reallotted to Thebans on ten-year leases in 426 B.C. A similar arrangement for Plataian land is implied by Isocrates for the period after their second exile in 373 B.C.[17]

The reconstruction of the urban center began after the battle of Chaironeia in 338 B.C. and is likely to have been accelerated after the destruction of Thebes. After the battle of Gaugamela in October 331 B.C., Alexander is reported to have promised a further subvention of direct support for the rebuilding effort.[18] As with his handling of Thebes, Alexander had the advantage of being able to combine military necessity and anti-Persian sentiment: Plataia was not just the site of the vanquishing of Xerxes; it was also situated in the best location to guard the passes over Kithairon, a factor made particularly relevant by Antipater's use of the land route through central Greece when he was combating the then-recent rebellion against Macedon led by Agis III of

Sparta. The location of the site, as well as its historical significance, explains the new, extensive fortification system there.

The redistribution of Theban territory allowed its neighbors to prosper, and the building materials available at Thebes, its extensive lower walls, and its satellite settlements could have provided a ready-enough supply to make a useful contribution to the rebuilding of Plataia. Additionally, the availability of animals as a result of the destruction of Thebes, particularly oxen, could have been incorporated into the reestablishment of Plataian agriculture and also could have facilitated the movement of building materials from Theban territory. The coincidence of Theban destruction and Plataian construction on an unprecedented scale also brings to mind the conspicuously generous contribution made by a Plataian to the Lykourgan building projects in Athens.

Eudemos of Plataia donated "a thousand yoke of oxen" to the construction of the Panathenaic stadium and the theater in time for the celebration of the Panathenaia in 329 B.C.[19] The account of the donation has caused some confusion because of the large numbers of animals involved. Explanations have included that the donation actually constituted a thousand days of ox labor, that it paid for the provision of oxen, or that Eudemos acted as a manager/subcontractor for the program.[20] But in these discussions there has been little consideration of the situation in Boiotia at the time. The destruction of Thebes, one of the largest poleis in the Greek world, would have released material wealth, land, and other resources, such as livestock, into surrounding areas. There may have been a large number of oxen taken from Thebes in 335 that were used in the rebuilding of Plataia, and with Alexander's continued support in 331/330, an exceptionally large number of oxen (from Thebes or elsewhere) could have been employed in the rebuilding in 330 B.C. When the work was completed, the redundant animals could then be liberated by canny operators such as Eudemos to send to Athens in time for the completion of the stadium by the summer of 329 B.C. Plataia would have benefited from the double windfall of Theban destruction and Macedonian patronage, providing individuals like Eudemos with the opportunity to siphon the available resources to provide lavish public benefactions in Athens for their personal benefit.

Eudemos is designated as a Plataian, but it is likely that he had spent most of his life in Athens, and the conspicuous donations noted in this inscription (and probably one other)[21] are clearly the acts of an individual keen to galvanize links with Athens only a few years after he had resettled on the north side of Kithairon.[22] The sudden availability of Theban resources and the need for skilled labor is likely to have encouraged even more settlers from Attica in the period after 335 B.C. We therefore have a situation where a community of mixed inheritance returned to a home territory in which the great majority of its members would never have lived and, within a few years after its return, saw the land available to it effectively enlarged to previously unknown size or productiveness. Allied to this was the more direct subvention of support for rebuilding from Alexander in 331 B.C., a suitable corollary to the destruction of Thebes, made possible by the wealth accrued in Asia.[23] This combination of a new population and great wealth underlay the construction of an enormous enceinte and the establishment of new festivals, the most prominent of which were the Greater Daidala and the Eleutheria.

The Greater Daidala is known principally from the long account given by Pausanias and was a festival created as a marker of Plataian exile and return that had the effect of integrating the new community into the changed physical and social landscape after 335 B.C.[24] The Eleutheria, celebrating the role of the Plataian landscape in the Persian Wars, is perhaps more interesting and important in the context of the role of Macedon in the recalibration of Boiotia. Although it is likely that some form of commemoration of the battle of Plataia took place before 338 B.C., it was a relatively local and sober affair, and it is unlikely to have been celebrated between 373 and 338 B.C.[25] The completion of the restoration of Plataia by Alexander as an act linked to his final victory over Darius at Gaugamela will have encouraged the festival to develop with greater ambition.[26] That the Plataians should aspire to make a monumental historical event on their territory a significant fixture on the Greek celebratory calendar is not surprising, especially if it could offer some protection against future threat of exile. The Eleutheria quickly became a major Panhellenic cult and agon, and the memory of the battle was an important element in Herakleides' report on Plataia.[27]

Taken together, the two festivals can be understood as creations designed to help integrate the community into the new Boiotia of the late fourth century. The Eleutheria and its concomitant grant of *asylia* made Plataia as a physical entity theoretically inviolable, in a sense making the Plataians the protectors of their own memorial landscape. The Greater Daidala, in turn, served to integrate the returning community into the new regional landscape, tracing a pilgrimage route to the distant, ancient Boiotian site of Alalkomenai and inviting to Plataia representatives and dedications from all other major communities in the region.[28] Within these two festivals lies the crux of Plataian self-presentation after 338 B.C., a community intent on emphasizing its place (and its permanency) within the region but also its unique position within wider Hellenic consciousness.

Orchomenos

Reconstituting Plataia was undoubtedly a complex social process, but it was only one of several similar but distinct processes occurring across Boiotia at the same time. Perhaps the most mysterious occurred at Orchomenos. It had always maintained traditions of its distinct "Minyan" identity, was listed separately in the Homeric Catalog of Ships, maintained unusual cultic links such as membership in the Kalaurian Amphiktiony, and was politically often distant from the rest of the region, though never, it seems, ethnically distinct.[29] It had no tradition of exile comparable to that of Plataia and, by welcoming the Persian forces in 480 B.C., had not even endured dislocation during the Persian Wars, unlike Thespiai and Plataia.[30] The *andrapodismos* visited on the city in 364 B.C. by Thebes was therefore not only completely unprecedented in the history of Orchomenos but also stands as the single most brutal act ever to have been exacted by one Boiotian community against another.

Epameinondas, absent in the Aegean, was reportedly surprised and unhappy at the annihilation of the large, famous, and strategically important polis.[31] This reaction recalls the unwillingness of the Theban leadership to take punitive action against Orchomenos in the aftermath of the victory at Leuktra, a policy that allowed Orchomenos to return peacefully to the fold.[32] The importance of its position at the northwestern corner of the region and the largest community on the *lieu de passage* of the Kephissos Valley often strained the relationship between Orchomenos and other Boiotian communities, but the massacre and enslavement of its inhabitants were unprecedented and also left a strategic defense problem for the region.[33] The site was not completely abandoned, but the ease with which it fell to the Phokian leader Onomarchos in 354 B.C. (as opposed to the resistance of stubborn Chaironeia) suggests that it was not strongly defended.[34] The subsequent course of the Third Sacred War, when the site of Orchomenos was used by the Phokians to make war very successfully within the region, demonstrates the problems caused by weakening this community.[35] At the end of the war the site was exposed to another *andrapodismos* together with Koroneia, but because these communities had been occupied by Phokians during the war, it is unclear whether this applied to just the Phokian occupiers or was a more general clearance of other Boiotians present at the site.[36]

Against this background of death, enslavement, and exile, the return of the "Orchomenians" after the battle of Chaironeia is far from uncomplicated. Some Plataians were able to maintain aspects of cohesive identity in Athens, and the majority of Thespians probably remained within Boiotia, but it is unclear whether Orchomenians survived in any numbers, where any survivors went, or what they were doing in the twenty-six years before Philip II permitted their return in 338 B.C.[37] Orchomenos was the second-largest community in Boiotia and after such upheaval is likely to have had the space to absorb significant numbers of settlers from elsewhere.[38] Orchomenos' location at the gateway between Lokris, Phokis, and central Boiotia makes it more likely that contingents could have come from any or all of these places.

Amid a very general picture, one specific detail is provided by a group of twenty-four cavalrymen returning to Orchomenos from Alexander's campaigns, probably after his victory over Darius at Gaugamela, who made a dedication to Zeus Soter.[39] If this "petit corps" joined him in the autumn or winter of 335 B.C., its members would have been part of the new polis for three years at most before leaving again for a further five years on the Asian campaign.[40] They would have needed to be skilled horsemen to make it that far with Alexander, and this suggests a continued ability to rear and train horses, something difficult to achieve in only three years. Maintaining horses in exile would have been similarly difficult, and these factors make it possible that these were entirely new Orchomenians in 338 B.C. rather than a group that had lived there before.[41] Returning to the rigor and restrictions of polis life for any Greeks who fought with Alexander must have been a strange and difficult experience, but for this group of horsemen, their polis would have been largely created while they were absent, and therefore, there would have been little familiarity with the community on demobilization. Similarly, a group of infantrymen from Thespiai joined Alexander and returned, perhaps at the same time as, or even with, the Orchomenian group, most probably after June 330 B.C., when the allied Greeks were demobilized by Alexander at Ecbatana.[42]

With Plataia, Thespiai, and Orchomenos made up of a disparate mix of individuals and small groups with limited experience of government or independent polis existence, the foundation of the third koinon becomes a strange event. Its formation would have been made even stranger because of the need to divide some of the spoils of Thebes among them. The koinon could have acted as a mechanism by which the new Boiotians could help one another articulate a regional identity, as well as confirm each community in its territorial and symbolic spaces. The economic aspects of this negotiation are somewhat secondary to the problems of learning to be "Boiotians," especially because "being Boiotian" was in many regards articulated traditionally around responses toward Theban predominance, an element that had been spectacularly withdrawn.

Changing Landscapes

If the community to which the Orchomenian cavalrymen returned was in the process of unprecedented social reformation, it was at the same time also undergoing radical changes in its physical territory. A system to regulate the drainage of Lake Kopais had been undertaken that sought to restore (and probably extend) the Bronze Age drainage system that had long ago fallen into disrepair.[43] The catalyst for the project is unclear, and Mackil has argued that it was a project of the nascent koinon.[44] However, Strabo, the only literary source for the work, implies otherwise: "And although the drainage holes filled up again, Krates, the miner from Chalkis, stopped clearing away the obstructions because of discord among the Boiotians, although, as he himself says in the letter to Alexander, many places had already been recovered" (Strabo 9.2.18). It is not possible to be conclusive, but the passage strongly suggests that the project was commissioned by Alexander III.[45] Krates is writing to Alexander to explain why the project has not been completed, an apology of an engineer producing a balance sheet of his achievements, as well as his failures. Little survives regarding Krates, but he was known well enough in antiquity that Plutarch might have included him among his *Lives*.[46] Alexander might have been interested in how effectively the new federation was overseeing its own drainage system and demanded updates on its development, but it is more likely that this was a project backed by Alexander and designed to accompany the reconstruction of the region in the wake of the loss of Theban predominance.

Managing the fluctuations of Lake Kopais would have several benefits, most obviously liberating a large amount of silt-rich land, but also helping lessen the deleterious effects of malarial marshes and regularizing the agricultural cycle.[47] It is worth noting that the only Boiotian communities that received grain from Kyrene in the 320s were the major Boiotian communities (Plataia and Tanagra) farthest from Lake Kopais and therefore least able to take advantage of its productivity.[48] But from the perspective of local inhabitants, the drainage would also have detrimental effects. Many of the signature products of the region (and its greatest delicacies) were found in and around Lake Kopais. The account of the Theban visitor to Athens in Aristophanes' *Acharnians* is instructive because the majority of the products he brings with him are products of wetlands. There are ducks, geese, and other aquatic birds, as well as "rush- mats" and lamp wicks, produced from plants that would have thrived in Lake Kopais.[49] The delicious Kopaic eel is also among the products the Theban in the *Acharnians* brings, and the eel was the most famous part of a substantial freshwater fishery, which was responsible for a significant part of the Classical Theban diet.[50]

In the upheaval and uncertainty of the post-Chaironeia era, when communities such as Orchomenos and Koroneia were repopulating, the importance to the region of the productivity of Lake Kopais would have been emphasized. As important as the lake itself was the fertile land near the upper boundaries of the lake that benefited from the annual deposition of silt brought down from the mountains of Phokis and Lokris, exposed with the seasonal changes in the level of the lake.[51] This system provided food throughout the year, allowing cultivation of high-yielding spring-sown cereals, as well as livestock husbandry, to take place alongside the catching of eels, fish, boars, and wildfowl.[52] The varied system had the other advantage of offering benefits to all communities around the lake, though in varying degrees. The east end of the basin would have seen the greatest benefits of any drainage, and a site such as Haliartos would have had access to significantly less land uncovered by seasonal changes in the lake level than Orchomenos.[53] The transference of this landscape to a managed pastoralism would be a major change and would require negotiation and a level of compromise and trust that might have been beyond the inhabitants of this new Boiotia.[54] Given the deprivations of the Third Sacred War and the Theban *andrapodismoi* of Orchomenos and Koroneia, it is unlikely that there would have been great internal pressure on land usage in northwest Boiotia. Furthermore, without the Thebans to feed, the edible resources of the lake had fewer demands on them.[55] In the social and political context of the 330s and given the natural productivity of the Kopaic wetlands, it therefore appears more likely that the attempted drainage scheme was the product of decisions made by Alexander and resisted by at least some of the locals who were attempting to integrate themselves into a landscape that had seen decades of upheaval.

If so, why would Alexander have wanted this project undertaken? He might have wished to emulate his predecessors; the most successful leaders of the century before Alexander, Archelaos I and Philip II, had both undertaken drainage projects in and around Macedon in order to reclaim marginal land for cultivation.[56] There is also the possibility that he was trying to compete with an even earlier ancestor, Herakles, who reputedly rendered ineffective the earlier drainage system for the glory and benefit of Thebes.[57] Alexander's detailed knowledge of Homer would also have provided him with the example of the famously wealthy Orchomenians, and he could add substantial new territory to the polis his father had helped reestablish. His own experiences in Boiotia are also likely to have influenced his perspective: 338 B.C. was a year of heavy rainfall that caused the land in the Kephissos valley to be flooded and marshy.[58] These difficult conditions in the most important land route into central and southern Greece would suggest the strategic drainage of the area to allow passage in all conditions. Similarly, a friendly, prosperous Orchomenian elite could act (like Plataia at the other end of the region) as a guarantee of the ability of Macedonian forces to enter and leave central Greece unmolested.

At a regional level, the changes brought about by the destruction of Thebes and the partially complete drainage of Lake Kopais seem to mirror each other. Both created a large new supply of highly desirable agricultural land surrounded by poleis, which would have appeared as if situated around the outside of a drained lake in both instances. Krates' work in Lake Kopais would have provided a parallel change to the destruction of Thebes, transforming the perilacustrine, fluctuating landscape into the best farmland in mainland Greece, with poleis situated around its perimeter.[59] The balance that would have been created by the changes helps emphasize the significance of Onchestos as a physical bridge between the two great basins of Boiotia. The high antiquity of its cult of Poseidon also offered a strong link with early Boiotia, and the combination of physical and symbolic factors helps explain Onchestos' choice as the political center of the new koinon.[60]

The engineering in Kopais may have been only part of a wider system of hydrological management that could have included other elements, such as the drainage and reservoir system at Thisbai. The dyke there helped provide a much larger cultivable plain for use by the community, and although there is an open debate about whether it was a Mycenaean or fourth-century system, it seems likely it was a combination of the two. This would mirror the developments at Lake Kopais with fourth-century engineering improving on a Bronze Age system.[61]

The Restoration of Thebes

If Alexander had a grand regional vision for how Boiotia without Thebes should look and function, it did not survive long after his death. After two decades of revolutionary change in the human and physical dynamic of the region, Cassander ordered the restoration of Thebes in 316 B.C. The practicalities of the process of gathering together surviving Thebans and rebuilding Thebes are unclear, but the reported resistance to the idea of Theban restoration is likely to have made the process of negotiation with other Boiotians difficult, and it was probably by threat of force the plan was carried through.[62]

The numbers of Thebans are unlikely to have been large (at least at first), given the slaughter of 335 B.C. and the deprivations of exile.[63] This may have gone some way to alleviate the pressures of recalibrating the landscape to accommodate the new inhabitants. From the extant sources, the process of rebuilding, physically and socially, seems to have been gradual. The description given in Diodoros (19.54) of many Greeks "sharing in the synoikism" is consistent with the picture we get in the most informative surviving inscription relating to the refoundation, now significantly improved with the publication in 2014 of a new fragment.[64]

The original fragment (*IG* VII 2419; *SIG* 337) contains the names of communities from Eretreia, Kos, Melos, and Aegina and perhaps individuals from Sidon and Athens, as well as King Demetrios, dedicating some of the spoils from the siege of Rhodes. There are Greek communities and Macedonian *basileis*, the use of that title being an indication that, as at Plataia, reconstruction was a gradual process that continued at least until the end of the century, as is implied also by literary testimony.[65] Other indications of this are that Cassander had to stop at Thebes later in the year to lend more assistance to the rebuilding of the walls.

The new fragment of the inscription adds to the wider geographical spread implied by Diodoros through two certain contributions from Cypriots and also nonroyal individual donors. The spirit of Diodoros' narrative is also confirmed, that the refoundation of Thebes was a Panhellenic enterprise whereby a famous and very old city was supported by new money from new bases of power. Indeed, in this respect, Thebes should be considered among the great new polis foundations of the early Hellenistic world.

By restoring Thebes, Cassander reversed an important event in Alexander's early kingship, one that he had consistently defended as correct and justified as part of a wider pro-Hellenic/anti-Persian campaign.[66] Alexander not only had destroyed Thebes but also had expressly prohibited the return of Thebans in the Exiles Decree.[67] Cassander's decision was met with complaints from his rivals, but as the inscription demonstrates, any hostility did not endure among the Macedonian kings.[68] In the case of Demetrios, the reflection of Alexander is even more striking. Alexander had increased assistance to Plataia after destroying Thebes as a Panhellenic sacrifice; Demetrios used the benefits derived from the siege of Rhodes to rearticulate his pro-Hellenic credentials by making a substantial donation to the refoundation of Thebes. For Cassander, more important than reversing Alexander's actions must surely have been concern with strengthening his control of central Greece, and this was likely also the cause of greatest concern among his rivals. Geographical considerations (Thebes as a node in Cassander's strategy for Greece) are again surrounded by history and symbolism, adding to the peculiar concoction of early Hellenistic Boiotia.

A further element in this was the establishment of a cult of Hektor, the only one in Greece, and one that looks like a unique, Theban addition to the anti-Alexander myth.[69] The bones of Hektor were recovered from the Troad, possibly in 316 B.C., and taken to Thebes, perhaps masking an earlier cult to another "Hektor." Schachter has ingeniously reconstructed the list of donors to the rebuilding of Thebes to include Ophryneion in the Troad, where there was a known grove dedicated to the hero (Strabo 13.1.29).[70] He suggests that these bones could have been part of a contribution to the refoundation of Thebes, an apt dedication given that Thebes and Troy suffered a similar fate, as well as the advertisement of opposition to Alexander implied in a dedication to Hektor.[71]

Thebes was a very ancient city, but the destruction of 335 B.C. had been brutal in both human and physical terms. Herakleides, visiting in the third century, reflected on the paradox of the refoundation: "Though an ancient city, its street-plan is new because, as the histories inform us, it has already been destroyed three times, because of the oppressiveness and arrogance of those living there" (Her. Krit. *BNJ* 369A F.1.12). Despite its antiquity, the reconstructed Thebes looked like a new city because of its wholesale destruction by Alexander.

* * *

Thebes was famous for its high antiquity, but in the third century B.C. it appeared like a new foundation. It was not alone. Plataia and Thespiai were both refounded in the 330s B.C., and Tanagra, the only major community in Boiotia not to suffer dislocation at the hands of Thebes, had already been rebuilt in the early fourth century on an impressive grid plan.[72] The drainage project overseen and partially completed by Krates would have brought significant changes to all the communities of the Kopais basin. Herakleides' statement about Thebes could therefore be applied to the region as a whole; Boiotia was ancient, but by the third century the region appeared very new. Recognizing that the fourth century witnessed massive physical change to the urban spaces of the major Boiotian communities, as well as significant upheaval in the landscape of the region, is interesting but not in itself revolutionary. What is more at issue is the possibility that this reconstruction, a complete refurbishment of a region, was only part of a wider phenomenon of change that was as much human as physical.

The returning Plataians could be considered, like their new city, an artificial element in the region. Their exile had extended longer than that of any other polis, long enough that they found it necessary to enact their local and regional identities through new cults, which linked them to the history of the site and of the region. Their reclamation of place marks the beginning of a fascinating dialogue between the new settlers and the history, myths, politics, and geography of the site. In the third century, they (in parallel to those from Oropos) could claim to be "Athenian Boiotians," a geoethnic oxymoron, but one that serves to articulate the ambiguous identity of the new inhabitants after 338 B.C. An individual such as Eudemos embodies this ambiguity at the earliest stage: a man probably born and raised in Athens and determined to retain (or establish) a position within that city. In Athens he had been a Plataian in exile; in Plataia his position was less clear, but by channeling some of the wealth provided by Theban destruction and Macedonian patronage, he was able achieve prominence in Athens.

In their two exiles, the Plataians did not suffer loss of life on a community-wide scale and had a recognized haven in Attica for historical reasons specific to them. The other two major communities to suffer as a result of Theban predominance in the fourth century, Orchomenos and Thespiai, had very different experiences. The *andrapodismos* of Orchomenos in 364 B.C. had significant long-term consequences, both locally and within the Kopais basin more widely.

Thespiai was a community used to upheaval and population disasters,[73] and although it did not suffer the dislocation of the other communities, its inhabitants still had to remake their polis after three and a half decades. It is not possible to see how this process worked in detail, but the cohorts of men from both poleis who fought with Alexander for many years in Asia only reinforces the view that this was a period of unprecedented turbulence.

The driver of this remarkable transformation came from without. Before 338 B.C. Macedonian influence in Boiotia had been indirect and limited, but after the battle of Chaironeia, Macedon and Macedonians came to play an extensive role in shaping and reshaping the physical and social landscape of Boiotia. From 338 to 336 B.C. Philip II undertook a program in the region that reversed in its totality the physical reorganization of Boiotia that had taken place during the period of Theban hegemony, a process that he had witnessed firsthand in its most dynamic period in the 360s B.C. The emasculation of Thebes allowed the major communities it had supressed, Thespiai, Plataiai, and Orchomenos, to begin the process of re-formation. The garrison placed on the Kadmeia would have had an unusually pernicious effect on the community.[74] Alexander continued the process, destroying Thebes and providing more support for Plataia as it was rebuilt. After Alexander's death Thebes was restored by other Macedonians, and by the early third century the settlement pattern of the region would have looked superficially much as it had in 432 B.C. or 386 B.C.

If Philip's program for Boiotia can be seen as a development of the pragmatic political style he had employed since the 350s, Alexander instead used Boiotia as a message board. The destruction of Thebes might not have been premeditated, but he would have been aware that the event could be turned to his advantage by justifying it as unfinished business from 479 B.C.[75] Here lies the crux. Boiotia was central to Greek myth and history, just as it was central to the mainland in geographical terms. Theban action across the region had been designed to make the region controllable, weakening the strength of the other Boiotian poleis. The Macedonians who usurped Theban control recognized this and attempted to use this plasticity to their advantage. The shift from pragmatism and fear of Theban revival to a dialogue based on symbolism and strategic geography was a marker of the changes occurring as a result of Macedonian influence and the reduced importance of central Greece in the wider political sphere. The restoration of Thebes was part of a game played among Alexander's successors, as the inscription relating to its gradual refoundation confirms.

Boiotia after 338 B.C. was a landscape built according to Macedonian actions and decisions, but the inhabitants, old and new, were not supine in its redesign. They resisted at least some of the drainage projects in the Kopais basin and opposed the refoundation of Thebes before being persuaded to acquiesce. The major poleis were all in some senses new foundations, and their response to this distance from the old was to behave as they expected Boiotians to behave, celebrating important events that had occurred in the region and integrating the re-formed communities with a new koinon and new cults. Much as the Greeks settled by Macedonians in the farthest reaches of the old Achaemenid Empire found value and cohesion in preserving their Greekness, the new Boiotians derived significant benefit from preserving or creating links with their inherited pasts. The pretense benefited all who took part: cities had resources and guarantees of safety to rebuild, and Macedonians had the political benefits of supporting this reconstruction and also defensive control of some of the most strategically important land routes in Greece. Boiotia was not created entirely anew in the late fourth century, but neither did it have direct continuity with its previous form.

This post-Chaironeian Boiotia can therefore be considered an exogenous construction, built around the changing dynamics and priorities of the Macedonian ruling class. It also manifested key characteristics of the early Hellenistic world: city destruction and foundation, population movements, hydrological engineering, and Panhellenic cult and festival creation. No other region in mainland Greece was so systematically affected by these currents; that all this happened in a little over two decades makes this period in many ways unique in mainland Greek history.

Epilogue

What If They Jumped? Rethinking Fourth-Century Boiotia

ROBIN OSBORNE

Were they always pushed? Did they sometimes jump? One way or another, those are the questions we are always wanting to answer about the Boiotians. Did they become Boiotians under external pressure, at whatever point in the Archaic period they did become Boiotians, or did they come for reasons of their own to feel the need to express some preexisting ethnic identity in more explicit forms? Did they simply crack in different ways under the conflicting pressures of the Hellenic League and the Persians, or were the Persian Wars a chance for those who chose to medize or those who chose to remain loyal to the Greek cause, or indeed both, to take the opportunity to break out of the constraints of Boiotian identity? Was it Athenian intervention that required the formation of the particular fifth-century federal arrangements, or was Athenian intervention simply an excuse for getting on and doing what everyone in Boiotia had already decided that he wanted to do?

This volume has offered a variety of views about the pushing and jumping experienced by the Boiotians in the fourth century, and it has shown how hard it is to distinguish pushing from jumping. As historians, we generally see it as part of our job to detect who or what is doing the pushing, and on the whole, claims that people jump are taken as a sign of a historian's naïveté. If we knew more, we would always be able to detect that someone or something is doing the pushing, or so we tend to think. And of course, there is a sense in which everything can be thought of as pushing. Those who jump push themselves to jump—often because they are following the example of others who have jumped (or been pushed) before them.

But what I want to do here is to resist that pressure always to postulate the invisible hand. I want to have a go at writing the history of fourth-century Boiotia on the basis that, rather than being thick-skinned pigs needing prodding with goads, the Boiotians may have been more like the Gadarene swine, taking their own direction—even if they did so in reaction to their own assessment of the options. If the Boiotians took their chances, what were the chances they thought they were taking?

What did residents of the cities of Boiotia want? In the face of pressure from outside, whether from north or south, there is little doubt that they wanted to be Boiotian. That is, they wanted to express the fact that they felt more in common with the other inhabitants of Boiotia than they did with any other Greeks, and at some point they had begun to display that by participating at common festivals. Or, to put it another way, faced with outside pressure, each community realized that it needed its neighbor, and the neighbors collectively realized that geography and numbers conspired to mean that no group smaller than Boiotia would be strong enough to resist the pressures from outside the group. In consequence, the communities constructed an identity for themselves and formed some common festivals.

Absent the pressure from outside, being Boiotian might become just one among many competing desirables, even at the level of the community. On the one hand, each community wanted to have its independent existence recognized—and this was true of rather small communities (Boiotia is particularly good for reminding us that city-states were frequently amalgams of would-be separate communities). On the other, one important way for the larger communities to defend their independent existence was to strengthen their own communities by adding other communities. And for the Boiotians as a whole, the question whether they were sufficiently strong as a group of independent communities making joint decisions on the basis of equal voices, or whether there needed to be a dominant partner, was one that different parties always felt differently about. In the terms used by John Ma in chapter 2, we might think that the Boiotian cities themselves, and not just Sparta, equivocated between settling for autonomy 1 and feeling that they needed autonomy 2.

But the communities also were not solidary. With agriculture as its primary asset, Boiotia faced the problems of every agrarian community. Landownership was the measure of status, as well as the source of wealth; but landownership produced social inequality that was hard to square with the community participation required for successful military action. The military might required to get the Boiotian voice heard outside Boiotia necessitated giving a political voice to a large proportion of the community, but if the political decisions taken led to war locally, local landowners were the ones who suffered (I will return to the significance of this point later).

Seen like this, the cities of Boiotia did not differ significantly in aims, but their aims came to be expressed in different actions depending on their size and on the nature of the wider geopolitical situation that they faced. Outside pressures were always liable to produce opposing reactions; every act of aggression by a party from outside, whether the outsider was Persian, Athenian, Spartan, or Macedonian, raised for every Boiotian community the question whether Boiotian identity came first, and the outsider should be resisted, or whether this particular outsider offered the chance to reassert local power in order to secure or protect the interests of the particular community within and against Boiotia as a whole. What decision any city took depended on its assessment of the strength of the foreign power, the willingness of that power to follow through on promises of support, the likely reaction of its Boiotian neighbors, its own ability to contain that reaction, and the internal political relations between landowners and potential soldiers at the time.

The defeat of Athens by Sparta and its allies, including its Boiotian allies, in 404 changed the situation for the Boiotians and demanded a reassessment of their relations both with each other and with those outside. The Spartans had been necessary allies in the face of Athenian aggression; now they became a potential threat, and initially that threat looked very serious indeed. What if, the Thebans at least seem to have worried, the Spartans took over the economic strength of Athens and simply added that to their own? Hence the demand from Thebes immediately after the end of the war that Athens be turned into a sheep pasture (Plut. *Lys.* 15.2; cf. Polyaenus *Strategemata* 1.45.5). Hence too the help for Athenians running from or resisting the Spartan puppet government of the Thirty (cf. Xen. *Hell.* 2.4.1–2, 30). What if the Spartans persuaded the rest of Greece that they were the only show in town, that resistance to Spartan power was futile, and that, in any case, improving the lot of the Greeks was a worthy goal and one that the Spartans could now reach? Hence the disruption by the boiotarchs of Agesilaos' epic-inspired sacrifice at Aulis (Xen. *Hell.* 3.4.4).

But if the defeat of Athens was a threat, it was also an opportunity. The danger was that the power vacuum created by the defeat would enable Sparta to grow more powerful; the opportunity was that the Boiotians themselves could expand. The Boiotians had already benefited economically from

Spartan occupation of Attica (*Hell. Oxy.* 17.3). Boiotia, like Corinth, could reasonably expect to step into at least some opportunities from which Athens had stepped out. Manpower was a major Boiotian asset, and once Athenian absence meant that it was soldiers, not sailors, who mattered, the Boiotians could produce a very large number of soldiers (more on this later).

Could the Boiotians seize the opportunity? In coming to a decision to jump, the Boiotians faced one major impediment: their past history. Thebes had taken the opportunities provided by the threat of Athens to press its own local advantage, first through the invasion and destruction of Plataia and then, in the aftermath of the battle of Delion, through action against Thespiai. For all that other Boiotians too might have been persuaded that action against Plataia was necessary, the treatment of these two cities could not but cast a shadow over any attempt to seize advantage for the Boiotians: for whose advantage was this really going to be? If unity had been impossible to achieve even in the face of Persian invasion and in the wake of Athenian aggression, how much less likely was Boiotian unity when it was a hard-to-adumbrate opportunity, not an all-too-distinct and precise threat, that was being dangled before Boiotian snouts?

In shedding light on what happened in fourth-century Boiotia, this volume has shown all sorts of ways in which Boiotians did manage to jump in the fourth century while making equally clear the opportunities never taken. Not the least remarkable and revealing initiative is represented by the Theban magistrates' coins, analyzed here by Albert Schachter. Although we cannot pinpoint the date at which this coinage began, Schachter's case for the coins starting at the end of the fifth century encourages the view that this was a coinage especially for the new world after Athens' defeat. Here was a simple mechanism for delivering an upsurge of Boiotian morale: a coinage for local use, produced in denominations suitable both for substantial transactions (the silver staters) and for relatively petty exchange (the obols), that paraded the Boiotian shield or the head of the local hero Herakles. Often restriking Aiginetan coins, this coinage offered a medium for local exchange that reaffirmed local identity with every transaction. Minted by Theban magistrates, it nevertheless could be sold to the other communities of Boiotia as a means of facilitating the Boiotian local economy from which all Boiotians could profit. Yet those were indeed Theban magistrates' names; for all that the other Boiotians could identify with the obverse, the reverse always reminded them of the true story—that being Boiotian meant being tied to Thebes. This generous facilitation of local exchange was actually the guarantee that Thebes remained the central market, that Thespiai did not take advantage of Kreusis to tie itself to Corinthian economic life, and that Tanagra and Anthedon would not sign up for the Euboic standard. An initiative that liberated Boiotia in one sense did not fail also to signal Boiotian dependency in another.

Similar issues arise over the Boiotian epigraphic habits analyzed by Nikolaos Papazarkadas. Did being Boiotian mean insisting on what was distinctive about local identity? Or did it mean playing a Boiotian part on an international scale and according to international rules? The way in which the cities of Boiotia stuck to the Boiotian epichoric script for the first quarter of the century tied in closely with the production of the Theban magistrates' coinage. It created a visible symbol of being Boiotian (in contrast, for instance, to the "Attikismos" advertised by the list of war dead on the *polyandrion* put up at Thespiai after the battle of Delion), but at the expense of displaying to the rest of the Greek world a local exclusivity. The change in the 370s to Ionic was effectively a decision that if Boiotia was to play a role on the stage of the Greek world as a whole, it must look the part.

Where Thebes led, the rest of Boiotia followed, and the Ionic script became the norm. But who was pushing and who was jumping? Are we dealing here with emulation, as I have proposed might be the case for the subject matter of public inscriptions in the various cities of the Boiotian League, or, with Mackil and Papazarkadas, should we be thinking of Theban coercion? Here, at least, it might be hard to tell. Few scholars would reckon that Theban control was so totalitarian that the subject matter of decrees of other cities in Boiotia was directly determined by its rulings—even Athens did not manage that in its empire, although Aristophanes, in replacing "coins" with "decrees" in his parody in *Birds* 1040–41 of the standards decree, could fantasize that it might. Broad control of what decision-making bodies in the Boiotian communities could and could not make decisions about was part of the price tag of autonomy 1; from this point of view, Papazarkadas' comparison of Thespiai with Oropos is telling, but what it tells is misleading. The enormous number of proxeny grants by Oropos is the story of a community caught in a unique place, not a Boiotian community more or less resistant to Thebes but a freelance community seeking to make the most of not being part of Attica or of Boiotia. For Oropos, unlike Thespiai or the other cities of the confederacy, autonomy 2 was (sometimes) an option. Close control by Thebes (or by "the confederacy" as a whole) of what decisions self-identifying Boiotian communities could make was another matter. What exactly would have been the mechanism for invalidating local decisions? And when it comes to script, are we really to suppose that Thebes would send in the masons to chisel out any epichoric letters? With regard both to the script and to the content of decrees, here is surely a case where the positive gains of doing what others were doing played much more of a role in determining what happened than any potential penalties for doing otherwise.

Jumping with the Thebans looked more and more attractive during the 370s and 360s. Who would not want to be on a bandwagon that was rolling so successfully? Thom Russell's exposition of Epameinondas' success in the Bosporus in the 360s only underlines this. With this crucial lifeline to Black Sea grain in their control and the massive revenues of Bosporus cities coming within their sights, Boiotian cities will have seen for the first time how their powerful resources of fighting men could be undergirded by economic resources that would offer the possibility of initiatives that had never previously been within reach. Here was a means of taking a grip on maritime trade without getting into bed with Athens—indeed, a means that could bypass Athens.

The equivocal attitude to Athens involved in Thebes' desire to see Athens wiped off the face of the map in 404 but support for Athenian refugees from the Thirty (an equivocal attitude reciprocated in Athens, most obviously over support for the recovery of the Kadmeia in 379) deeply affected the jumps that Thebes made. Plataia and Thespiai both had major strategic assets (access to ports on the Corinthian Gulf, control of land routes into and out of the Peloponnese and over Helikon into northwest Greece) that might be traded for Athenian support. These were potentially weapons threatening such mass destruction that they could be made to justify a preemptive strike. The Theban moves to destroy Plataia (Pausanias 9.1.5–8—Pausanias' entry point to fourth-century Boiotia, cf. Gartland in chapter 6 of this volume) and Thespiai (Diod. 15.46.6, 15.51.3; Xen. *Hell.* 6.3.1, 6.3.5, 6.4.10) in the 370s, which seem on the face of it entirely destructive of Boiotia, could be presented as required by the circumstances, the necessary preliminaries not to Theban dominance in Boiotia (itself hardly in question) but to Boiotian dominance in the wider Greek world.

It is in the context of this calibration of what it would be to rewrite the history of Greece with Boiotia as the central place in political as well as geographical terms that the issue of democracy in Boiotia, explored by P. J. Rhodes in chapter 4, needs to be visited again. For whom does an attempt to make Boiotia dominant on these conditions make sense? No doubt the prospect of becoming the most powerful political unit within the Greek world would have widespread appeal—few object to being at the top of the power structure. But no one could have had any illusions about the potential cost of achieving that position. When Xenophon has Socrates take the would-be politician Glaukon through a list of what every politician needs to know (*Memorabilia* 3.6), he lays down not simply the prerequisites for exercising personal political influence but also the prerequisites for any city aiming at asserting itself against others: identifying sources of revenue, having some idea of costs, knowing one's own military resources and those of the enemy, and considering systems of defense.

Epameinondas' Bosporan activities answered the question of revenue sources, but Boiotian strength necessarily rested in the final analysis on its land and its manpower. Boiotian standard army strength amounted in the early fourth century (*Hell. Oxy.* 19.4) to 11,000 heavy infantry and 1,100 cavalry—to which a similar or larger number of light troops needs to be added (cf. Thuc. 4.93.3), giving a standard total of around 25,000, one perhaps capable of some expansion (cf. M. H. Hansen 2006: 84). Any attempt to put Boiotia in control of the Greek world was bound to involve these troops. But these troops will also have been a significant proportion of the agricultural labor force required to turn Boiotia's other great asset, its land, into an effective resource. And although deployment of troops against invaders was complementary to, and indeed required for, the effective exploitation of the land, deployment of troops elsewhere in the Greek world would compete with the needs of the land.

The conservatism of landowners was taken as a given in ancient sources. *Hellenika Oxyrhynchia* 6.3 observes of Athenian politics in the 390s that "moderates and men of property were content with the present circumstances," and Aristotle (*Pol.* 1292b25–40, 1318b9–15) commends the democracy of farmers because farmers are too busily involved in their tasks to meddle. It was no doubt the far-from-conservative politics pursued by the Thebans that led Polybius to assume that their constitution was radically democratic (Polybius 6.44.9). But that was no foolish assumption. However charismatic we take Epameinondas and Pelopidas to have been—and Polybius credits Theban achievements entirely to these leaders—Pausanias (9.1.5) tells us that meetings were long, and there is no reason to think that policy was not strongly debated. Those who voted for policies that involved aggression against Plataia and Thespiai might reasonably be reckoned to have voted for their own material interest (although see Snodgrass in chapter 1 for the evidence that all that was taken from Thespiai was its political organization), and in this case those who already had property and those who did not would have shared the same material interest. But when it came to decisions that involved military action outside Boiotia, the interests of different groups diverged. Where was the interest of significant landowners in engaging their agricultural labor force in campaigns away from Boiotia and of unknowable duration? For all the absence of specific information about who could vote, either at Thebes or elsewhere in Boiotia, we should hesitate before reckoning Polybius wrong.

The defeat of Athens in 404 presented the Boiotians with new opportunities. Not only did they no longer have need of the Spartans, but they could even see the way to becoming rivals of the Spartans. What happened over the next forty years was certainly not determined by the Boiotians alone, but we should not tell a story in which they were merely reactive, however much other Greeks wanted to delude themselves that this was the case (cf. *Hell. Oxy.* 7.2 for Boiotians taking Timokrates' gold in the 390s). The decisions about coinage, about script, and about their epigraphic habits charted in this book give us some small insights into the ways in which the Boiotians took measures to shape their own future and to strengthen themselves against the wider world. Some of the further directly political initiatives taken by the Boiotian koinon have become apparent in the last decade with the expanding list of federal resolutions preserved on stone (Papazarkadas in chapter 8). But if we allow ourselves some empathy with the Thebans, we can see how their actions were part of a concerted plan to jump before they were pushed.

Fourth-century Boiotia has few admirers. The Boiotian confederacy is seen as a sham, resistance to Philip as equivocal and too little too late, the revolt of Thebes on Philip's death as a massive political misjudgment. What this volume reveals, however, is the way in which, however much hindsight labels their decisions unwise, the politically empowered residents of Boiotian cities, and not merely Thebes, attempted to balance personal, community, and ethnic self-interests in a world from which the one stable factor—that all politics had to be carried out in relation to the great powers of democratic Athens and antidemocratic Sparta—had been removed. We understand that story better if we allow ourselves to imagine that the individuals and communities involved actively shaped their futures and did not merely react to outside forces.

NOTES

INTRODUCTION

Abbreviations follow Simon Hornblower, Antony Spawforth, and Esther Eidinow, eds., *The Oxford Classical Dictionary*, 4th ed. (Oxford: Oxford University Press, 2012), and J. H. M. Strubbe, ed., *Supplementum Epigraphicum Graecum, Consolidated Index for Volumes xxxvi–xlv (1986–1995)* (Amsterdam: J. C. Geiben, 1999): 677–88. Abbreviations not found in those sources include:

I.Oropos	V. Petrakos, *Οἱ Ἐπιγραφὲσ τοῦ Ωρωποῦ* (Athens, 1997)
I.Thespiai	P. Roesch, *Les Inscriptions de Thespies*, online corpus (2007)
NIO	P. Siewert and H. Taeuber, eds., *Neue Inschriften von Olympia (Die ab 1986 veröffentlichten Texte)*, Tyche Sonderband 7 (Vienna, 2013)

1. See Ma, chapter 2 in this book.

2. Cooper 2000.

3. See Russell, chapter 5 in this book.

4. Disruption caused by the Macedonian garrison: Din. 1.19.

5. For the destruction of Thebes, see Gartland, chapter 9 in this book.

6. Ma (2008) suggests a late fourth-century date for the construction of the lion memorial.

7. Bintliff 2005: 5, with reference to Bintliff 1997. Beloch (1886) estimated 150,000 to 200,000 for the population. Hansen's shotgun method offers useful parallels with estimates ranging from 125,000 to 250,000: M. H. Hansen 2006. A useful update to the shotgun method considers Boiotian poleis in detail: M. H. Hansen 2008.

8. Vika, Aravantinos, and Richards 2009. Up to half the entire area of Boiotia might have been under cultivation (for cereals, olives, and legumes) in the fourth century: Bintliff 1993: 139. Shiel (2000) summarizes the arguments over whether the intensity of Boiotian land use in the early fourth century was unsustainable.

9. Vika (2011) provides the dietary information from a diachronic study of Theban osteological information. The reduction in fresh fish consumption in the Hellenistic period could also have been an effect of the draining of Lake Kopais.

10. The figures given at Pausanias 10.20.3 (10,000 infantry, 500 cavalry) for early third-century Boiotia suggest a certain amount of demographic similarity with the figures provided for the late fifth century (*Hell. Oxy.* 19.3).

CHAPTER 1. THESPIAI AND THE FOURTH-CENTURY CLIMAX IN BOIOTIA

1. Schachter 1996: 115–17.

2. Larsen 1955.

3. Schachter 1996: 118 and n. 70.

4. Tuplin 1986.

5. Seymour 1922.

6. Tuplin 1986.

7. Schild-Xenidou 1972: nos. 52, 60, 62–65, 70.

8. Roesch 2007: 4:208.

9. Schachter 1981: i, 216–17 with n. 2.

10. Roesch 1982: 467–68, 474. See also Scott, chapter 7 in this book.

11. Fossey 1988: 136.

12. Leake 1835: 479.

13. See Jamot in Homolle 1891: 449.

14. Leake 1835: 2:479.

15. Ulrichs 1863: 2:84.

16. Konecny, Aravantinos, and Marchese 2013: 112–18, Abb. 85–87.

17. Plassart 1926: 390n1.

18. Plassart 1926: 448–49, no. 85.

19. C. Müller 1996: 180–82.

20. Schachter and Marchand 2013: 295–99, no. 6.

21. See Bintliff 2005.

22. On their respective treatments, see Buckler 2003: 276–77.

23. Pleket 2010: 219.

24. See Bintliff, Howard, and Snodgrass 2007: 205, fig. LSE 3/16, and 229, fig. LSE 6/16, with Appendix B1 (on the CD), for the individual finds.

25. See Bintliff, Howard, and Snodgrass 2007: 26–34 with table 4.2.

26. Bintliff, Howard, and Snodgrass 2007: 172, table 10.1.

27. Stamatakis 1883: 86.

28. Roesch 2007: 1:40–41, no. 34.

29. For Plataia, see now Konecny, Aravantinos, and Marchese 2013: 57–118, 213–19.

CHAPTER 2. THE AUTONOMY OF THE BOIOTIAN POLEIS

1. Thuc. 1.113; Diod. 12.6; Plut. *Per.* 18 (the last two affirming that Tolmides fell at Koroneia); Plut. *Agesilaos* 19.2 (location and trophy; see Krentz 1989). On these events, see Beloch 1914: 179–81 (connecting the Boiotian victory with the foundation and institutionalization of the Boiotian League); Lewis 1992: 133 (decoupling the victory and the league); Mackil 2013: 35, 192–93 (on the significance of the trophy, interpreted as monumental and part of a pan-Boiotian imagined community). The two sites, Chaironeia (captured by the expedition) and Koroneia (where the battle took place), were occasionally confused in nineteenth-century narratives or travelers' accounts; Koroneia has been the object of sustained fieldwork by J. Bintliff as part of the Leiden-Ljubljana Ancient Cities of Boeotia Project, with findings being regularly reported in the journal *Pharos*. Tolmides: Nauhaud 1986.

2. Thuc. 1.108; 3.62.5, 67.3 (speech of the Thebans after the surrender of Plataia); 4.92.6 (speech of Pagondas before Delion).

3. E.g., Roesch 1965; Larsen 1968: 39–41, 71–72; Schachter 1989; Buck 1994; Corsten 1999: 27–60; Cartledge 2000; Knoepfler 2000; Mackil 2013, notably 330–41.

4. *NIO* 122–23, 127–28; Arist. *Rh.* 1407a1.

5. Hansen and Nielsen 2004: 432; Mackil and van Alfen 2006: 219–31.

6. Cartledge 2000.

7. M. H. Hansen 1995; Hansen and Nielsen 2004; generally, *IACP* 87–94.

8. *NIO* 5; *IAGC* 222 (Thespiai), 205 (Eutresis), 223 (Thisbai), 202 (Chorsiai), 218 (Siphai).

9. Thuc. 4.76.3; unnamed historian (*FGrH* 4 F 81, under Hellanikos as in Steph. Byz, but assigned tentatively to Theopompos, whence *FGrH* 115 F 407, dubitative) on events of 446; *IACG* 201.

10. Edwards 2004 on Hesiod as documenting a tense moment of the structuration of the Thespian landscape (on which Bintliff, Howard, and Snodgrass 2007).

11. For a later example, see the relations of Chorsiai and Thisbai in the early second century: *ISE* 65–66, with Knoepfler, *BE* 2008, 244; Migeotte 1984: nos. 10–11; H. Müller 2005; Ma 2013.

12. Hdt. 5.74–80; *IG* I^3 501 (*ML* 15); Aravantinos 2006; Papazarkadas 2014b (publishing the already famous inscription concerning the dedications of Kroisos; I suspect that the context is a Theban expedition against Athenian-held Oropos).

13. M. H. Hansen 1995; Keen 1996.

14. Xen. *Hell.* 3.2; Roy 2009. See Ruggeri 2004 and Taita 2007 on Elis and its neighbors.

15. Plut. *Lys.* 28.2.

16. Xen. *Hell.* 6.3.7.

17. Xen. *Hell.* 5.2.11–24; 5.3.26 (although Xenophon's account, after attributing the autonomy motive to the Akanthians and Apolloniates who appealed to Sparta for help against the Olynthians, does not explicitly mention these cities' autonomy as a Spartan demand); Zahrnt 1971; Psoma 2001.

18. Ducat 2008 on the Spartan formation and its structure.

19. Xen. *Hell.* 3.4.6.

20. Xen. *Hell.* 4.8.15.

21. The exploitation of ambiguity in terminology is also to be seen in the absorption of Helisson by Mantineia: Helisson in fact lost its polis status but was allowed to "stay a polis as before" by avoiding the relocation of its population and by keeping its existence as a town, which is one of the meanings of "polis." See Mack 2015: 218–21 on Rhodes and Osborne 2003: 14.

22. Xen. *Hell.* 5.4.15, 20, with Wickersham 2007; *IG* VII 1904, same document *I.Thespiai* 999. The gravestone, with the rather roughly carved epitaph of the Spartan Hip(p)okles (photo in *LSAG*^{2}, plate 75.5), bears a much earlier, smaller, and more elegant epitaph (Ἀριστοκράτες, c. 500 or early fifth-century B.C. on the basis of the script: *IG* VII 1903, same document *I.Thespiai* 515), inscribed on the same face but at a 180-degree orientation. In other words, an earlier gravestone was flipped over and reused for a Spartan garrison soldier or officer (in or after 378 rather than the 380s, as proposed in *I.Thespiai*). I suggest that this stone comes from the plot of an exiled, pro-Theban family, and that this plot was desecrated and demolished and its stones were reused when the family was exiled. (I saw the stone in the epigraphic reserve in the Thebes Museum in 2003, on the eve of the great reorganization and reexploration that has borne such rich fruit, alongside rescue excavations—Papazarkadas 2014a; although I rejoiced at seeing the Spartan epitaph, I must admit that I did not notice the older, upside-down inscription.)

23. Xen. *Hell.* 5.4.46.

24. Mantineia: Plut. *Pel.* 4.4–5 (the context is quite clear and can only be the reduction of Mantineia after the King's Peace; it is worth noting that the experience of Pelopidas and Epameinondas, located in the defeated allied wing and witnessing the victorious Spartan contingent coming to the rescue, exactly matches, while giving a worm's-eye view, the account of Spartan tactics at the battle of Nemea in 394, where the allied spear fodder was defeated by the

coalition contingents, but the latter were flanked and swept away piecemeal by the victorious Spartan wing: Xen. *Hell.* 4.2.13–23). Boiotians at Olynthos: Xen. *Hell.* 5.2.27, 37, 40–41 (and conversely, Olynthian cavalry served under Spartan leadership against the Thebans: 5.4.24).

25. This is suggested by a fragmentary inventory of sacred vessels, found on the site of Chorsiai (*I.Thespiai* 38, also published as Platon and Feyel 1938, *SEG* XXIV 361; studied in Vottéro 1996: 166–70; and Iversen 2010). The vessels are described as belonging to the Thespians and are listed across various places: the nonpolis harbor settlement of Kreusis, the small polis of Siphai, and a place called Heraion, which I suspect might be Chorsiai itself, under a toponym that denies its polis identity and hence was imposed after absorption by Thisbai or Thespiai. The inventory thus would affirm Thespian presence (the concrete ownership of the vessels would act as a metaphor for an implicit claim) across a whole landscape of settlements—polis, nonpolis, former polis (Chorsiai), and smaller polis (assuming that Thisbai appeared in the inventory)—each one marked and related to the others by a copy of the inventory, which might also have been inscribed at Thespiai as the center of this landscape (*I.Thespiai* 39). The meaning of the document turns on its dating. Both copies of the inventory are inscribed in the Ionic-Attic alphabet, which may point to a date in the 370s (see now Aravantinos and Papazarkadas 2012; Knoepfler, *BE* 2012, 196bis). In this case, the inventory represents an effort at constructing symbolic forms of dependency around Thespiai. On the other hand, the Ionic-Attic alphabet might not constitute a firm chronological pointer to the 370s, so that the document could simply represent formal links of dependency before the King's Peace (Iverson 2010, also on the possibility of a gradual introduction of the Ionic-Attic alphabet; see further Schachter, chapter 3, and Papazarkadas, chapter 8, in this book). The preceding interpretation was sketched out in Ma 2013, but incompletely.

26. Aravantinos and Papazarkadas 2012 for a possibly early (377/376 B.C.?) example of Theban leadership in war, in an alliance with Histiaia.

27. Xen. *Hell.* 5.4.63; cf. 6.1.1, 6.3.1; 6.4.6.

28. See Arrian 1.8.8, Diod. 17.13.5, Plut. *Alex.* 11.11, and Justin 11.3.8 for the most complete list of victims of Thebes taking part in the sack of 335 (Bosworth 1980 on Arrian 1.8.8); Knoepfler 2000 on lingering suspicions of Thebes into the early Hellenistic period.

29. Ma 2013.

CHAPTER 3. TOWARD A REVISED CHRONOLOGY OF THE THEBAN MAGISTRATES' COINS

I would like to thank Samuel Gartland for inviting me to contribute this chapter. I am also grateful to Emily Mackil for helpful criticism. I am particularly indebted to Jack Kroll for his invaluable help, criticism, and encouragement; this chapter would have been a lot worse than it is without his wise and generous counsel.

The magistrates are listed according to the sequence developed by Hepworth 1998 in the appendix at the end of the chapter.

1. Imhoof-Blumer 1877: 6–12; Head 1881: 61–72; 1911: 351–52; Babelon 1914: 253–56; Kraay 1976: 112–14; Martin 1985: 167.

2. Hepworth 1998: 63n13.

3. Hepworth 1998: 63.9.

4. Hepworth 1998: 63n14.

5. Hepworth 1998: tables I–XIV.

6. Hepworth 1998: 63.

7. Hepworth 1998: 65 for ΚΑΙΩ(Ν), 66 for ARKA/APKA, and 67 for ΠΟΛΥ.

8. ΞΕΝΟ: see Hepworth 1998: 67.

9. Hepworth 1998: 63.

10. In 338: Head 1881: 61–72; 1911: 351–52; Kraay 1976: 114 ("either in 338, after the battle of Chaeronea, or shortly before"). In 335: Martin 1985: 167–68; Hepworth 1998: 63n16.

11. Threatte 1980: 27–31.

12. D15 ΗΙΣΜ (Ἰσμεινίας II) could be regarded as an archaism, although it would not be impossible even in the 360s.

13. Hepworth 1989: 37–38; Vottéro 1996.

14. See Schachter 2014: 316 and 329. ΘΕ appears on coins of the Theban electrum issue, now dated by Samuel Gartland to the mid-360s: Gartland 2013: 23–24.

15. See below, n. 25, on the change from the epichoric to the Attic-Ionic alphabet in Boiotia.

16. Hepworth 1998: 61n1.

17. Hepworth 1989.

18. Cited by Kraay 1976: 114n1, who rejects it because of the supposed date of deposit of the Myron-Karditsa hoard (360/350). This argument is disposed of by Hepworth 1989. On the significance of raising the date of the hoard, see the discussion later in this chapter.

19. Hepworth 1989: 39.

20. Illustrated in Head 1897: plate 36.

21. Hepworth 1989: 39.

22. Hepworth 1989: 39.

23. Hepworth states that "the two issues may refer to the same individual, although the likely full name—Ismenias—was common in Boiotia": Hepworth 1998: 64n25.

24. Xen. *Hell.* 5.2.35–36.

25. A point already made by Imhoof-Blumer 1877: 9 but ignored except by Babelon 1914: 253–54 ("on a ΨΑΡΟ(πος) ou ΨΑΡΟ(πῖνος)," although in the preceding paragraph he lists Charon as one of the magistrates). Denis Knoepfler (Knoepfler 2008: 635) uses the coins of ΨΑ-ΡΟ/ΧΑ-ΡΟ to date the change from the epichoric to the Attic-Ionic alphabet in Boiotia to early in the 370s; cf. Knoepfler 2009: no. 244; 2012: no. 196bis; and Aravantinos and Papazarkadas 2012: 249n51. His argument depends on identifying the magistrate as Charon. Most people—e.g., Knoepfler as cited here; Vottéro 1996: 179–80; Aravantinos and Papazarkadas 2012: 249; and Nikolaos Papazarkadas in this volume—maintain that the change to Attic-Ionic resulted from legislation passed during the 370s. I am not entirely convinced by this and have more sympathy with the position taken on this subject by Paul Iversen (Iversen 2010: 262–64) that it was a gradual process, dictated more by utility and fashion than by any political motivation.

26. See, for example, Vlachogianni 2004–2009: 367–68.

27. If one were looking for symbolism, the shield—also a *hapax*—on the reverse of one of the five Epameinondas varieties might be even more interesting: Hepworth 1998: 81, table 6, no. 35.

28. Issues A1, B4, B5, B7, C1, C2, C3, C4, ΚΑΙΩ(Ν), ΠΟΛΥ, D1, D3, D4, D5, D6, D7, D8, D10.

29. Club: A2, A3, A4, A5, A6, D14, D18, D21, D22; grapes: D10, D11, D12, D13, D14, D15, D16; leaves: A3, A4, A5, A6, D9, APKA; wreaths: A5, A6, A8, B2, B3. Symbols appearing once: corn grain (A7), boukranion (A7), caduceus (B1), incense burner (B2), rosette (D2), shield (D2), crescent (D12), helmet (D17), dolphin (D20), arrow (ΞΕΝΟ).

30. At Thebes (Head 1881: 40–41 and 54–55), Chaironeia (Head 1881: 44), Mykalessos (Head 1881: 47), and Tanagra (Head 1881: 52–53) and in the BO-IΩ series (Head 1881: 77–78).

31. In Boiotia at Thespiai (Head 1881: 55) and in the BO-IΩ series (Head 1881: 77–78).

In Euboia at Chalkis (Babelon 1914: 185–88: caduceus, corn grain, rosette [which Babelon qualifies as βαλαύστιον, that is, flower of the wild pomegranate]) and at Histiaia (Babelon 1914: 203–6: caduceus). The dolphin appears in Euboian coinage that W. P. Wallace dates c. 270/267 (W. P. Wallace 1956: 107–8, 173–76, and 34 and 65–66 for the date).

32. Note that the abbreviation on the reverse of a tetartemorion, H-I, accompanies a bunch of grapes on a vine: BCD 2006: 105 Lot 570.

33. Flament 2010: 53–63.

34. Buckler 1989a (=Buckler and Beck 2008: 224–32); 1989b: 50–53.

35. See Schachter 2014: 326–27.

36. In 351: a "gift" of three hundred talents from the king in reply to a request by the Thebans: Diod. 16.40.1. In 344/343: Boiotian troops hired by the king for a campaign against Egypt: Diod. 16.44.1. See Schachter 2016: 124.

37. Koroneia 353: Buckler 1989b: 71–73; Arist. *Eth. Nic.* 3.8.9; Ephoros *FGrH* 70 F 94; Diod. 16.35.3. Recapture of Orchomenos and Koroneia by the Thebans in 353: Buckler 1989b: 52–54; Demosthenes 16.4, cf. 16.26. Phalaikos' reconquest in 349 of Koroneia, Tilphosssaion, Chorsiai, and Orchomenos: Buckler 1989b: 101–5; Koroneia: Demosthenes 3.27 and schol.; Diod. 16.56.2; Tilphossaion: Diod. 16.56.2, cf. 58.1; Demosthenes 19.141 and 148; Theopompos *FGrH* 115 F 301; Chorsiai: Demosthenes 19.141; Theopompos *FGrH* 115 F 167; Diod. 16.56.1 and 58.2; Orchomenos: Demosthenes 19.141 and 148; Diod. 16.56.2 and 58.1.

38. Rhodes and Osborne 2003: 57=Tod 1948: no. 160=*IG* VII 2418. The date was proposed by M. Guarducci; see below, n. 92. The superscription: [τοὶ χρε]ίματα συνε[βάλονθο ἐν τὸν πόλεμον] | [τὸν] ἐπο⟦λέμιον⟧ Βοιωτοὶ περ[ὶ τῶ ἰαρῶ τῶ ἐμ Βελφοῖς] | [π]ὸτ τὼς ἀσεβίοντας τὸ ἰαρὸ[ν τῶ Ἀπόλλωνος τῶ] | [Π]ουθίω *vac.*

39. Hepworth 1998: 66.23. Presumably he bases this at least in part on the evidence of the so-called Alexander-Eagle hoard found in Thessaly in 1992 and published by Ute Wartenberg (Wartenberg 1998). The coins that she saw—there is some doubt about the actual number of coins in the hoard—consisted of about 35 Philip II staters, 3 Alexander III "Eagle" tetradrachms, 1 or 2 normal Alexander III tetradrachms, 57 Theban magistrates' staters, 16 Sikyon staters, 13 Opountian Lokris staters, and 1 Larissa stater. The non-Theban coins in the hoard are assigned dates between 365 and 330, and the deposit date of the hoard is given as c. 330–300 (Meadows and Wartenberg 2002: 86). The Theban magistrates' staters in this hoard run from the beginning of Hepworth's Group B to the penultimate issue of Group D; four magistrates are represented from Group B (ΘΕΟΓ, ΧΑΡΟ, ΠΕΛΙ, ΠΥΘΙ), two from Group C (ΠΤΟΙ, ΔΑΙΜ), as well as ΚΛΙΩ(Ν) (largest number of specimens—seven—by far) and ΑΡΚΑ, and fourteen from Group D (ΚΑΒΙ, ΕΠΠΑ (D2), ΔΙΟΚ, ΑΓΛΑ, ΚΑΛΛ, ΘΕΟΤ (D3), ΦΙΔΟ, ΑΠΟΛ, ΕΥϜΑΡΑ, ΚΡΑΤ, ΔΙΟΓ, ϜΕΡΓ, ΑΝΤΙ (2), ΔΑΜΟΚΛ). Wartenberg notes that the commonly accepted range for the series is 379/338 and observes (1997: 180) that "the last issue in Hepworth's arrangement with the name ΑΣΩ(Π) is missing, which confirms his interpretation that it was a later issue in this large group," and that "the staters in our hoard show some degree of wear, from which one should assume a certain period of circulation. The fact that most names which come late in the series are represented in the hoard makes a date in the 330s likely." The fact that the Theban coins show a degree of wear suggests that they could have been in circulation for longer than most of the others, and that the hoard was amassed over a period of time, possibly from different sources.

This collection of coins does not add materially to our knowledge of the date of their issue. Even the absence of ΑΣΩ(Π) is not necessarily significant, because, of the thirty-five—or thirty-six—issues from B1 to D22, thirteen (eight in Group D alone) are not represented here, which is a high proportion. The collection was put together in a haphazard rather than a conscious manner. Compare this to the BO-IΩ and magistrates' coins in the Myron-Karditsa hoard, where every issue of the former and every issue in Groups A, B, and C of the latter is represented. Here there was a systematic setting aside of coins, no doubt over a long period of time.

40. Early in the year 2000 a small hoard of silver staters was found in Boiotia "near a sanctuary of unknown identity." It was published by Katerina Liampi in 2008 (Liampi 2008; Hoover, Meadows, and Wartenberg 2010: 27). Four of the coins are from Sikyon, three dating from c. 431–400, the fourth c. 360s/350. Three of the Theban coins have the shield on the obverse and on the reverse Θ-E and a volute amphora in a square incuse. They are dated c. 425/400 B.C. The remaining seven staters are from the magistrates' series, three from Group A (ΔΑΜΟ, FΑΣΤ [two examples]), two from Group B (both ΨΑΡΟ), one example of ΚΛΙΩ, and one of ΑΣΩ, the final issue of Group D. Five of the coins were incised with graffiti: one of the Sikyonian coins (no. 4) carries the letters ΛΕΙΑ, and one of the early Theban ones (no. 5) NIKA, while the ΔΑΜΟ coin (no. 8) has A, one of the FΑΣΤ ones (no. 9) has ΟΝΑΣΙΜ, and the ΚΛΙΩ coin (no. 10) has N. The alphas of nos. 4 and 8 and the epsilon of no. 4 appear to be archaic in form, the N of no. 5 is retrograde, and in no. 9 the sigma has three bars. All of this may be due to the difficulty of incising graffiti on small hard surfaces. Katerina Liampi suggests that this hoard was deposited in a sanctuary by victorious soldiers as a tithe of the booty (λεία) won in a battle (νίκα). The isolated A and N and ΟΝΑΣΙΜ are interpreted as abbreviations of their names. This all seems reasonable. She argues further, on the basis of Hepworth's placing of ΑΣΩ(Π) at the end of the magistrates' series, whose end she accepts as 338 or shortly before, that the victory in question was the one at Chaironeia and that the dedicators were Macedonians. But there are other possible occasions as well if we admit that the series could have ended earlier. For example, in 354 and 353 the Phokians captured Orchomenos and Koroneia, respectively, and took them again in 349, in addition to Tilphossaion and Chorsiai (see above, n. 37). I suggest later that the coin issue of ΑΣΩ(Π) could have been one result of the so-called gift of three hundred talents given by Artaxerxes III to the Thebans. In that case, the campaign of 349 might have provided the occasion for the dedication of this hoard. See below, n. 98.

41. A hoard from Boiotia or Euboia to which a burial date of c. 400 B.C. has been given contains Theban didrachms with the heads of Dionysos and Herakles on the reverse, but no magistrates' coins and no BO-IΩ coins (W. P. Wallace 1956: 49–50=Thompson, Mørkholm, and Kraay 1973: 42=Kraay 1976: 111). This in itself need not be conclusive, but it is well to be cautious. H. B. Mattingly 1989: 230–31 argues that "the hoard's burial date may be as late as 390."

42. Buckler 1989b: 148–95.

43. Plut. *Gen. Socr.* (597A–C). *LGPN* 3B: Καβίριχος (1) (the magistrate on the coins) and (3) (the "federal archon").

44. Svoronos 1916: 296–312, nos. 464–986 (the magistrates' coins). The hoard: Thompson, Mørkholm, and Kraay 1973: 62.

45. Hepworth 1998: 65 on the ΚΛΙΩ(Ν) issue: the Myron(-Karditsa) hoard has specimens of every name in Groups A, B, and C. "In addition the hoard contains 19 specimens of the ΚΛΙΩ(Ν) issue which is asymbolic and not die-linked to any other issue. The ΚΛΙΩ(Ν) issue has three die-linked varieties: ΚΛ-ΙΩ, ΚΛΙΩΝ, and ΚΛ-ΙΩΝ. The linkage shows that the two ΚΛΙΩΝ

variants are later. All 19 specimens in Myron are from the earlier ΚΑΙΩ variety, mostly in unworn condition. . . . The Boiotian issues in the Myron hoard were clearly completed mid-way through the ΚΑΙΩ(Ν) issue, before either of the two ΚΑΙΩΝ varieties were in common circulation. This fortunate end-date for the Myron magistrates allows us to place the ΚΑΙΩ(Ν) issue immediately after the last issue in Group C (ΔΑΙΜ)."

46. Hepworth 1998: 66: "Like ΚΑΙΩ(Ν) the ARKA issue is not die-linked to any other magistrate. *Termini post* and *ante quem* are established by the absence of ΑΡΚΑ from the Myron hoard and its presence in the Thessaly 1978 hoard whose linked magistrate sequence ends seven issues after those of Myron. It seems logical to place both the unlinked issues together and ARKA is therefore tentatively positioned between the ΚΑΙΩ(Ν) and KABI issues." Hepworth 1998: 67: "The other unlinked issues—ΞΕΝΟ and ΠΟΛΥ—should be regarded as probable forgeries until any further specimens appear, preferably from a certain hoard provenance. However, if ΠΟΛΥ—known from only a single museum example—is genuine, it would probably belong on stylistic grounds to the same period as the ΚΑΙΩ(Ν) and ΑΡΚΑ issues."

47. Xen. *Hell.* 5.2.29 (θέρους δὲ ὄντος), and Aristeides i p. 419 Dindorf xix=xxii Keil (τοῦτο μὲν Πυθίων ὄντων ἡ Καδμεία κατελήφθη). See Schachter 1981–1994: 3.48–49.

48. Xen. *Hell.* 5.2.31.

49. The Olynthians, for example: Xen. *Hell.* 5.2.15.

50. See for now Robinson 2011: 56–57.

51. Θηβαίοις συντελεῖν: Isokrates 14.8 (*Plat.*); συντελεῖν εἰς τὰς Θήβας: Isokrates 14.9, and *Hell. Oxy.*=*FGrH* 66 F1 265 (referring to an earlier occasion); Diod. 12.41, 15.38–39, 50, 70.

52. Aravantinos and Papazarkadas 2012.

53. Head 1881: 77–78; 1911: 352; Kisseoglou 1955; Kraay 1976: 113.

54. BCD 2006: 15 Lot 6.

55. BCD 2006: 94 Lot 496.

56. Cf. BCD 2006: 17 Lot 20 and possibly 94 Lot 495.

57. Hepworth 1989: 36.

58. See Roesch 1965: 157–78.

59. Later practice shows just how flexible the Thebans could be in assigning magistrates to supervise the coinage. Bronze coins of the first and early second centuries A.D. bear on the reverse the legends ΕΠΙ ΑΡΧΙ—ΠΕΜΠΤΙΔΟΥ, ΕΠΙ ΠΟΛΕΜ Γ Κ ΜΑΚΡΟΥ, and ΕΠΙ ΜΑΡΚΟΥ ΠΟΛΕΜ ΘΗΒΑΙΩΝ (Head 1881: 95, 96, and 97, respectively). Pemptides was probably chief priest of the Imperial cult (see Koumanoudes 1966 and *LGPN* 3b Πεμπτίδης 2). So we see that within a relatively short time span (one of the Pemptides coins is on the reverse of a head of Galba, the coin of Marcus on the reverse of Trajan; Head 1881: 95, who suggests that ΜΑΡΚΟΥ is a mistake or misreading for ΜΑΚΡΟΥ, in which case they would belong together) not only a magistrate but also a prominent private citizen held the office.

60. The abbreviations should properly be expanded into the genitive case. Nikolaos Papazarkadas has pointed out to me that ΛΥΚΙΝΩ on a bronze issue (Head 1881: 70) is obviously in the genitive, giving the meaning "in the year/tenure of Lykinos."

61. The leaders of the anti-Spartan faction in Thebes during the earlier years of the fourth century B.C. are named by Xenophon as Androkleidas, Ismenias, and Galaxidoros. It was they, according to Xenophon, who accepted money from Timokrates of Rhodes, the Persian agent (Xen. *Hell.* 5.2.31). The Oxyrhynchos historian identifies the leaders of the two opposing factions at Thebes as Hismenias, Antitheos, and Androkleidas, who were said to have been pro-Athenian; and Leontiades, As<t>ias, and Koiratadas, who favoured the Lakedaimonians

(*Hell. Oxy.* 20.1 Chambers). Plutarch identifies the recipients of the Persian money in 395 as Androkleidas and Amphitheos (Plut. *Lys.* 27.1). Pausanias names them as Androkleidas, Ismenias, and Amphithemis (Paus. 3.9.8). Androkleidas occurs in all the lists, Hismenias in all but one. They were clearly the leading members of their faction, both in the 390s and at the time of the coup of 382. Of the other names—Galaxidoros, Antitheos, Amphitheos, and Amphithemis—we can probably dismiss Amphithemis as a mistaken reading for Amphitheos. Amphitheos was an important figure of the opposition to the pro-Spartan government; he was imprisoned under sentence of death by Leontiades in 379 but was set free by the liberators (Plut. *Gen. Socr.* 577D, 586F, 594D, 598A, 598B). Galaxidoros, whom Xenophon names, was another member of the anti-Spartan faction. He apparently stayed behind in Thebes after the coup but seems—like Epameinondas—not to have come to any harm (Plut. *Gen. Socr.* passim). There is ample room for confusing the names of the third member of the triumvirate. The clue comes from the fact that the opposing leaders are named in groups of three, whereas it is obvious that there were two dominant leaders on the anti-Spartan side and one—Leontiades—on the pro-Spartan side. What we seem to have are the names of colleges of polemarchs—there were always three of them—and it is not impossible that we have, on the anti-Spartan side, the names of sets of polemarchs of three different years. If this is so, there is no reason to reject any of them except Amphithemis.

62. *LGPN* 3B: Ϝαστίας (2). Of the other two members of Wastias's cohort, Leontiadas (*LGPN* 3B: Λεοντιάδας [2]) is best known as the instigator of the coup of 382 and one of the leading members of the junta that ran Thebes from the middle of 382 to the end of 379, the others being Archias (*LGPN* 3B: Ἀρχίας [14]) and Philippos (*LGPN* 3B: Φίλιππος [23]), who were polemarchs in 379 (we do not know the name of the third polemarch, although Xen. *Hell.* 5.4.5 and 5.4.7 makes it clear that there were three), and Hypatas (*LGPN* 3B: Ὑπάτης [1]), who is known only from Plut. *Pel.* 11.1 and *Gen. Socr.* 596C, where he is the last of the group to be killed. Kabirichos, the eponymous archon, was at most a friendly neutral. The third member of Wastias' cohort, Koiratadas (*LGPN* 3B: Κοιρατάδας [2]), was at the siege of Byzantion in 408 (Xen. *Hell.* 1.3.15–17, 21–22) and served as a mercenary general in Asia in 400 B.C. (Xen. *Anab.* 7.1.33). He appears in *Hell. Oxy.* 20 Chambers as Κορραντάδας: the emendation is undoubtedly correct.

63. *LGPN* 3B: Ἀνδροκλείδας (2). Plut. *Pel.* 5.3, 6.3; Xen. *Hell.* 5.2.31 and 35. He left money in Athens to his fellow exile Pherenikos, son of Kephisodotos: Lysias fr. XXIV.1 Gernet-Bizos.

64. *LGPN* 3B: Ἀμφίθεος (1), where Antitheos and Amphithemis are both reduced to incorrect readings. See above, n. 61.

65. *LGPN* 3B: Ηισμεινίας (9). Plato *Rep.* 1.336a; *Meno* 90a; Plut. *Tranq. anim.* 472D; *Cupid. divit.* 527B; cf. *Praec. ger. reip.* 823E.

66. Xen. *Hell.* 5.2.25.

67. Xen. *Hell.* 5.2.35–36; Plut. *Pel.* 5.3.

68. *SEG* XXXIV 355, for Athenaios of Macedon, and *IG* VII 2407, for Nobas of Carthage. The stone bearing *IG* VII 2407 is lost; R. Pococke read TIMOM in line 12, and Dittenberger restored this to Τίμωνο|ς, but Denis Knoepfler has restored Τιμόλαος instead of Τίμωνος: Knoepfler 2005: 84–85, fig. 16 ("Tableau des béotarques des années 371–362"); see too Knoepfler 2009: no. 261 and *SEG* LVIII 448. Timolaos might have been related to—perhaps the father of—Philip II's friend Timolaos, who was killed as being a Macedonian sympathizer in the uprising before the destruction of Thebes in 335 B.C. Three Theban friends of Philip—Timolaos, Anemoitas (*LGPN* 3B [1]), and Theogeiton (*LGPN* 3B [5])—were excoriated by Demosthenes for being the ruin of Thebes: 18.48 and 295; cf. Theopompos, *FGrH* 115 F 203, Dinarchos 1.74, and Polyb. 18.4.4. Two of them—Timolaos and Anemoitas—were murdered in 335 by insurgents

before Alexander's siege: Arrian *Anab.* 1.7.1. (called Amyntas and Timolaos, two members of the garrison on the Kadmeia). For these, see Berve 1926: 31.62 Ἀμύντας (=Anemoitas) and 374.752 Τιμόλαος.

69. Plut. *Pel.* 8.2.

70. Plut. *Gen. Socr.* 594D.

71. Plut. *Gen. Socr.* 597C.

72. *IG* VII 2462=*CEG* II 632*=Tod 1948: no. 130=Rhodes and Osborne 2003: no. 30.

73. Paus. 6.6.2 (at Olympia): Πολύκλειτος δὲ Ἀργεῖος, οὐχ ὁ τῆς Ἥρας τὸ ἄγαλμα ποιήσας, μαθητὴς δὲ Ναυκύδους, παλαιστὴν παῖδα εἰργάσατο Θηβαῖον Ἀγήνορα. ἀνετέθη δὲ ἡ εἰκὼν ὑπὸ τοῦ Φωκέων κοινοῦ· Θεόπομπος γὰρ ὁ πατὴρ τοῦ Ἀγήνορος πρόξενος τοῦ ἔθνους ἦν αὐτῶν (Polykleitos of Argos, not the one who made the cult image of Hera, but the one who was a student of Naukydes, made a statue of a boy wrestler, Agenor of Thebes. The statue was dedicated by the Phokian Koinon because Agenor's father, Theopompos, was a proxenos of their ethnos). There were not many occasions during the fourth century B.C. when a Theban would have become a proxenos of the Phokians. The one that springs to mind is the period soon after the battle of Leuktra, when the Thebans formed an alliance with them: Xen. *Hell.* 6.5.23, 7.5.4, and cf. *Ages.* 2.24. The statue of his son Agenor could have been put up between 370 and 357, in which case the sculptor could have been either Polykleitos II or III: *LGPN* 3B: Θεόπομπος (4) (5), Ἀγάνωρ (1).

74. Buckler 1980: 135. On his career, see Schachter 2004: 359–60; and Mackil 2008: 164.

75. Plut. *Pel.* 27–29; Diod. 15.71.2.

76. Plut. *Artaxerxes* 22.8; Aelian *VH* 1.21.

77. *CID* 2.43.21–22.

78. *LGPN* 3B: Ἰσμεινίας (11). Mackil 2008; *SEG* LV 564bis and LVIII 448.

79. Arist. *Rh.* 2.23.11 (1398b).

80. Arrian *Anab.* 2.15.2–4; Schachter 2004: 359–60.

81. Vlachogianni 2004–2009 (*SEG* LVIII 447).

82. Vlachogianni 2004–2009: 363.

83. Plut. *Pel.* 35.2. *LGPN* 3B: Διογίτων (10).

84. *SEG* LV 564bis and LVIII 448. For his probable ancestry, see Mackil 2008: 164–65. The exact date of this decree is open to question, but it belongs in the 360s.

85. *IG* VII 2407, where his name is restored by Knoepfler 2005: 81–83.

86. Plut. *Pel.* 8.2. See the earlier mention of these exiles.

87. Paus. 9.13.6. *LGPN* 3B: Δαμοκλείδας (2).

88. Asopodoros: an Asopodoros was one of the boiotarchs in *IG* VII 2408, the proxeny decree in honor of a Byzantine (*LGPN* 3B: Ἀσωπόδωρος [10]); another was *hieromnemon* at Delphi in 340 (*CID* 2.43.47; *LGPN* 3B: Ἀσωπόδωρος [3]); and a third was one of the Thebans who loaned money to the Karystians during the second quarter of the fourth century (*IG* XII 9.7; Migeotte 1984: 73). Asopichos: there are two Thebans known by this name, unless they are the same person: one was the father of Timokles, who won horse races at the Basileia and the Herakleia, and whose statue, carved by a Polykleitos, was rescued from the ruins of Thebes and set up again (*IG* VII 2532=*CEG* II 630 [Timokles] and 2533=*CEG* II 786 [Korbeidas]; *LGPN* 3B: Ἀσώπιχος [8]); the other was ἐρώμενος of Epameinondas, fought at Leuktra, and dedicated his shield at Delphi to commemorate the affair; this must have been some time after the battle because it had a copy of the trophy on it (Theopompos, *FGrH* 115 F 247 [Athenaios 13 (604F–605A)]). He also fought alongside Epameinondas at Mantineia and survived (Plut. *Amat.* [761D]; *LGPN* 3B: Ἀσώπιχος [12]). Asopoteles: an Asopoteles was a boiotarch in another of the proxeny decrees (*SEG* XXXIV 355; *LGPN* 3B: Ἀσωποτέλης [1]).

89. Hepworth 1998: 67.

90. Paus. 9.13.6–7; cf. Diod. 15.53.3.

91. See above, n. 72.

92. See above, n. 38. The date proposed by Guarducci 1930: 321–25 is generally accepted. Tod 1948 2.177–179.160 is more circumspect and dates it "355–1 B.C." Roesch 1965: 79 is even more cautious: "au cours de la Guerre Sacrée entre 355 et 346."

93. BCD 2006: 99.527a–b; Head 1881: 70.

94. Hepworth 1998: 66.23.

95. Hepworth 1998: 66.24.

96. See Munn 1993: 137.

97. *LGPN* 3B ΕὐϜάρατος (1).

98. Diod. 16.40.1–2; Buckler 1989b: 100, who suggests that the money was given in payment for the provision of hoplites to assist the king in his unsuccessful campaign to regain Egypt. See too n. 40 above.

99. For the process, see Kroll 2011.

100. As early as the Myron-Karditsa hoard, which I think was deposited by a Theban, 326 out of some 1,650 coins—just under 20 percent—were Aiginetan. Cf. too *CID* 2.13 line 15 of 340 B.C.—Aiginetan coinage for donations (in common with others).

101. Hepworth 1989: 37: "The ΕΠΠΑ/ΕΠΑΜ(Ι) issue is the twenty-third in the series, and the third after the deposition of the Myron hoard." He dates the Epameinondas coins to 364, which would give 367 for the deposit of the hoard. Warren 2000: 204: "Sikyon's output of staters falls decisively into two groups, those which are extensively represented in the Myron hoard (*IGCH* 62), and those struck subsequent to its burial, which is probably to be dated to c. 364 BC[22]"; and 204n22: "The hoard contained in large numbers half the known magistrate-varieties of the Theban staters with Boiotian shield and krater [*sic*]. A burial date of c. 364 BC seems more likely than c. 350 BC (as *IGCH* 62), if these staters were struck to finance the campaigns of Pelopidas and Epaminondas in the period of the Theban hegemony down to 362 BC. Robert Hepworth, who is publishing a study of this series, independently arrived at a similar dating. It is important to note that wear and other reasons point to the output of Sikyonian staters in the hoard having stopped well before the burial of the hoard."

CHAPTER 4. BOIOTIAN DEMOCRACY?

My thanks to Samuel Gartland for inviting me to contribute to this book.

1. Main features, Thuc. 5.38.1–3, *Hell. Oxy.* 19.2–4 Chambers; for the characterization, cf. Thuc. 3.62.3. This constitution is described as oligarchic by Thuc. 5.31.6; cf. 4.76.2; see Larsen 1955, arguing that in the late fifth century there were dissidents who would have preferred democracy.

2. *Hell. Oxy.* 19.2 Chambers was willing to include under the term *politai* the poorer men who failed to satisfy the property qualification.

3. Probably only nine units until 427, when Thebes added to its original two units two for the destroyed Plataia and its dependencies.

4. It is often thought that these four groups influenced the four groups within the council proposed in the "future constitution" promulgated for Athens by the oligarchs in 411: *Ath. Pol.* 30.3.

5. Xen. *Hell.* 5.1.30–3; cf. Diod. 14.110.3–4.

6. Occupation of Thebes, Xen. *Hell.* 5.2.23–36, Diod. 15.20, Plut. *Ages.* 23.6–24.1, *Pel.* 5–6; tyranny in Thebes, Xen. *Hell.* 5.4.2; *dynasteiai* in other cities, Xen. *Hell.* 5.4.46 (and for the significance of the word, cf. Thuc. 3.62.3).

7. Xen. *Hell.* 5.4.2, Diod. 15.25.1, Plut. *Pel.* 7–12.

8. *IG* II^2 43=Rhodes and Osborne 2003: 22.24–25, 79; negotiations, 72–77.

9. Plut. *Pel.* 13.1, 14.2.

10. Isoc. 14.29 (*Plat.*).

11. Thirteen years, Plut. *Pel.* 34.7; not boiotarch in 371, Paus. 9.13.6–7 (but boiotarch every year, Diod. 15.81.4).

12. E.g., Busolt 1920–1926: 2.1424, 1425, 1428; Larsen 1968: 175–78 (but with qualifications); Buckler 1980: 33, 34–45 (emphatically, and suggesting Athenian influence, despite stressing the power of the boiotarchs at 24–30); M. H. Hansen, in Hansen and Nielsen 2004: 455 (of Thebes; at 432 he does not characterize the post-379 federation).

13. E.g., Rhodes 2010: 284.

14. Xen. *Hell.* 5.4.46; Diod. 15.34.2; 37.2; Plut. *Pel.* 13.6–7.

15. Polyb. 6.43.4–7 says that the rise of Thebes was due to its leading men rather than to its constitution; in 6.44.7 he writes of the power of the mob (*ochlos*), which could be a comment on the use of an assembly rather than a council; in 8.35.6, with reference to Pelopidas' action against the tyrants of Pherai, he states that Pelopidas persuaded Epameinondas to champion the democracy not only of the Thebans but of the Greeks (on which Walbank 1957–1979: 2:111 remarks that "the extent of democracy should not be exaggerated").

16. Xen. *Hell.* 5.4.46 (cf. this chapter at n. 6).

17. In the translation of Warner 1979, "as previously in Thebes" would imply that the *dynasteiai* were set up after the liberation of Thebes, but "previously" corresponds to nothing in the Greek text (ὥσπερ ἐν Θήβαις).

18. This was one of the qualifications of Larsen 1968: 178. Buckler 2003: 215 wrote that "The criteria for citizenship, whether local or federal, remains [*sic*] unknown."

19. Paus. 9.1.6. He writes of the Thebans (cf. Diod. 15.46.4–6), but the decision to destroy Plataia may technically have been a decision of the federation (cf. this chapter following n. 26).

20. There may have been an archon in the previous federation, but there is no evidence for one.

21. E.g., Busolt 1920–1926: 2:1429; Larsen 1968: 178–79; Buckler 1980: 23–24.

22. Buck 1994: 108–9 with 159–60n40: the inscription that he cited for non-Theban boiotarchs (*SEG* XXV 553) is to be dated after 338 (*SEG* XXXII 476, L 486).

23. E.g., Sordi 1973: 79–82; Knoepfler 2000: 351–55; cf. *SEG* L 481. Knoepfler argues that after 335 there were seven *tele* (for a time eight), each of which supplied one boiotarch, and suspects that while the number seven was inspired by the seven gates of legendary Thebes, the continuation of seven boiotarchs after Alexander's destruction of Thebes suggests that the *tele* were created as districts, but not as electoral units, perhaps in the 370s (2000: 358–59). Samuel Gartland reminds me of the seven liberators of Thebes in Xen. *Hell.* 5.4.1.

24. The *koinos synodos* of Diod. 15.80.2 is the federal assembly.

25. Lebadeia, *IG* VII 3054, 3055; Thebes, *BCH* 94 (1970): 140–44 no. 1 (cf. *SEG* XXVIII 465, XXXII 430), *SEG* XXVIII 466.

26. Xen. *Hell.* 7.3.5(–12); on Diod. 17.9.1 in a revolutionary situation in 335, see discussion later in this chapter, with n. 36.

27. *SEG* XXXIV 355, *IG* VII 2407=Rhodes and Osborne 2003: 43, *IG* VII 2408 with *SEG* XXXIV 355; *SEG* LV 564 bis, *SEG* LVIII 447. *SEG* LV 564 bis exceptionally names the pro-

poser, Ismenias; he was a prominent man, but he was not a boiotarch when he made the proposal if D. Knoepfler is right to restore in *IG* VII 2407 the archon of *SEG* LV 564 (2005: 77–87).

28. Buckler 1980: 25 with 283–84nn27, 29. For the incident in 421/420, see Thuc. 5.38.2–3. But Plut. *Pel.* 12.6–7 refers to the time of the liberation in 379, when there was not even an established Theban constitution; otherwise, the only text that might support this view is Diod. 15.79.5, where turncoats in Orchomenos betrayed their fellow conspirators to "the boiotarchs," and "the *archontes*" arrested the Orchomenian knights and brought them before the (presumably federal) assembly, which condemned them and their city (which could have happened without their having a formal probouleutic role).

29. In 411, Thuc. 8.67.3, *Ath. Pol.* 29.5; 411/410, Thuc. 8.97.1–2, *Ath. Pol.* 33.1; 404/403, Xen. *Hell.* 2.3.18; 321–318, inscriptions, e.g., *IG* II^2 380; 317–307, inscriptions, e.g., *IG* II^2 450.

30. Argos used *aliaia* both in the early fifth century when it was oligarchic and in the later fifth century when it was democratic: *SEG* XIII 239, XXXIII 275. In Boiotia, Lebadeia in fact used *polis*: cf. the discussion earlier in this chapter, with n. 26.

31. In 370, e.g., Plut. *Pel.* 24–25; Diod. 15.72.2. Cf. Fröhlich 2004; Rhodes 2005: 1–7.

32. Paus. 9.14.7. In Athens in 411 the Four Hundred chose their *prytaneis* by lot: Thuc. 8.70.1.

33. Buckler 1980: 32.

34. Plut. *Pel.* 25.7–14, discussed by Buckler 1980: 32–33.

35. Just. *Epit.* 9.4.7–10.

36. Arr. *Anab.* 1.7. 2 (<καὶ αὐτονομίαν> Abicht, preferable to <καὶ παρρησίαν> Krüger); Diod. 17.9.1.

37. Diod. 15.79.3–6. The federal assembly, Stylianou 1998: 498.

38. *IG* V.ii 1 = Rhodes and Osborne 2003: 32.3–4.

39. E. Meyer, in *RE* Supp. XV (1978), 136–55 at 151. Hellenistic decrees were enacted by an assembly that could be referred to as "demos" (*IG* V.i 1425.4–5), "the Messenians" (*SEG* XII 371.14), or *polis* (*IG* V.ii 1419.9–10; cf. *SEG* XII 371.11); G. Shipley in Hansen and Nielsen 2004: 563 goes too far in writing of "democratic institutions."

40. Xen. *Hell.* 7.1.44–6,3; cf. Diod. 15.70.3. Buckler 1980: 183 remarks on "tacit approval of Euphron's moves towards radical democracy in Sikyon," but the Boiotians accepted oligarchy before and after, and in his summing up of Epameinondas, p. 221, he comments, "Nor did Epameinondas try to use democracies against oligarchies."

41. Xen. *Hell.* 7.1.41–43; the brief mention in Diod. 15.75.2 says nothing about that.

42. Just. *Epit.* 16.4.1–4. Cited as evidence for support of democracy, Buckler 1980: 183; but contrast 172.

43. Beck 2000: 344.

44. *Hell. Oxy.* 19.4 Chambers. Some have taken this as a statement that the councilors had to pay their own expenses, but that seems unlikely; see Bruce 1967: 108 (numbering this passage 11.4).

CHAPTER 5. DIODOROS 15.78.4–79.1 AND THEBAN RELATIONS WITH THE BOSPORUS IN THE FOURTH CENTURY

All dates are B.C. Thanks are due to Samuel Gartland for the invitation to submit this chapter, to the anonymous reviewer, who made a number of useful observations, and to David Whitehead, who read and offered helpful comments on an earlier version. All errors remain my own.

1. Cf. Buckler 1980: 160–75; Jehne 1999: 328–29; Ruzicka 1998; J. Roy, *CAH* VI², 200–2; Buckler 2000a: 359–61; Buckler 2000b: 438–40; Buckler and Beck 2008; Hornblower 2011: 260–63; Mackil 2008: 181–85; Mackil 2013: 80–81, 84; Tejada 2015.

2. Stylianou 1998: 494–95. In Diodoros' account, the Athenian general Laches, in command of a στόλος ἀξιόλογος, was overawed by Epameinondas' force and refused to fight. If this means that the force with Epameinondas was significant enough to discourage Athenian resistance, then presumably the one hundred triremes had already been built before 364/363. To allow for this, attempts have been made to push back the genesis of Epameinondas' policy to 367/366, and Persian gold has been invoked to explain how the Thebans could have afforded such a venture: cf. Buckler 1980: 161; Sealey 1993: 90; Buckler 1998: 192; Roy, *CAH* VI², 201; Buckler 2000a: 359; Buckler and Beck 2008: 180, 182. Yet it is more likely that Laches refused to fight for political reasons, since resisting Epameinondas would entail breaking the peace of 366/365: cf. Cawkwell 1972: 271; Ruzicka 1998: 61; Stylianou 1998: 496. Schachter 2014: 325–27 makes the plausible suggestion that money to pay for the fleet came from or was expected to come from the three cities visited by Epameinondas.

3. On the cleruchy, cf. Cargill 1983. On its connection to the voyage, cf. Cawkwell 1972: 271–73, and Hornblower 2011: 260–62.

4. So Ruzicka 1998: 62–63, noting that the recent rejection of Pelopidas' Theban-sponsored peace made the Thebans' claim to leadership of Greece shaky at best: Xen. *Hell.* 7.1.39–40.

5. Diod. 16.7.3–4, 22.1–2. For this chronology, see Cawkwell 1962: 43–49; Buckler 1980: 171; Cargill 1981: 178–79; Cawkwell 1981: 53–55; Hornblower 1982: 209; and Peake 1997.

6. Roy, *CAH* VI², 202: "no lasting gains for Thebes seem to have been made, except perhaps to detach Byzantion from alliance with Athens"; Buckler 1980: 173: "Despite the glory of sailing the Aegean unopposed and thereby defying the Athenian navy, Epameinondas returned home without having accomplished anything of note." Stylianou 1998: "The naval enterprise, therefore, came to very little" (497). Cf. Buckler 1998: 195 for similar sentiments. On Keos, cf. below. By contrast, see Ruzicka 1998 for the opposite extreme: Epameinondas' expedition was what sparked the Social War.

7. Isoc. 5.53: the Thebans sent triremes to Byzantion "as if [ὡς καὶ] they would rule by land and by sea."

8. Plut. *Phil.* 14.1.

9. Stylianou 1998: 494–95, discussing these pieces of evidence, points out that Epameinondas' rhetoric was probably exaggerated in Athens and our sources. See also Cawkwell 1972: 270.

10. Xen. *Hell.* 4.8.27–28, 31 (Chalkedon). For Thrasyboulos' activities in the period before the King's Peace, cf. Seager 1967; Perlman 1968; and Cawkwell 1976.

11. Plut. *Per.* 37; cf. Braund 2005.

12. Thuc. 1.94–96.

13. *IG* I³ 259.III.7; 261.V.29; 263.V.16; 279.II.32; 281.III.18. Across the whole empire only Aegina and Thasos, the two contributors of thirty talents, paid consistently more than Byzantion: noted by Merle 1916: 20n5.

14. See Heskel 1997: 65. Buckler 1980: 172 suggests that Epameinondas sailed on through the straits to Herakleia, although Justin implies that the Herakleiots' appeals were unsuccessful.

15. Kraay 1976: 114n1; Hepworth 1989: 39–40; Hornblower 2011: 262; but cf. Schachter, chapter 3 in this volume.

16. *SEG* XLIV 901. Cf. Blümel 1994; Buckler 1998; and Schachter 2014: 326.

17. Tod 1948: no. 142. See Cartledge 1987: 311; and Hornblower 2011: 263. During the revolt the Keans allied with Histiaia on Euboea, a Boiotian ally: Tod 141. It may therefore be that this is the context of an inscription from Thebes published in 2012, which preserves an alliance between Histiaia and the Thebans, and which accords "hegemony by land and sea" to the Thebans. The editors, however, prefer on the basis of letter forms to date this inscription to 377/376, when the Thebans occupied Histiaia (Xen. *Hell.* 5.4.56), although they note that a post-Leuktra date remains possible: Aravantios and Papazarkadas 2012.

18. Roesch 1965: 75–76, 101; Roesch 1984b links the decrees with the Theban naval programme of 364/363. Glotz (1933) suggests that the Carthaginian was given proxeny in exchange for technical help with the shipbuilding: cf. Rhodes and Osborne 2003: 43. Athenaeus son of Demonicus of Macedon may have come from a trierarchic family: cf. Arr. *Ind.* 18.3, with Hornblower 2011: 262. Schachter 2014: 326–27 with n. 58 makes a link between the Byzantine honored with proxeny here and Byzantine financial help to Thebes in connection with Epameinondas' shipbuilding project. For the connection between these decrees and the naval expedition, and for the view that they illustrate that the voyage was considerably more ambitious than often thought, see Mackil 2008: 181–85, and Mackil 2013: 420–26.

19. Vlachogianni 2004–2009. The ethnic is restored at l.5, which reads . . . ινθίως. The restoration Perinthos is discounted by the editor as being unlikely on historical grounds (p. 365), but Epameinondas' presence at Byzantion would put him in close proximity to the city at this time. On the Lakonian Timeas, cf. Mackil 2008. Epameinondas' voyage might also have had a destabilizing effect in cities in the Black Sea and the Hellespont: Tejada 2015 discusses the evidence of political instability in the region from Aeneas Tacticus.

20. Ruzicka 1998.

21. Busolt 1874: 803; Accame 1941: 179n3; Bury and Meiggs 1975: 546n16; Stylianou 1998: 496; Hornblower 1982: 200–201; Jehne 1994: 116; Ruzicka 1998: 60–61; Jehne 1999: 338–39; Hornblower 2011: 262; Tejada 2015: 53. For some examples of the ways this phrase has been interpreted, cf. Miller, *RE* III (1897) s.v. Byzantion, col. 1133 ("wandte sich Epaminondas mit Erfolg auch B."); Merle 1916: 38–39 ("die Byzantier nahmen ihm auf"); Cawkwell 1972: 271 ("made the cities friendly to the Thebans"); and Buckler 1998: 194 ("he procured the independent cities for the Thebans").

22. An early revolt might explain a detail in Nepos, *Timoth.* 1.2, according to which Timotheos conquered Byzantion and Olynthos. However, the conquest of Byzantion is not mentioned by Isoc. 15.7–14; cf. Busolt 1874: 811; Merle 1916: 39–40n8; Cawkwell 1972: 270–71n4; Ruzicka 1998: 67 with n. 27; Jehne 1999: 339.

23. Diod. 16.7.3; cf. Cawkwell 1972: 270n4.

24. [Dem.] 50.6–7 (implicating also the Kyzicenes), 17–19; cf. Dem. 5.25 and [Dem.] 45.64. *On the Peace* was delivered in 346, and *Against Stephanus I* was composed in 349. Evidently, the Byzantines' beaching of grain ships was not a one-off occurrence limited to 362, but recurred many times after Epameinondas' reception in the city. Possibly it became a regular occurrence after 362. It may also have been directed more generally against ships passing between the Black Sea and Greece, not just Athens-bound ships.

25. [Dem.] 50.6: ἕνεκα τῆς ἰδίας χρείας τοῦ σίτου.

26. [Arist.] *Oec.* 1346b29–33. See Gabrielsen 2007: 312.

27. Miller, *RE* III (1897) s.v. Byzantion, col. 1133, identifies both episodes.

28. Buckler 2000b: 440: "Tensions existed between Athens and Byzantion before 357 BC, but the Athenians did not consider these differences to amount to acts of war"; Roy, *CAH* VI^2,

202n17: "unfriendly"; Cawkwell 1972: 323n86: "The beaching of corn-ships does not necessarily argue more than bad relations." Cf. Hornblower 1982: 203; and Ruzicka 1998: 67, who takes this episode as evidence that the Byzantines remained alienated from Athens.

29. Properly stressed by Berthold 1980: 42n44.

30. Xen. *Hell.* 1.1.35–36; 2.2.1–2, 5–9. It also prompted a rise in grain prices in Peiraieus: [Dem.] 50.6.

31. Xen. *Hell.* 5.1.1–31.

32. Didymus, *Dem.* 10.34–11.5=*FGrH* 115 F 292; 328 F 162; cf. Dem. 18.71–72, 138; [Dem.] 11.1 et schol. Only Diod. 16.77.2 fails to mention the ships. As told by Demosthenes (18.241), Philip's aim was to become "lord of the grain supply of the Greeks" (τῆς σιτοπομπίας τῶν Ἑλλήνων κύριος).

33. Polyb. 4.38.1–10.

34. Buckler 1980: 170–71; cf. Fossey 1979.

35. On the view that Byzantion revolted in response to Epameinondas' visit, cf. also Mackil 2013: 80 with n. 129, and 285 with n. 171. For the connection between Epameinondas' visit and the beaching of the grain ships, see also Hornblower 2011: 262.

36. Dem. 15.26: τί δήποτ' ἐν Βυζαντίῳ οὐδείς ἐσθ' ὁ διδάξων ἐκείνους μὴ καταλαμβάνειν Χαλκηδόνα, ἣ βασιλέως μέν ἐστιν, εἴχετε δ' αὐτὴν ὑμεῖς, ἐκείνοις δ' οὐδαμόθεν προσῆκε· μηδὲ Σηλυμβρίαν, πόλιν ὑμετέραν ποτὲ σύμμαχον οὖσαν, ὡς αὑτοὺς συντελῆ ποιεῖν καὶ Βυζάντιον ὁρίζειν τὴν τούτων χώραν παρὰ τοὺς ὅρκους καὶ τὰς συνθήκας, ἐν αἷς αὐτονόμους τὰς πόλεις εἶναι γέγραπται; trans. Vince, Loeb.

37. *FGrH* 115 F 62=Athen. 12.526e. For hostilities between Byzantion and Chalkedon, note also Aen. Tac. 12.3 and Polyaen. 6.25.

38. Miller, *RE* III (1897) s.v. Byzantion, col. 1134 ("B. benützte den glücklichen Ausgang des Kriegs [i.e., the Social War], um seine Macht über Kalchedon und Selymbria auszudehnen, gegen die Verträge"); Merle 1916: 42–43; Gehrke 1985: 37, dating the installation of democracy in Chalkedon to 354/353; Isaac 1986: 220, seemingly connecting these episodes to the Social War; Shrimpton 1991: 68–69 ("The grab for territory is most naturally associated with the annulment of Athenian authority in the region, in other words, the Social War"); Radicke 1995: 142; Łajtar and Loukopoulou, *IACP*, 917 (354/353 "or slightly later"). The episode is dated to 357, the outbreak of the Social War, by Merkelbach (1980: 94), and A. Avram, *IACP*, 980. Stylianou 1998: 497 also makes mention of a policy of aggrandizement in the region, connecting the beaching of ships with the taking of Chalkedon, but without settling on a date.

39. *IG* II^2 1437.16–17. Cited by Radicke 1995: 142; cf. also Merle 1916: 43n5.

40. Xen. *Hell.* 5.1.31; Diod. 14.110.2–4.

41. Note, however, the possibility (discussed earlier) that a Theban proxeny decree published in 2010 relates to Perinthians.

42. Polyb. 18.2.4, 44.4. For this document's authenticity, see Treves 1940; J. Robert and L. Robert, *BE* 1946–47: 24; Robert 1962: 64n2; Wankel 1976: 487–88; and Canevaro 2013: 261–67. Merle 1916: 43–44 with n. 8 also connects Byzantion's acquisition of the port of Phileas on the Black Sea (Steph. Byz. s.v. Φιλέας; Ps.-Scym. 723) to the same period as the annexation of Chalkedon, though gives no arguments.

43. *FGrH* 70 F 83=Steph. Byz. s.v. Χρυσόπολις.

44. Stylianou 1998: 95, 497; cf. Buckler 2000b: 446n32.

45. Diod. 14.31.4; Xen. *Hell.* 1.1.22 (τῆς Καλχηδονίας εἰς Χρυσόπολιν); Strab. 12.4.2. Buckler 2000b: 446n32 notes that Chalkedon belonged to the King, and considers it unlikely the Persians would have assented to the gift of Chrysopolis to Byzantion. But Artaxerxes had re-

cently adopted a pro-Theban stance, and might have agreed to the Thebans' request if it was likely to threaten Athens. Furthermore, Chalkedon, despite being bound by the terms of the King's Peace, was nevertheless found seizing Athenian grain ships in 362.

46. Dion. Byz. 109 (ed. Güngerich).

47. Xen. *Hell.* 1.1.22; Diod. 13.64.2–3; cf. Polyb. 3.2.5, 4.44.4–5, 52.5. Possibly the two are synonyms, and both tolls were levied on shipping sailing into and out of the Black Sea: Walbank 1957–1979: 1:497–98. Perhaps the better explanation is that in Polybius' day the Pontus was no longer principally an exporter: Rübel 2001: 41n9. On the *dekateuterion* at Chrysopolis, note also Gabrielsen 2007: 293–95. The toll was revived during the Corinthian War by Thrasyboulos: Xen. *Hell.* 4.8.27–28, with Buckler 2000a: 160.

48. Rhodes and Osborne 2003: 270.

49. *IG* II^2 43.106; Xen. *Hell.* 6.5.23. See Rhodes and Osborne 2003: 270; and Buckler 2000b: 438.

50. Note *IG* II^2 233, Athenian honors for Tenedos in 340/339. See Buckler 2000b: 438.

51. Lewis 1990: 71–73, against Buckler 1980: 222–23 and Buckler 1982: 84–86, 88–89. Note already Swoboda 1900: 465–67; Merle 1916: 38–40 ("Im συνέδριον der thebanischen Bünder war Byzantion durch Abgesandte [i.e., the σύνεδροι] vertreten"); Tod 1948: 2: 178.

52. Plut. *Pel.* 24.3 (ἄνευ δόγματος κοινοῦ καὶ ψηφίσματος), 4 ('Αργεῖοι καὶ 'Ηλεῖοι καὶ 'Αρκάδες, ἐν τοῖς συνεδρίοις ἐρίζοντες καὶ διαφερόμενοι πρὸς τοὺς Θηβαίους ὑπὲρ ἡγεμονίας). On this evidence, see Buckler 2000b: 432–33.

53. Cf. Buckler 2000b, rejecting Lewis' "phantom synedrion." Among those who accept the existence of Lewis' *synedrion* are Cargill 1981: 169; Hornblower 1982: 200–201; Bakhuizen 1994: 308; Dreher 1995: 64; and Hornblower 2011: 262; it is rejected by Cartledge 1987: 310; Roy, *CAH* VI^2, 202; and Beck 1997: 216.

54. Lewis 1990: 72.

55. Buckler 2000b: 435–37; cf. Beck 1997: 216n15 and Jehne 1994: 22–23n74.

56. Note Jehne 1994: 22 ("Rätselhaft, aber auch isoliert, bliebt die Terminologie der Inschrift").

57. So Buckler 2000b: 441, who notes that the Arkadian envoys sent to Thebes in 362 are also called πρεσβεῖς, not *synedroi*: Xen. *Hell.* 7.4.39.

58. Jehne 1999: 330, 335. The reference is to Const. Porph. *De. Them.* 46 (p. 85, Pertusi), where Byzantion is called a colony of Megara, Sparta, and Boiotia. Cf. also Fossey 1994: 109, 111.

59. Megara: Ps.-Scymnus, 715–16; Philostr. *VS* 529; Suda s.v. Βυζάντιον; Eustathios comm. in Dion. Per. *GGM* II §803; John Lydus *De Mag.* 3.70; George Cedrenus 112A–B (p. 197, Wünsch); Miletos: Vell. Pat. 2.7.7; Megarians, Karystians, Mycenaeans, Corinthians, and "many others": Genesius 12b (p. 27, Lachmann: ἄλλων τε πολλῶν); Athens: Amm. Marc. 12.8.8 (*atticorum colonia*); Pausanias the Spartan: Justin 9.1.3 and Orosius 3.13.2; Argos: Hesychios of Miletos, *FGrH* 390 F 1.3. Dionysios of Byzantion mentions Megarians alongside others, including Corinthians, Arkadians, and Rhodians: 14–15, 19, 32, 34, 47, 53 (ed. Güngerich). Tacitus (*Ann.* 12.63), Herodotus (4.144), and Strabo (7.6.2) are unspecific (Tacitus: *Byzantium in extremo Europae posuere Graeci*). Modern writers tend to accept Megara or posit a mixed foundation with contingents from various poleis, including perhaps Boiotians, alongside a majority of Megarians: e.g., Merle 1916: 6–7; Hanell 1934: 123–28, 132–36; Isaac 1986: 218; A. J. Graham, *CAH* III^3, 120; Malkin and Shmueli 1988: 21.

60. See Jehne 1999: 330–31.

61. Jehne 1999: 329–30, 335–36, citing Xen. *Hell.* 1.3.15, a passage that mentions Megarian and Boiotian contingents stationed at Byzantion with their Spartan allies during the siege of

408. Diod. 14.12.3 also mentions thirty Byzantines called "Boiotians," who were strangled in public by Klearchos. Jehne (1999: 336n119) calls this a textual corruption of "Byzantine," but as Basset 2001: 6 notes, the participle ὀνομαζομένους makes this unlikely: why should these men be "named" Byzantines?

62. Lewis 1990: 71.

CHAPTER 6. ENCHANTING HISTORY

1. Habicht 1985: 165–75. P. 97 provides a conciliatory approach: Pausanias was not a historian, but if he had been, he would have been a successful one.

2. For instance, Pausanias' narrative of Olympia is "liturgically structured" following the traditional progression around the altars followed by locals (Elsner 1992: 13). This is the structure that baffled and humiliated Wilamowitz-Moellendorff when he was acting as a tour guide to German grandees, provoking his attacks on Pausanias.

3. Snodgrass (1987: 76–87) discusses Pausanias' treatment of Boiotia and emphasizes both the inescapable gravity of Thebes and the "relentless linearity" of his progression around the region.

4. On the relationship of Epameinondas and Philopoimen within the *Periegesis*, see Vincent 2010.

5. All translations of Pausanias are adapted from W. H. S. Jones.

6. Knoepfler 2004. Most important here is the contention that Pausanias employs Polybius as a source for book 8 but did not discover the *Histories* until after he had written book 9. This means that the transition between those books is an even greater disjunction than would otherwise be the case.

7. Hutton 2005: 274. Advertisement of biography elsewhere: Paus. 3.15.10; 6.3.8; 6.12.9. Pausanias also sometimes advertises future treatments of history: 6.2.4. Moggi (1993: 402–4) notes Pausanias' plentiful use of cross-references.

8. Orchomenos is not the last community in book 9, but it is the last to be used as a base from which to explore the local area, and its narrative takes up significantly more space than do those of Chaironeia and Lebadeia, which succeed it.

9. Paus. 9.36.4. Paus. 8.33.2 echoes Homer *Iliad* 9.381 directly by using Orchomenos and Egyptian Thebes as exemplars of legendary wealth.

10. A variable phenomenon within the *Periegesis*: Pretzler 2007: 79.

11. Pausanias saves an extended narrative of the war until he has left Boiotia for Phokis at the beginning of book 10 (10.2–3). Knoepfler (2004: 485–87) argues that the absence of post-316 material in the *Boiotika* is due to Pausanias' ignorance of Polybius during that book's composition.

12. Roesch (1982: 214n37) argues that Pausanias here means a monument to the memory of Lysander, not a tomb.

13. Austin 1931: 209. See also Pritchett 1999: 148–49.

14. Prominent opportunities include the first mention of his death at 3.5.3; a statue dedicated in his honor at Olympia: 6.3.14; and the victory dedication for Aegospotami: 10.9.7.

15. Habicht (1985: 103–4) notes that the account of Cassander here picks up from various references in book 1.

16. Hutton 2005: 95: "by choosing a certain site to use as a primary hub, Pausanias places the focus of an entire region on that site and emphasizes its importance and noteworthiness.

Usually, these primary hubs are the cities which are the preeminent economic and political centers of the region, although in the case of Thebes, which was in a poor state in Pausanias' day, the conclusion is inescapable that mythological and historical considerations play a major role."

17. Bermann 2002: 84.

18. Pretzler 2007: 9.

19. See above, n. 9.

20. Ameling (1996: 123) calculates the length of treatments of different periods overall in the *Periegesis*, with the fourth century receiving many times more coverage than the fifth century, and a similar amount (per century) to the Hellenistic period.

21. Alcock (1995: 328–29) on "hegemonic" Pausanias.

22. Tuplin (1984) provides the best exposition of the sources for the biography of Epameinondas.

23. The language of Pelopidas' epigram from the statue dedicated by the Thessalians at Delphi (*SEG* XXXV 480), though echoing the headline achievement in humbling Sparta, is more focused on the individual record rather than the pan-Hellenic benefactions of Epameinondas.

24. Neither is among those recorded as contributors to the restoration of Thebes in either *IG* VII 2419 (or the new fragment published in Buraselis 2014) or Diod. 19.54.2, but both records are partial. At Diod. 19.63.4 the walls are the specific focus of Cassander's attention.

25. Paus. 9.9. See also 4.3.4 for early links between Thebes and Messene.

26. Paus. 9.9.1: "The war between Argos and Thebes was, in my opinion, the most memorable of all those waged by Greeks against Greeks in what is called the heroic age." Pausanias found many heroic monuments in Argos connected to Thebes: Pariente 1992: 218. Musti (1988) sees further links in the presentation of Argos and Thebes because of the legendary traditions that link the two cities. For Sacadas' presentation in Pausanias, see Bowie 2014, especially 40–41. Epameinondas' formative influence on Messenian culture might have extended to tripods: Papalexandrou 2014: 135.

27. For dating of the life and statue of Pronomos, see Wilson 2007.

28. For the Argive monument at Delphi, see Scott 2010: 115–17. Scott also notes here the visual prominence of Herakles in the Argive monument, and the Theban-born hero played an important role in articulating relations between Messene and Thebes: Luraghi 2008: 230–32. The Arkadian gate at Messene, added to the fortifications in the Hellenistic period, closely echoes the shape of the Argive monument at Delphi, presumably deliberately.

29. As the site of the great helot revolt against Sparta of the 460s, Mt. Ithome had practical and romantic appeal as a site of resistance against Sparta, and the remnants of fortifications from that event may have been reused in the new foundation: Luraghi 2008: 217.

30. The wall at Ambrossos is another that Pausanias credits with Theban design, but thirty years later than Messene: 10.36.3 (with 10.3.3), where its physical appearance is described: black and strong (ἰσχυροῦ). Typaldou-Fakiris (2004: 207–8, 326–29) dates the fortification of Ambryssos/Ambrossos to 339/338 B.C.

31. Music was also part of celebratory destruction, such as that of the walls of the Peiraieus: Xen. *Hell.* 2.2.23.

32. There is one other occurrence in Pausanias of a νύκτα ἀσέληνον, at 8.50.8 (Philopoimen attacking the Spartan dockyards at Gytheion).

33. Thuc.3.22.1: οἱ δ', ἐπειδὴ παρεσκεύαστο αὐτοῖς, τηρήσαντες νύκτα χειμέριον ὕδατι καὶ ἀνέμῳ καὶ ἅμ' ἀσέληνον ἐξῇσαν·

34. Winter (1971: 132n25 and 139n43) cites Thuc. 3.23.2 as evidence that the battlements of the Plataian fortifications were not strong.

35. Russell 1999: 35. The experience of the escape does, however, focus Thucydides on the haptic description of the slippery mud under the Plataian feet.

36. Diod. 15.46.6 does not allude to the significance of intervisibility but does add the participation of cavalry, essential for the success of this attack, which relied on speed and a long, circuitous route to avoid detection. Hdt. 9.59.1 also understands the importance of this limited visibility between Thebes and the plain south of the Asopos.

37. Hutton 2005: 88–90.

38. An early date for the foundation of the festival, perhaps before the refoundation of Thebes, is preferable: Iversen 2007: 406. Contra Knoepfler (2001b), who argues that the festival cannot have been established before Thebes reentered the confederation, an event he dates to 287 B.C. Other studies of the Daidala include Chaniotis 2002; Strasser 2004; Pirenne-Delforge 2008: 223–26; and Mackil 2013: 225–32.

39. Suggestion of evacuation before Leuktra: 9.13.6; Mantineians: 9.14.4; Orchomenians: 9.15.3.

40. The idea of assigning refugees a new nationality is extraordinary, but it is passed over or accepted without comment by most historians, e.g., Hammond 1997: 370.

41. Epameinondas is presented as calm and free from anger at 8.49.3. He also captures Thespians who had fled to the stronghold of Keressos, another instance of city abandonment in Boiotia, and another example of Epameinondas fulfilling a prophecy: Paus. 9.14.4.

42. Pretzler (2007: 79) discusses this alternative account of his death as one that incorporated local traditions.

43. Elsner 1992: 16–17.

44. Paus. 4.28.5–6. Xenophon relates Epameinondas' call for Arkadians to paint clubs on their shields to make it appear as though they were Thebans: Xen. *Hell.* 7.5.20. Pausanias also relates the visual manipulation of the shield of Aristomenes before the battle of Leuktra: Paus. 4.32.4–6 (cf. 9.39.14).

45. E.g., Xen. *Hell.* 6.4.7.

46. E.g., Isoc. *Plataikos* 53–55: The Argive supplication at the walls of the Kadmeia is invoked as an argument to encourage the Athenians to assist them in returning from exile.

CHAPTER 7. THE PERFORMANCE OF BOIOTIAN IDENTITY AT DELPHI

In this chapter, Scott+bold number refers to monument reference numbers in Scott 2010. Jacquemin+bold number refers to monument reference numbers in Jacquemin 1999. Numbers for monuments in the figures refer to those in Scott 2010.

1. In particular, the narrative of Theban hegemony within Greece beginning with Thebes' victory over Sparta at the battle of Leuktra in 371 B.C. and Thebes' involvement in the lead-up to, and during, the Third Sacred War fought over Delphi; cf. Buckler 1980, 1985; Markle 1994; Munn 1997; Buckler 2003; and Buckler and Beck 2008.

2. A statue group by the southeast entrance to the Apollo sanctuary, next to an Athenian statue group (Scott **186**; Jacquemin **322**); a stoa opposite their new statue group (Scott **187**; Jacquemin **654**); a set of gold stars within the stoa (Scott **188**; Jacquemin **325**); an ivory offering (Scott **189**); a statue of Lysander (Scott **190**; Jacquemin **330**): Scott 2010: 107. See Figure 7.2. Agesilaos of Sparta also dedicated a percentage of the hundred talents worth of

war booty extracted from his campaigns in Asia Minor at the occasion of the Pythian Games in 394 B.C.: Parke and Wormell 1956: 209.

3. Dionysios of Syracuse: Diod. 15.13.1. Jason of Pherai: Xen. *Hell.* 6.4.29–32; Diod. 15.48.1–4. Iphikrates: Diod. 16.57.2. Cf. Parke and Wormell 1956: 210–12; Sordi 1957: 41–48; and Scott 2014.

4. Parke and Wormell 1956: 214; Amandry and Hansen 2010: 147–51; Scott 2010: 114.

5. Boiotian commander on the Spartan monument: Paus. 10.9.9; *FD* III 1 52. The Boiotians had, however, been active in the area around Delphi during a military scrabble with the Phokians in 395 B.C.: Buckler and Beck 2008: 45–49.

6. Diodorus (17.10.5) mentions a story in which blood was said to have run from the roof of the treasury of the Thebans, which had been built with booty taken from the war with Phokis (the Third Sacred War). Some argue that this treasury is a second Theban treasury constructed somewhere else in the sanctuary after 346 B.C. (for which there is no archaeological evidence), or else that Pausanias was mistaken in attributing the treasury in the southwest corner of the Apollo sanctuary to Theban celebrations of victory at Leuktra, and it should instead be dated to after 346 B.C. For discussion: Jacquemin 1999: 60n174.

7. *FD* III 62 (*CID* II 81). South side and north side: Bousquet 1952: 27–28. East side only: Jacquemin 1991. East side more likely: Amandry 1981: 691.

8. Preferred place for dedication of monuments related to military victory: Scott 2010: 118–19. Occasional exceptions of statue dedications placed on the temple terrace in the immediate aftermath of the earthquake: Scott 2010: 114n9.

9. Scott 2010: 143. Cf. Amandry 1945; Partida 2000: 192.

10. Eastern orientation of the treasury: Bommelaer 1991: 129.

11. On the ability for dedicators to choose where they wanted to put their dedications: Scott 2007; 2010: 29–40.

12. Bommelaer 1991: 128.

13. The "Boiotian" niche: Bommelaer 1991: 128; Scott 2010: 108.

14. The names: Partida 2000: 19. For the most recent assessments of the development of a collective Boiotian identity in the sixth and fifth centuries, see Larson 2007; and Mackil 2013: 22–45. The koinon is better known after 447 B.C., when the collective name *Boiotoi/Boiotios* begins to be used in a strictly political sense: *Hell. Oxy.* 11.2, 3–4; Buck 1985; Larson 2007: 10–11, 191; Mackil 2013: 22–45, 185–91.

15. Unlikely existence of a koinon behind this monument: van Effenterre 1997. Not a Boiotian structure: Bourguet 1929: 220.

16. Delphi Museum inv. 3078; Larson 2007: 137–38. Similar dedications have been found using this collective ethnic within Boiotia during this period, e.g., at the sanctuary of Apollo Ptoion and Athena Itonia near Koroneia: Larson 2007: 140.

17. 500–450 B.C.: *SEG* XLI 506; 450–400 B.C.: *FD* III 1 574; Larson 2007: 145, 147. In contrast, the earliest attested epigraphic example of *Boiotoi/Boiotios* used by Boiotians at Olympia is in 296 B.C. (and then not again until 106 B.C.): Larson 2007: 146. On display instead at Olympia from the sixth century were dedications offered to commemorate military victories of Boiotian poleis over other Boiotian poleis: Mackil 2013: 333.

18. Other sanctuaries particularly important for expressions of Boiotian community in this period: the sanctuary of Athena Itonia (near Koroneia), the sanctuary of Poseidon at Onchestos, and the sanctuary of Apollo Ptoios: Mackil 2013: 157–71.

19. Orchomenos had sided with Sparta and Lysander in the run-up to the battle of Haliartus (395 B.C.) and afterward remained Thebes' bitterest rival; cf. Andocides 3.20. Thebes refused to sign the peace negotiations instituted by the Persian king in 386 B.C. specifically

because it was not allowed to sign on behalf of the Boiotians: Xen. *Hell.* 5.1.25–31. It was eventually forced to accept these terms, and with them, the official dissolution of the Boiotian confederacy: Munn 1997: 75. That confederacy was reconstituted after the Theban revolution of 378 B.C.: Plut. *Pel.* 13.1, 14.1; Munn 1997: 80–81; Buckler 2003: 273–76; Buckler and Beck 2008: 87–98. Theban supremacy resulted in the battle of Leuktra (having insisted this time on signing a peace treaty on behalf of all Boiotia), in the forceful takeover of Boiotian cities like Plataia and Thespiae in 373, and in the destruction of others (including Orchomenos from 370 B.C. onward): Xen. *Hell* 6.3.1; Buckler 2003: 271, 276. Within a year after Leuktra, the Thebans could count almost all of central Greece as allies: Xen. *Hell.* 6.5.23; Buckler 1980; Munn 1997: 71–72, 74, 80–81, 86; Buckler and Beck 2008: 127–39; Mackil 2013: 71–84, 338, 366. For the importance of this treasury dedication as strengthening Theban claims to legitimacy of (their leadership of) the Boiotian koinon: Mackil 2013: 210–11.

20. Such spatial mirroring or spatial opposition had been a key component of how dedications gathered meaning at Delphi throughout the fifth century B.C.: Scott 2010: 108–10. For the importance of this construction of identity through opposition especially for the articulation of Boiotian identity: Larson 2007: 11.

21. For the entrance to the Apollo sanctuary in the southwestern corner: Bommelaer 1991: 128. Given the fact that the polis of Delphi surrounded the Apollo sanctuary, I argue that visitors would have been equally likely to enter the sanctuary from the southwest and the southeast.

22. Roesch 1984a: 187–88; Jacquemin 1999: 32–33; Scott 2010: 24; 2014: 246.

23. For the construction of a staircase at the back of the Athenian treasury, for instance: Laroche and Nenna 1992: 111–14. For a staircase in the northern section of the sanctuary constructed as part of the post-373 B.C. rebuild: Courby 1927: 216. For a staircase leading to the area of the "aire" in front of the stoa of the Athenians: Bommelaer 1991: 146.

24. E.g., *FD* III 1 457.20; Jacquemin 1999: 35, 101, 245.

25. E.g., Bommelaer 1991: 129.

26. Discussions of this new orientation: Jacquemin and Laroche 2010: 3, 5; 2012–2013: 106–114.

27. Bourguet 1929: 191–92.

28. Athenian treasury in the Apollo sanctuary, 490 B.C.: cf. Bommelaer 1991: 133–38; Rups 1986: 133; Neer 2004. Possible Athenian treasury in the Athena sanctuary: Daux 1936: 64; Amandry 1984: 191. It is disputed whether the Syracusans built a treasury in the late fifth century at Delphi to oppose spatially the Athenian treasury and whether the Acanthians built a new treasury or refitted an old one opposite the temple terrace around the same time: Bommelaer 1991: 160; Partida 2000: 103; Scott 2010: 105.

29. Cf. Scott 2010: 108–10.

30. Monument at the battlefield of Leuktra, the first battlefield memorial to a Greek victory over Greeks: Cic. *Inv. Rhet.* 2.23; Munn 1997: 84–85. If Pausanias' information on Theban commemoration in Thebes can be trusted (occurring at the temple of Demeter), it may indicate the Theban desire to echo Spartan occupation of the Kadmeia in 382 B.C., which occurred during the celebration of the Thesmophoria at Thebes; cf. Xen. *Hell.* 5.2.29.

31. Cf. Bommelaer 1991: 123–43.

32. Michaud 1973: 16, 20, 25. Indeed, only one other treasury at Delphi sits on the boundary wall in the same way, the Kyrenean treasury, also built during the fourth century B.C.: Bommelaer 1991: 156–58.

33. Michaud 1973: 21.

34. Michaud 1973: 20n2, 21, 94; Partida 2000: 192.

35. Cf. Michaud 1973: 21–24. The significant and solid bastion would also have helped the structure survive on this more unstable side of the sanctuary. Indeed, the original excavation reports note that the treasury was built extremely solidly throughout, perhaps with this purpose in mind: Michaud 1973: 93; Partida 2000: 192.

36. Michaud 1973: 94; Bommelaer 1991: 130; Partida 2000: 192.

37. E.g., Partida 2000: 193.

38. Jacquemin and Laroche 2012–2013: 113–4.

39. Cf. Jacquemin 1999: 145; Jacquemin and Laroche 2012–2013:113.

40. For wider discussions of the purpose of treasuries: Rups 1986.

41. For discussion: Michaud 1973: 73–74; Jacquemin 1999: 145; Partida 2000: 193.

42. Siphnian Treasury: Bommelaer 1991: 123–26; Picard 1991: 44–49; Scott 2007.

43. Cf. Audiat 1933; Bommelaer 1991: 133–38.

44. Michaud 1973: 93; Bommelaer 1991: 129.

45. Michaud 1973: 93–94.

46. Michaud 1973: 94. The Theban treasury was constructed according to exacting and innovative architectural ratios that can be paralleled in other structures at Delphi built around this time, such as the limestone temple in the Athena sanctuary, to the extent that scholars have argued that they must have been built by the same team: Bommelaer 1991: 130; Frey 1992.

47. E.g., Partida 2000: 196–98.

48. Bommelaer 1991: 108–9.

49. Not unlike the Plataian "serpent" column, with its list of Greek poleis who had fought against the Persians carved onto the monument, set up after 479 B.C.: Paus. 10.13.9; Meiggs and Lewis 1988: 27.

50. *FD* III 1 351–67.

51. Jacquemin 1999: 224. The second-century B.C. reappearance of a Boiotian koinon (*FD* III 1 366) is discussed later in this chapter. *FD* III 1 362, which ran the entire length of the north side of the Theban treasury, is, on the face of it, not about Thebes but about a dispute between the Boiotian communities of Boumeltia and Halai over land boundaries, but this dispute was eventually arbitrated by the Thebans, who used this inscription also to lay out their decision: Bourguet 1929: 210–16.

52. For the unusual nature of the Boiotian koinon in this period: Mackil 2013: 338, 366. Similar notes of mixed communality and Theban supremacy can be seen elsewhere in the makeup of the koinon after 378 B.C.; all boiotarchs, for example, were Theban from 378 to 355 B.C.: Mackil 2013: 338.

53. Cf. Jacquemin 1999: 259; and Jacquemin and Laroche 2010: 3. More ironically, the Spartan general Lysander had, back in 395 B.C. in preparation for the battle of Haliartus, assembled half of his allied troops at Delphi, from where they began their march south. The Thebans' emphatic celebration of their victory over Sparta, specifically at Delphi, would as a result have had even greater resonance: Xen. *Hell* 3.5.3–5; Munn 1997: 71.

54. Cf. Parke and Wormell 1956: 223–27; Sordi 1957; Roux 1976: 192; Buckler 1985; Munn 1997: 94–98; Buckler 2003: 385–429; Buckler and Beck 2008: 213–23; Deltenne 2010.

55. *SIG*[3] 176 / *FD* III 4 375, normally dated to 360/359 B.C., offering the Thebans *promanteia* ahead of all others except the Delphians. For debate over the reason for granting this *promanteia*: Buckler 1985: 241. For debate over the date at which this *promanteia* was granted (linked to debate over when the treasury of the Thebans was completed), see Michaud 1973: 2–7, 94n1; and Buckler 1985: 241–42. For discussion of the fulsome nature of the *promanteia*: Pouilloux 1952, 1962.

56. For discussion of these two monuments: Bommelaer 1991: 113–15. For discussion of the link with Thebes: Jacquemin 1999: 259.

57. For the way in which the changing relationship between Argos and Thebes would have been understood by visitors moving past these two monuments: Salviat 1965: 314.

58. Pelopidas' statue is the first for which the evidence is indisputable: Jacquemin 1999: 198. For discussion of the fragmentary surviving inscription (which attributes the work to Lysippus): Bousquet 1963: 206–8. The inscription also makes very clear the enemy over which Pelopidas had been successful: Sparta is the first word; cf. Mackil 2013: 423.

59. *FD* III 4 196; Diod. 15.54.1 (as Leandrias). For discussion of his role at Leuktra: Jacquemin 1999: 57, 131, 258. In addition, we know that Asopichos of Thebes placed a shield in the Athenian stoa (Scott **225**) that was later melted down by the Phokians in the Third Sacred War: Athen. 13.604.

60. Dedicatory inscription: *FD* III 1 6. This is despite the fact that the Arkadians had no real role at Leuktra: Rhodes and Osborne 2003: no. 30. The monument relates better to Theban and Arkadian involvement in raids on Sparta in 370–368 B.C.: Xen. *Hell.* 6.5.3–7.1.26; Roy 2000: 310; Scott 2008. At the same time, the sculptors creating these monuments seem to have been happy to work for both sides: Antiphanes of Argos worked on the Spartan monument to victory at Aigospotamoi, the semicircular Argive monument to victory over Sparta, and the Arkadian statue group: Jacquemin and Laroche 2010: 8.

61. Even the fabric of Delphi seems to have been pro-Theban at this time: according to Plutarch, the golden stars placed in the Spartan stoa after Spartan victory at Aigospotamoi were said to have fallen to pieces after Leuktra, as did one of the statues in the Spartan statue group opposite and even Lysander's statue on the temple terrace: Plut. *Lys.* 18.1; Plut. *Mor.* 397E–F.

62. Athen. 13.591B–C.

63. Cf. Jacquemin 1999: 204. According to Paus. 10.15.1, Phryne dedicated it herself. According to Athenaeus, the "neighbors" (perhaps the polis of Delphi) dedicated it (13.591B).

64. Cf. Paus. 10.15.1; Plut. *Mor.* 401A–D; Athen. 13.591B.

65. Cf. Plut. *Mor.* 400F–401B.

66. Keesling 2006: 67.

67. For discussion of the two known courtesan dedications at Delphi: Keesling 2006: 61–65 (Rhodopis' iron spits), 66–71 (Phryne's statue).

68. For discussion of Thespiai and its relationship to the Boiotian Confederacy in this period: Roesch 1965: 43–46, 100–102, 124–25; Tuplin 1986.

69. *FD* III 5 3 I, 75–79.

70. Theban: *SGDI* 2747. Thespian: *FD* III 5 26, I A, 1.10.

71. *Hieromnemones*: Theban (*FD* III 5 22.47), Thespian (*FD* III 22.1–2). Thebans in other capacities: *FD* III 5 19.75; *FD* III 5 19.74, 92, 93; *FD* III 5 20.9. For discussion: Roesch 1982: 463–67.

72. Roesch 1982: 447. For further discussion of the Boiotians involved in the Amphiktionic administration of Delphi: La Coste-Messelière 1949: 242.

73. *FD* III 5 19.93; 19.100; 19.102 (344–343 B.C.); Roesch 1982: 467.

74. Parke and Wormell 1956: 227; Jacquemin 1999: 238; Scott 2010: 124–25. For the total value of the dedications melted down: Diod. 16.56.6.

75. The destructive force of the Phokians seems to have focused on the expensive dedications by the Lydian kings and those of community victory celebrations or athletic victories. For example, the shield dedication of Asopichos of Thebes was melted down by the Phokians. For the possible religious overtones of Phryne's dedication: Keesling 2006: 70–71.

76. *CID* II 34 II.56–62 (343 B.C.). For discussion of the importance of removing dedications from sanctuaries: van Straten 2000.

77. Pausanias 10.13.6. Cf. Jacquemin 1999: 185n225.

78. Space for performance of ceremonies, e.g., *FD* III 3 238 1.8–21. For discussion: Bourguet 1914: 124–27; Bergquist 1967: 131–32; Amandry 2000. Despite its absence of dedications, it was the space in which to bury dedications during sanctuary renovations: Amandry 1977.

79. Hdt. 8.27.

80. For discussion of this possibility: Defradas 1954: 146.

81. For the Panhellenic and Boiotian aspects of Herakles: Schachter 1979.

82. For all the inscriptions found on this monument: Daux and Salac 1932: 61–80. For discussion of the almost total reconstruction of the dedicatory inscription (*FD* III 3 77): Daux and Salac 1932: 64.

83. Cf. Roesch 1984a: 194.

84. Roesch 1984a: 187.

85. Roesch 1984a: 189.

86. Cf. Bommelaer 1991: 144.

87. Cf. Scott 2008.

88. For discussion of the events of this period: Munn 1997: 98–104. For discussion of the change in the nature of the Boiotian koinon after 338 B.C.: Mackil 2013: 340, 405.

89. Roesch 1979; 1982: 468.

90. Roesch 1982: 447, 469. Indeed, it is these inscriptions that prove the reconstitution of the Boiotian Confederacy after the victory of Philip at the Battle of Chaironeia: Roesch 1982: 463.

91. *FD* III 3 89, 90, 92, 93, 95, 96, 99, 100. There is some difficulty in dating these inscriptions due to uncertainties over the chronology of Delphic archons. Some of them (*FD* III 3 89, 90, 99, 100) could also date to 292–288 B.C.: Roesch 1982: 462.

92. Roesch 1965: 46–70, 103–8, 125–26; 1982: 417–38, 462, 497–98; 1984a: 192.

93. For the placement of these inscriptions in chronological batches on different parts of the north face of the monument: Roesch 1984a: 193–94.

94. E.g., *SGDI* 2674 (316 B.C.) for Boiotians (from Tanagra) and *FD* III 1 356 (324/323 B.C.) for a Theban: Roesch 1982: 469, 471. On the Theban treasury: *FD* III 1 356 (327/326 B.C.) identifies the individual as a Theban. The inscription of *FD* III 1 360 (263 B.C.) identifies the individual as *Boiotios ek Theban*.

95. E.g., *FD* III 1 96 (a Thespian honored for services as a *naope*, 327/326 B.C.); *FD* III 5 52 (a citizen from Orchomenos as *hieromnemon* in 332 B.C.); *FD* III 5 57A (a citizen from Tanagra as *hieromnemon* in 326 B.C.); *FD* III 5 20 and 60 B (a citizen from Plataia as *hieromnemon* in 325 B.C.). The reasoning is that for these offices, it mattered to know the exact polis of origin rather than the wider ethnic identity. For further discussion: Roesch 1982: 441–42, 474–75.

96. A similar distinction seems to have been made with *auletes* players, who never used the ethnic "Boiotian," possibly because Theban players were renowned across the ancient world for their skill, and it was more useful to plug into that identity as a professional (e.g., *FD* III 3 115): Roesch 1982: 444–45.

97. The last inscription placed on the Theban treasury, *FD* III 1 366 (c. 150 B.C.), speaks of the *koinan pasi Boiotois* (line 1); Bourguet 1929: 218. Cf. Paus. 7.16.10. This inscription is argued to be proof that the Boiotian koinon was allowed to re-form, at least for a short time, after the battle of Pydna: Roesch 1982: 417. For further discussion of the Boiotian koinon in the Hellenistic and Roman periods: Cloché 1952; Mackil 2013.

98. Cf. Larson 2007: 12.

99. Cf. Hall 1997: 32; Larson 2007: 11. For Delphi being particularly good at identity display: Scott 2010: 219–40. Boiotians not at Olympia in the same way: Roesch 1982: 463–89; Larson 2007: 146.

CHAPTER 8. THE EPIGRAPHIC HABIT(S) IN FOURTH-CENTURY BOIOTIA

I am grateful to Samuel Gartland for inviting me to participate in this collection. I am equally grateful to Robin Osborne for sharing with me his article "Thespiai: The Epigraphic City down to 171" before publication. For help with questions concerning Pindar, I would like to thank Leslie Kurke. I am also grateful to Randy Souza for critically reading a draft of this chapter. Basileios Petrakos, secretary of the Archaeological Society at Athens, generously granted me permission to publish photographs of inscriptions from his Oropian corpus. Likewise, the Ephorate of Boiotia allowed me to publish photographs of inscriptions kept in the Museum of Thebes; Ephor Alexandra Charami and the archaeologist Yannis Fappas were both instrumental. Finally, I am indebted to Yannis Kalliontzis, Georgia Malouchou, and Angelos P. Matthaiou for their advice on the script of *IG* VII 2462 (see the appendix).

1. MacMullen 1982.

2. Hedrick 1999; the reader may note the lengthier adjectival form.

3. Sickinger 2009.

4. Osborne 2009. See, however, the examination of the epigraphic production of an entire multipolis region in Chaniotis 2004.

5. Petrakos 1997.

6. Roesch 2007.

7. For the sources, see Roesch 1965: 45; and Hansen and Nielsen 2004: 457.

8. For a diligent analysis of the epigraphic production of Thespiai, see Osborne forthcoming. The first, Thespian, part of my chapter should ideally be read together with Osborne's analysis, which has a longer chronological scope. As concerns the fourth century, Osborne believes that "what Thespiai inscribes seems to be what her neighbours are also inscribing," whereas I am of the opinion that what Thespiai inscribed seems to have been what her neighboring rival, that is, Thebes, allowed it to inscribe, especially between 371 and 335.

9. For instance, Vottéro 1996: 166–70 and Iversen 2010.

10. Platon and Feyel 1938, in particular the discussion of Feyel at 164–66.

11. There are, for instance, five fourth-century dedications to Hermes (*I.Thespiai* 280, 281, 282, 283 bis, and 284), one of the least popular members of the Olympic pantheon elsewhere. For his cult in Boiotia, see Schachter 1981–1994: 2:40–54.

12. *I.Thespiai* 455, 456, 457, for all of which Guy Vottéro proposes a date in the third century B.C.

13. Schachter and Marchand 2013, esp. 278–80, no. 1.

14. Fraser and Rönne 1957: 92–94.

15. Adolf Wilhelm in *SEG* II 186 was the first scholar to propose a date in the Corinthian War. Taillardat and Roesch (1966: 79–83) suggested 395 as the year of the battle in which the dead of the left column fell, and 394 as the year for the casualties of the right column. Their interpretation has become almost canonical, although Pritchett (1985: 141–43) contested it and hesitantly suggested 378/377 B.C. Without reference to Pritchett's treatment, Vottéro (1996: 164–66) has not excluded a date between 378 and 374 B.C.

16. A very insightful comparative analysis of the Thespian funerary monument for Delion is offered by Low 2003; note, in particular, her remark "Those commemorated in this monument died fighting against Athens, for an oligarchic against a democratic system" (108).

17. *I.Oropos* 539, 621, 665, 666, 673, 727.

18. Samos: Shipley 1987: 140–43. The similarities between Oropos and Samos were detected and exquisitely investigated by Knoepfler 2010 [2012].

19. This and related issues are discussed in detail in Faraguna 2012.

20. Papazarkadas 2009. Knoepfler 2010 [2012]: 449–50, while approving many aspects of my analysis, has endorsed Louis Robert's well-known thesis that the *Nea* is Oropos rather than a part of its territory. Although the exact identification is not of importance for the purposes of this chapter, if Robert and Knoepfler are right, this would strengthen even more the point I am making here.

21. Thuc. 3.104: Τοῦ δ' αὐτοῦ χειμῶνος καὶ Δῆλον ἐκάθηραν Ἀθηναῖοι κατὰ χρησμὸν δή τινα. ἐκάθηρε μὲν γὰρ καὶ Πεισίστρατος ὁ τύραννος πρότερον αὐτήν, οὐχ ἅπασαν, ἀλλ' ὅσον ἀπὸ τοῦ ἱεροῦ ἐφεωρᾶτο τῆς νήσου· τότε δὲ πᾶσα ἐκαθάρθη τοιῷδε τρόπῳ. θῆκαι ὅσαι ἦσαν τῶν τεθνεώτων ἐν Δήλῳ, πάσας ἀνεῖλον, καὶ τὸ λοιπὸν προεῖπον μήτε ἐναποθνῄσκειν ἐν τῇ νήσῳ μήτε ἐντίκτειν, ἀλλ' ἐς τὴν Ῥήνειαν διακομίζεσθαι. . . . καὶ τὴν πεντετηρίδα τότε πρῶτον μετὰ τὴν κάθαρσιν ἐποίησαν οἱ Ἀθηναῖοι τὰ Δήλια (In the same winter the Athenians also purified Delos, in accordance with some oracle. There had been some purification by Pisistratus the tyrant, not of the whole island but of as much as could be seen from the sanctuary, but on this occasion the whole island was purified. This is how it was done. The Athenians removed all the tombs of those who had died on Delos and proclaimed for the future that no one was either to die or to give birth on the island, but that they were to be conveyed across to Rhenea. . . . The Athenians then celebrated the quadrennial festival of the Delia for the first time after the purification). Translation from Rhodes 1994: 155–57. See Parker 1983: 163, 277.

22. These are *I.Oropos* 341, 348, 355, 356, 357, 358, 359.

23. *I.Oropos* 355: Μειδίας Κηφισοδώρου Ἀ[[- - -]] | Ἀμφιαρά[[ωι]].

24. E.g., the inscribed sundial *I.Oropos* 359, ll. 4–6: Θεόφιλος | [[- - -]] | Ἀθηναῖος.

25. See Petrakos 1967: 13 and 1968: 30–31, noting that whenever Oropos gained its independence, the Oropians would not allow Athenian dedicants to "sign" their dedications other than as "Athenians."

26. *I.Oropos* 276, ll. 4–5: ἐμβάλ<λ>οντα εἰς τὸ[ν | θησαυρὸν μὴ ἔλαττον δρα]χμῆς βοιωτίης (dropping into the offertory box no less than a Boeotian drachma); see Petropoulou 1981.

27. They are *I.Oropos* 278 and 279; for the former (=*SEG* LIII 466), see also the detailed treatment of Lupu 2003.

28. Petrakos, in *I.Oropos* 277, suggests a possible date between 387 and 377 B.C.

29. *I.Oropos* 277, ll. 39–43: τὸ ὄνομα τοῦ ἐγκαθεύδον|τος, ὅταν ἐμβάλλει τὸ ἀργύριον, γράφεσθαι τ|ὸν νεωκόρον καὶ αὐτοῦ καὶ τῆς πόλεος καὶ ἐκ|τιθεῖν ἐν τοῖ ἱεροῖ γράφοντα ἐν πετεύροι σ|κοπεῖν <τ>οῖ βολομένοι.

30. Wilhelm 1909: 285. See the comprehensive treatment of Hedrick 2000, who aptly notes in relation to *I.Oropos* 277: "The influence of Athenian texts can be seen in the language and organization of many documents from the shrine [sc. of Amphiaraus]. Consequently, it is not surprising that this formula is attested here. . . . The use of the formula conforms to the pattern we have discerned in the Athenian texts."

31. Thus Rhodes and Osborne 2003: 135.

32. See Knoepfler 1993.

33. *I.Oropos* 520 seems to be the earliest extant catalog of its sort in the comprehensive monograph of Manieri 2009. Manieri discusses *I.Oropos* 520 and other aspects of the Great Amphiareia at 35–36 and 219–28.

34. See now Humphreys 2004–2009 [2010].

35. For instance, *I.Oropos* 281: Ἱστίης ("Ionic-Eretrian," according to Petrakos ad loc.); *I.Oropos* 283: Ἥρης | τελέης. *I.Oropos* 281, a cippus with a smooth band for the inscription placed slightly below the top edge, is reminiscent of Tanagran funerary monuments; see Fossey 1991b: 198–201.

36. *I.Oropos* 286–87: hόρος | hoδô.

37. *I.Oropos* 291–92.

38. *I.Oropos* 309–20.

39. See Habicht 2002, with insightful remarks on Petrakos' corpus of Oropian documents.

40. I follow Habicht 2002 in omitting fragmentary texts. Obviously, their inclusion would make for an even more impressive picture by further increasing the actual number of Oropian proxeny decrees.

41. Full demonstration in Knoepfler 2001a: 367–89.

42. For these two, see the useful edition by Rhodes and Osborne 2003: no. 75, who adopt Knoepfler's chronological reconstruction.

43. See the thorough analysis of Morpurgo Davies 1993, especially 276.

44. For Lykourgos' policy in Oropos, see Humphreys 2004: 82–84, 95–96, 112–14.

45. Vottéro 2001: 39–40 (but Vottéro's 6 percent must be a typo).

46. Full analysis of the new text can be found in Aravantinos and Papazarkadas 2012. *IG* II^2 14 is chronologically earlier; however, it is a treaty made between Athens and the Boiotian koinon, not Thebes alone.

47. See now Mackil 2013: 69n63; Knoepfler, in *BE* (2013) no. 170.

48. For the Lebadeian "epigraphic wall," see Turner 1994 and Pitt 2014.

49. Arrington 2012, especially figure 3 at p. 73.

50. Dow 1961.

51. Lambert 2002, especially 356n17.

52. Plut. *Vita Pel.* 7.1–2, with Georgiadou 1997, ad loc., who aptly observes that Pelopidas and Thrasyboulos are associated in Plutarch, *Non posse* 1098A. That the Theban exiles would have spent considerable time in Athens' agora—and would have marveled at the institutions and monuments of the Athenian democratic system—is implied by Pelopidas' exhortation to his fellow men not to rely exclusively on Athenian decrees and not to fawn over the Attic orators in the aforementioned extract of Plutarch.

53. Thorough analysis of the decree and of the political career of Archinos can be found in D'Angour 1999. Archinos, an upper-class Athenian with moderate democratic leanings, would have been an obvious source of inspiration for Pelopidas and the young aristocratic Thebans who had sought refuge in Athens.

54. Knoepfler 1992: 423–24, no. 24; cf. Knoepfler in *BE* (2009) no. 244.

55. See now Matthaiou 2009.

56. Luraghi 2010. For the Boiotian dialect, rather than script, as an indicium of Boiotian ethnicity already in the sixth and fifth centuries B.C., see Larson 2007.

57. Vottéro 1996: 177–78; followed by Luraghi 2010: 83 with n. 32, who observes that "the last decades of the fifth century had seen a decline in the importance of alphabet as a symbol of ethnic identity."

58. The minute analysis of Vottéro 1996: 161–64 is indispensable.

59. For useful observations on the various categories of Athenian lists, see Dow 1983: 95–98.

60. For the importance of lists in the context of the civic ideology of fourth-century Athens, see Liddel 2007: 182–98.

61. *Editio princeps* of the Theban dedication: Ducrey and Calame 2006 (=*SEG* LVI 551); observations on the lettering: Aravantinos and Papazarkadas 2012: 243.

62. See the similar observations made by Michael Scott in chapter 7 of this book with regard to Thebes' post-Leuktra presence at Delphi, especially the construction of the Theban treasury ("the Delphic monumental landscape now reflected the realities of a Greek world in which Thebes was the new power to be reckoned with") and the Thessalians' dedication of a statue of Pelopidas (once again, made by Lysippus), which "continued to reinforce the message of Theban power and authority within Greece at this time."

63. For instance, Paul Iversen 2010: 262–63 leans toward the idea that the trend started in Boiotian regions, such as Thespiai, that were traditionally culturally oriented toward Athens and spread from there throughout Boiotia. Iversen has formulated his theory commendably carefully, although I am less inclined to accept his categorical rejection of the idea of a formal decree qualifying the introduction of the Ionic alphabet: just as in the case of Athens, a political decision to shift to a new alphabet might have been partly influenced by very real unofficial developments. Similar to Iversen's is the view taken by Albert Schachter in chapter 3 of this volume in his analysis of the Theban magistrates' coins, which appear to bring out a complicated picture of coexisting epichoric and Ionic inscriptions. I will point out only that even after the adoption of the Ionic script by Athens, the Athenians intentionally preserved the Attic version AΘE on their celebrated coinage.

64. See now Mackil 2013: 337–39.

65. Editio princeps by Papazarkadas 2014b.

66. See now Mackil 2013: 71–85.

67. See the up-to-date discussion by Fossey 2014: 3–22.

68. See *SEG* XVIII 465, reporting the restoration of Knoepfler 1978: 387–92, and the criticism of Roesch 1978: 20–21.

69. Editio princeps: Mackil 2008.

70. Vlachogianni (2004–2009) expresses her preference for the restoration of the ethnic [- - - Ὀλυ]νθίως, adducing as a possible historical context Theban endeavors to obtain Macedonian timber for their fleet. Note that the stele is crowned by an *anthemion*, a morphological feature that has some good Attic parallels. Fossey 2014: 20–22 has ingeniously suggested restoring the ethnic [- - -Ἀμαρυ]νθίως. Although Fossey acknowledges the difficulty in his theory (Amarynthos is never attested as as independent Euboean polis), he also points out that Amarynthos' naval significance would still fit the pattern highlighted above.

71. For this material, see Wolters 1940.

72. The inscribed sherds from the Herakleion are published in Aravantinos 2014.

73. Especially in the context of Peter Rhodes' chapter in this volume, which argues that the Boiotian constitution was not democratic at all, even after 379/378 B.C.

74. For a first concise report, see Matthaiou 2014.

75. Such inferences should not come as a surprise. Millender 2001, for instance, has shown that the alleged Spartan distaste for the written word was to a large extent an ancient construct and that the Spartans did make considerable use of public documents. Besides, Pindar's

city of birth could not possibly have been such a cultural backwater. In order to assess questions of Theban literacy, it would be interesting to know the city's role in the collection, preservation, and transmission of Pindar's works. Understandably, the relevant discussion has been very Athenocentric (see, e.g., Irigoin 1952: 11–28, an erudite work), although Hubbard 2004: 82–83 has briefly drawn attention to Thebes.

76. Note, however, that the famous epigram for Leuktra, *IG* VII 2462, is irrelevant to my discussion since it most probably dates after the refoundation of Thebes by Cassander; see the appendix to this chapter.

77. I have unashamedly borrowed the idea of a short century from Eric Hobsbawm's famous *The Age of Extremes: The Short Twentieth Century, 1914–1991* (1994). My short fourth century overlaps to a large extent with the period of the Theban hegemony.

78. As we have just been reminded by the discovery of a new fragment of *Syll.*^{3} 377: Buraselis 2014. See also the appendix to this chapter.

79. Once more the concept is adopted from Eric Hobsbawm's "long nineteenth century," i.e., 1789–1914. In the case of Boiotia, the long third century might well be the period between 335 and 172/171, i.e., the dissolution of the Boiotian koinon by the Romans.

80. The text was first published in the Greek daily *Παλιγγενεσία* on May 17, 1877. That first edition was reprinted in the scholarly review *Athenaion*: Koumanoudes 1877: 151–52.

81. Egger 1878. It is possible that the anonymous scholar commenting on the script was either Paul Foucart or Klon Stephanos, who in the same volume, *BCH* 2 (1878): 27–28, gave a description of the monument based on autopsy in the Museum of Thebes and concluded that "il servait à couvrir un tombeau d'époque récente."

82. Kaibel 1878: xvi–xvii, no. 768a: "sed et hoc et inscita narrandi ratio, dictionis inconcinnitas et obscuritas, dialecti inconstantia (v. 5. δουρί) eo magis ducit ut epigramma non IV saeculo sed tempore aliquanto recentiore scriptum putemus."

83. Dittenberger ad *IG* VII 2462: "Litteratura titulum eo qui est de pecuniis ad bellum sacrum Phocense collatis (n. 2418) paullo antiquiorem indicat, ita ut nulla causa sit, cur monumentum posteriore demum aetate, quae est Kaibelii opinio, non proximo post proelium Leuctricum tempore erectum statuamus."

84. P. A. Hansen 1989: 107–8, no. 632: "Kaibel pp. xvi sq. n. 768a (qui de aetate epigrammatis concepti incisique male iudicat)."

85. Tod 1948: 92–94, no. 130.

86. Fraser and Rönne 1957: 36n9.

87. Pritchett 1985: 142n146.

88. Shrimpton 1971: 313.

89. Tuplin 1987: 95.

90. Vottéro 1996: 157: "le changement d'alphabet a eu lieu entre la bataille de Délion en 424 et celle de Leuctres en 371, puisque les textes relatifs à ces deux faits, l'épitaphe des Thespiens *IG* VII 1888 pour l'un, l'épigramme des combattants de Leuctres *IG* VII 2462 pour l'autre, utilisent des alphabets différents."

91. Rhodes and Osborne 2003: no. 30.

92. See the discussion earlier in this chapter.

93. Fossey 1991a: 86–87 ("Appendix 3: Orkhomenian Soldiers with Alexandros of Makedonia (*IG* vii 3206)") with plates 22–23.

94. *IG* VII 2419 with the new fragment published by Kostas Buraselis (2014, esp. p. 160 fig. 1).

95. See Holleaux 1895. All subsequent discussions rely heavily on Holleaux's article.

96. See Meiggs and Lewis 1988: 28–29, no. 15.

97. See Page 1981: 330, and Wilson 2007: 141–42, 145.

98. In other words, there might originally have been other epigrams mentioning Theopompos and Mnasilaos, which would not have been reinscribed in the post-315 B.C. resurrected monument. Georgia Malouchou has suggested to me that this omission could mean that the reinscribing was a private rather than a public enterprise.

CHAPTER 9. A NEW BOIOTIA?

1. Demand 1990; Mackil 2004.

2. Athens: Paus. 9.7.1; Justin 11.4.8; Akraiphiai: Paus. 9.23.5. The Corinthian Gulf may have provided further opportunities for escape (cf. Din. 1.18). The description of Theban cavalry "flooding out over the plain" (Arrian *Anab.* 1.8.7) might indicate that those with access to horses had better opportunities to escape. A Theban serving with Athenians at Panakton in the period of exile has been identified: Munn 1996: 53–55.

3. Plut. *Alex.* 11.12 and Aelian *VH* 13.7 echo the numbers given by Diodoros, all of which probably draw on Kleitarchos: Gullath 1982: 65n1. Arrian (*Anab.* 1.8.8) and Diodoros (17.13.1–5) provide vivid descriptions of the scene.

4. Arrian *Anab.* 1.9.9; 2.15.3.

5. The population of the region is discussed in the introduction. See also Vottéro 1998: 83.

6. Cf. McKechnie (1989: 56–57), who considers that the Thebans are likely to have still been present and to have needed only Cassander's summons to reform the polis.

7. Justin 11.4.7 reports that local motivations to enslave old enemies inflated prices.

8. Aeschin. 3.157; Din. 1.24; Gullath 1982: 69n2 on Macedonians taking Theban captives. For Phila, see Plut. *Mor.* 849D; Idomeneus, *FGrH* 338 F 14 (=Athenaeus 13.590d). The high price was unusual; if all Theban captives were as expensive, the 440 talents reported for the entire sale would have represented only 1,320 slaves sold.

9. Pliny *NH* 34.8 reports on a chandelier taken by Alexander to Kyme, hinting at a wider distribution of Theban loot. Given Alexander's reported care over the house of Pindar (Arr. *Anab.* 1.9.10; Plut. *Alex.* 11.6; Aelian 13.7; Pliny *NH* 7.109), it is tempting to suggest this dedication could have been a link to another Boiotian poet, Hesiod, whose father was from Kyme.

10. M. H. Hansen (2008: 269–70) suggests 5,000 to 7,000 for the population of Plataia while highlighting the problems associated with the calculation. A more recent estimate suggests a population of around 3,000 in 430 B.C.: Konecny, Aravantinos, and Marchese 2013: 34n153. There are several major difficulties in calculating the numbers of Plataians in exile and where they were, one of which is the use of Plataian citizenship grants by Athens (e.g., Ar. *Frogs* 693–94). Another issue is the relocation of Plataians to Skione (Thuc. 5.32.1; Isoc. 4.109). They are usually presumed to have returned to Athens after the Spartans took control of the settlement at the end of the Peloponnesian War (Xen. *Hell.* 2.2.9; Plut. *Lys.* 14.3), but this process is not clear in our sources.

11. Lysias 23.2–3. Lysias claims that the Plataians would gather each month at the cheese market in Athens (23.6). See also Kalliontzis (2014) on an inscription commemorating Plataian war dead, perhaps in a fourth-century encounter in northern Greece, which may relate to the period in Athenian exile. On some of the problems associated with the sources for the grant of Athenian citizenship, see Canevaro 2010.

12. Her. Krit. *BNJ* 369A F.1.7: ἀρνούμενοι τοὺς Βοιωτοὺς Ἀθηναῖοί εἰσι Βοιωτοί. "Boiotian Tanagrans" are sent grain from Kyrene in the well-known early Hellenistic decree (*SEG*

9.2=Rhodes and Osborne 2003: 96), an unusual qualifier for Tanagrans, perhaps signifying the liminal status of this community between Attica and Boiotia in the period after the destruction of Thebes and the return of Oropos to Athenian control.

13. See Konecny, Aravantinos, and Marchese 2013: 33–35.

14. Demosthenes 19.326 for the Athenian garrison of Panakton in the 340s. The contiguous border between Athens and Plataia was famously exploited for symbolic purposes before the battle of Plataia in 479 B.C.: Plut. *Arist.* 11.3–8.

15. The claim to be colonists of the Athenians might have been only one of the identities of this group. As Thebes had long demonstrated, it was possible to have overlapping and contradictory identities based on different foundation myths (Kadmos, Amphion, and Zethus, migratory Boiotoi) without any difficulty. For useful overviews of some of the issues related to plural Theban foundation narratives, see Berman 2004; and Kuhr 2006: chap. 4, esp. 247–56.

16. Farinetti 2011: 191–200 for the high fertility of Theban land. Sources for division of land of Thebans: Arrian. *Anab.* 1.9.9; Justin 11.4.7; Diod. 18.11.3–4; Hyperides 6.17 and Paus. 1.25.4 seem to imply neighbors moving in with less regulation. Din. 1.24 clearly refers to the city center being used as farmland.

17. Isoc. *Plat.* 7: "For who does not know that our land has been portioned out for grazing and our city utterly destroyed?"

18. Konecny, Aravantinos, and Marchese (2013: 35–36) suggest that conspicuous improvements to the fortifications with up-to-date defenses may have resulted from this increase in support.

19. For the problem of the attribution of "Panathenaic" to the theater rather than the stadium, see Rhodes and Osborne 2003: 477 and Lambert 2012: 354.

20. Isager and Skydsgaard 1992: 104–5.

21. *IG* II^3 1 345.

22. The war to which Eudemos donated four thousand drachmas is likely to have been the abortive Athenian participation in the revolt of Agis III of Sparta. Eudemos' anti-Macedonian subscription is in contrast to Plataia's stance in the Lamian War, where the resettlement of Thebans by Athens was seen as the greater evil (Diod. 18.11.3–5). It is not unlikely that the ability to hold land granted in the decree might have confirmed Eudemos as legitimate owner of property he had already secured in Attica during his time there.

23. Plut. *Alex.* 34.1; Plut. *Arist.* 11.9.

24. See the discussion in chapter 6 of this volume.

25. Boedeker (2001: 151–52) adroitly makes the case for an earlier festival at Plataia from archaeological evidence. Rigsby (1996: 27) places the foundation of the Eleutheria alongside the refoundation of Thebes in 316 B.C., seeing it as a way of marking the symbolic centrality of the mainland states in a world where power and geography had become plural and disparate.

26. Schachter 1981–1994: 4:125–43 on the cult of Zeus in Plataia, with 126–32 providing a plausible reconstruction of the historical development of the Eleutheria.

27. Plut. *Arist.* 21.1 records the creation of the agon but misplaces it to the 470s. Rigsby (1996: 54–84) reflects on the grant of *asylia* for the festival and the unparalleled success of Boiotian poleis in attaining similar status for their cults in the third century. Her. Krit. *BNJ* 369A F.1.11 (quoted earlier).

28. For discussion of the Daidala, see chapter 6 in this volume.

29. Kalaurian Amphiktiony: Strab. 8.6.14; *IG* IV 842. The membership is not uncontroversial but has received support in recent years: Forrest 2000: 284; Breglia 2005; Constantakopoulou 2007: 29–37.

30. Destruction of Thespiaia and Plataia in 480 B.C.: Hdt. 8.50.2. Thespiai sought new settler-citizens after 479 B.C. (Hdt.8.75.2), a practice that might offer a parallel to the resettlement after 338 B.C.

31. Paus. 9.15.3, although this is in keeping with Pausanias' encomiastic portrayal of Epameinondas throughout the *Periegesis*, on which see chapter 6 in this volume.

32. Diod. 15.57.1. Buckler 1980: 66; Bakhuizen 1994: 316.

33. Ma 2008: 72. A *theorodokos* was appointed in Orchomenos in 360/359: *IG* IV^2.1 94.a.8. This has encouraged a suggestion that there may have been a resettlement by pro-Thebans (Hansen and Nielsen 2004: 447), whereas Buckler (1989b: 55–56) opts for a scenario that saw a partial enslavement of the population and a dismembering of the polis into villages. Thuc. 4.76 (424 B.C.), documenting the breakup of the political unit of Orchomenos and Chaironeia by the koinon, is perhaps the best example of action taken because of fear over Orchomenian control of the Kephissos valley.

34. Diod. 16.33.4, although it may have been fortified: Diod. 16.58.1.

35. The control of the site may have changed hands several times during the course of the war: Buckler 1989b: 82–84.

36. Dem. 19.112; 19.325.

37. That Orchomenians were present at the destruction of Thebes suggests that a return had begun by this stage; Diod. 17.13.5 names Thespians, Plataians, and Orchomenians. Justin 11.3.8 has Phokians as well. Plutarch (*Alex.* 11.5) and Arrian (*Anab.*1.8.8) have Phokians and Plataians only.

38. If the political and military contributions outlined at *Hell. Oxy.*19.3 (Chambers) are proportional, Orchomenos and its dependencies would have had a population of around 25,000 at the beginning of the fourth century (one and two-thirds of the eleven federal units, which represented 165,500 population across the region. For this figure, see the introduction).

39. *IG* VII 3206, discussed in Fossey 1991a: 86–87 and Knoepfler 1992: 495 no. 170.

40. Diod. 17.17.4: 600 Greek cavalry accompanied Alexander. *Hell. Oxy.*19.3 states Orchomenos had responsibility for supplying one and two-thirds of the eleven units of federal forces, theoretically meaning a cavalry contingent of around 166 horse.

41. Raising horses was specifically banned in Phokis as part of the peace terms of the Sacred War: Diod. 16.60.1.

42. *Anth. Pal.* 6.344. As Foucart (1879: 457–58) suggests, the absence of dialectal forms indicates that this was probably a reinscription of a later period, but there is no reason to doubt that there was an authentic original. Demobilization of allied contingents: Arrian *Anab.* 3.19.5–6; Plut. *Alex.* 42.5; Justin 12.1.1–3; QC 6.2.17. Diod. 17.74.3; Bosworth 1989: 97.

43. The extensive investigation undertaken by the Munich research project is the foundation for understanding the Bronze Age system: Knauss, Heinrich, and Kalcyk 1984; Knauss 1987, 1990.

44. Mackil (2013: 306) considers some of the economic and political problems the drainage might have caused and suggests that it was an early project of the koinon.

45. There is physical evidence to support Strabo's testimony, but the extent and location of fourth-century work is debated (Krasilnikoff 2010: 117). In the last decade, the old claim

that the tunnel constructed in the east of the Kopais basin may have been the work of Krates has been revisited: Hope Simpson and Hagel 2006: 204; Koutsoyiannis and Angelakis 2007.

46. Krates is no. 37 in the "Lamprias Catalog." It is also possible that he is the person mentioned by Diogenes Laertius (4.23) who accompanied Alexander as a "miner-sapper." Ps.-Call. 1.33 also mentions a Krateros who took part in the building of Alexandria. Cf. P. W. Wallace 1979: 76–78.

47. Furthermore, when Alexander stopped at Onchestos in 335 B.C., the marshes there were reported to be "bellowing": Diod. 17.10.4. There have been suggestions of a natural, cyclical basis of the flooding: Repapis 1989. When the land was drained in the twentieth century, there was a layer of four meters of peat on the lake bed before it oxidized and eroded: Rackham 1983: 297 with n. 8. Theophrastus (*Hist. Pl.* 4.11.3) implies that the lake was associated with sickness, and Corvisier (1985: 10–22) considers Kopais and the spread of malaria. Cf. Herakleides Krititikos (*BNJ* 369A F.1.25), who characterizes Onchestos as having "τὸν πυρετόν."

48. *SEG* IX 2=Rhodes and Osborne *GHI* 96.

49. Aristophanes *Acharnians* 860–80. The animals mentioned have been identified with modern species, some of which can still be found in central Greece: Gonzalez 2010. Although ψιάθως (rush mats) and θρυαλλίδας (lamp wicks) are "processed," they are both principally products of Lake Kopais (*Plantago crassifolia* can be used for lamp wicks and thrives in brackish water in modern Greece).

50. The osteological evidence is discussed in the introduction, n. 9.

51. Farinetti (2008) discusses fluctuations in the level of the lake and the issues surrounding this.

52. Theophrastus *Hist. Pl.* 8.4.5–6; *Caus. Pl.* 4.9.5. For sowing of spring wheat, see Michell 1940: 55.

53. See Hope Simpson and Hagel 2006: fig. 11 and Farinetti 2008: fig. 2 for projections of the basin showing the relative amount of land that would be revealed by a drop in the water level. Strabo's mention of the ancient site of Orchomenos being drained (9.2.18) may imply that the completed part of the work focused on the northwest of the basin, but the identity and location of this site are not secure: Wallace 1979: 165–66.

54. Although arguments over use of the lake might also have caused conflict; rights to exploit the lake for fishing could have caused a third-century boundary dispute recorded in a rupestral inscription between Akraiphiai and Kopai (*IG* VII 2792, *SEG* XXXVI 441). See Mackil 2013: 445–46 (T31). Alexander had to arbitrate in arguments over land caused by the drainage projects in Macedon undertaken by Philip II: Hatzopoulos 1996: 2: 25–28, no.6.

55. For discussion of Theban fish eating, see the introduction.

56. On possible drainage projects of Archelaos: Greenwalt 1999: 167–69. Theophrastus states (*Caus. Pl.* 5.14.6) that Philip II reclaimed the waterlogged plain of Philippi. Cf. Pliny *NH* 17.30; and Horden and Purcell 2000: 248.

57. Polyaenus 1.3.5; Diod. 4.18.7. Frazer (1898: 5:194–95) notes principal Bronze Age *katavothras* blocked by fallen rocks. Bosworth (1996: 98, 182–83) discusses Alexander's later desire to compete with Herakles.

58. Theoph. *Hist. Pl.* 4.11.2; Pliny *NH* 16.169; Frazer 1898: 5:119.

59. Farinetti 2008.

60. The importance of Poseidon's grove at Onchestos in the *Homeric Hymn to Apollo* (230–39) is similarly likely to be a reflection of its early delimitation of the boundary between Theban and Orchomenian areas of influence.

61. Knauss (1992, 1993) believes in an initial Mycenaean phase followed by improvement/repair alongside the Kopais system after 338 B.C. Hope Simpson and Hagel (2006: 222–23) date the work to the fourth century only.

62. Diod. 19.54.1. Diodoros obliquely states that the Boiotians were persuaded (πείσας) to acquiesce. See Knoepfler 2001c: 12–13 for some discussion of what this might have meant in practice.

63. McKechnie (1989: 57) considers that the Thebans are likely to have been in situ on the basis of Cassander's "summoning" of them after he passed Thermopylai, and of the thought that Athens would restore them. It is probable that many with a claim to being "Theban" and who could stake a claim in the new city had remained on the land in some capacity, and these were reinforced (presumably by a lot of elite members of society) from Athens and elsewhere.

64. Buraselis 2014.

65. Knoepfler 2001c: 13–18.

66. Alexander's stance on the city of Thebes was consistent, but his treatment of individuals might have been less punitive (Arrian *Anab.* 2.15.3–4). It is worth noting that both the individuals treated leniently had personal attributes that appealed to Alexander.

67. Diod. 18.8.4 for the general provision and Plut. *Mor.* 221a for the specific clause relating to Thebans. See Worthington 1990: 194n3 for summaries of explanations of Diodoros' omission of the clause.

68. See Miller 1996 for the relationship more broadly.

69. There is no physical evidence for the cult, but Pausanias (9.18.5) records it as a response to an oracle promising blameless wealth (ἀμύμονι πλούτῳ), an understandable desire in the context of the fourth century.

70. Schachter 1981–1994: 1:234.

71. Alexander visited Ilion and prayed to Priam as a descendant of Neoptolemos. Arr. *Anab.* 1.11.7–8. An argument has been made for a late sixth-century foundation of the cult of Hektor: Federico 2008.

72. Roller (1989: 90–91) suggests that the period after the King's Peace of 386 would provide a logical juncture for the reconstruction. He also reflects that Tanagra, with its fourth-century construction of a grid plan attractively arranged over a sloping site, anticipates Priene's development later in the century: Roller 1987: 229.

73. See chapter 1 by Snodgrass in this volume.

74. See the introduction in this volume.

75. Flower 2000: 96–97, emphasizing how popular the destruction of Thebes would have been in many Greek communities.

REFERENCES

Accame, S. 1941. *La lega ateniese del sec. IV A.C.* Rome: A. Signorelli.

Alcock, S. 1995. "Pausanias and the Polis: Use and Abuse." In *Sources for the Ancient Greek City-State,* ed. M. Hansen, Acts of the Copenhagen Polis Centre, vol. 2, 326–44. Copenhagen: Munksgaard.

Amandry, P. 1945. *Note sur l'aire delphique.* Rapport: Delphes 1945-I. Athens: Archives—EFA.

———. 1977. "Statue de taureau en argent." *BCH Suppl.* 4: *Etudes delphiques*: 272–93.

———. 1981. "Chronique delphique 1970–81." *BCH* 105: 673–769.

———. 1984. "Notes de topographie et d'architecture delphiques VIII: Eléments d'architecture archaïque et classique." *BCH* 108: 177–98.

———. 2000. "La vie religieuse à Delphes: Bilan d'un siècle de fouilles." *BCH Suppl.* 36: *Delphes: Cent ans après la Grande fouille; Essai de bilan*: 9–21.

Amandry, P., and E. Hansen. 2010. *Fouilles de Delphes II 14: Le temple d'Apollon du IVième siècle.* Paris: De Boccard.

Ameling, W. 1996. "Pausanias und die hellenistische Geschichte." In *Pausanias Historien,* ed. J. Bingen, 117–160. Geneva: Fondation Hardt.

Aravantinos, V. 2006. "A New Inscribed Kioniskos from Thebes." *Annual of the British School at Athens* 101: 369–77.

———. 2014. "The Inscriptions from the Sanctuary of Herakles at Thebes: An Overview." In *The Epigraphy and History of Boeotia: New Finds, New Prospects,* ed. N. Papazarkadas, 149–210. Leiden: Brill.

Aravantinos, V., and N. Papazarkadas. 2012. "hαγεμονία: A New Treaty from Classical Thebes." *Chiron* 42: 239–54.

Arrington, N. T. 2012. "The Form(s) and Date(s) of a Classical War Monument: Re-evaluating *IG* I^3 1163 and the Case for Delion." *ZPE* 181: 61–75.

Audiat, J. 1933. *Fouilles de Delphes II 2: Le trésor des Athéniens.* Paris: De Boccard.

Austin, R. P. 1931. "Excavations at Haliartos, 1931." *Annual of the British School at Athens* 32: 180–212.

Babelon, E. 1914. *Traité des monnaies grecques et romaines.* Vol. 2, pt. 3. Paris: E. Leroux.

Bakhuizen, S. C. 1994. "Thebes and Boeotia in the Fourth Century B.C." *Phoenix* 48 (4): 307–30.

Basset, S. 2001. "The Enigma of Clearchus the Spartan." *AHB* 15: 1–13.

BCD. 2006. *Triton IX: The BCD Collection of the Coinage of Boiotia.* Lancaster, Pa.: Classical Numismatic Group.

Beck, H. 1997. *Polis und Koinon: Untersuchungen zur Geschichte und Struktur griechischen Bundesstaaten im 4. Jahrhundert v. Chr.* Stuttgart: F. Steiner.

———. 2000. "Thebes, the Boiotian League, and the 'Rise of Federalism' in Fourth Century Greece." In *Presenza e funzione della città di Tebe nella cultura greca: Atti del Convegno Internazionale (Urbino 7–9 Luglio 1997)*, ed. P. A. Bernadini, 331–44. Pisa: Istituti editoriali e poligrafici internazionali.

Beck, H., and A. Ganter. 2015. "Boiotia and the Boiotian Leagues." In *Federalism in Greek Antiquity*, ed. H. Beck and P. Funke, 132–57. Cambridge: Cambridge University Press.

Beloch, J. 1886. *Die Bevölkerung der griechisch-römischen Welt.* Leipzig: Duncker und Humblot.

Bergquist, B. 1967. *The Archaic Greek Temenos: A Study of Structure and Function.* Lund: Gleerup.

Bermann, D. W. 2002. "'Seven-Gated' Thebes and Narrative Topography in Aeschylus' *Seven against Thebes.*" *Quaderni urbinati di cultura classica* 71: 73–100.

———. 2004. "The Double Foundation of Boiotian Thebes." *TAPA* 134 (1): 1–22.

Berthold, R. 1980. "Fourth-Century Rhodes." *Historia* 29: 32–49.

Berve, H. 1926. *Das Alexanderreich auf Prosopographischer Grundlage.* Vol. 2. Munich: Beck.

Bintliff, J. 1993. "Forest Cover, Agricultural Intensity and Population Density in Roman Imperial Boeotia, Central Greece." In *Evaluation of Land Surfaces Cleared from Forests in the Mediterranean Region during the Time of the Roman Empire*, ed. B. Frenzel, 133–43. Stuttgart: Gustav Fischer Verlag.

———. 1997. "Further Considerations on the Population of Ancient Boiotia." In *Recent Developments in the History and Archaeology of Central Greece*, ed. J. Bintliff, 231–52. Oxford: BAR.

———. 2005. "Explorations in Boeotian Population History." *Ancient World* 36 (1): 5–17.

Bintliff, J. L., P. Howard, and A. Snodgrass. 2007. *Testing the Hinterland: The Work of the Boeotia Survey in the Leondari South-East and Thespiai South Sectors, 1989–1991.* Cambridge: McDonald Institute for Archaeological Research.

Bintliff, J. L., and A. M. Snodgrass. 1988: "Off-site Pottery Distributions: A Regional and Interregional Perspective." *Current Anthropology* 29: 506–13.

Blümel, W. 1994. "Two New Inscriptions from the Cnidian Peninsula: Proxeny Decree for Epaminondas and a Funeral Epigram." *EA* 23: 157–59.

Boedeker, D. 2001. "Paths to Heroization at Plataea." In *The New Simonides: Contexts of Praise and Desire*, ed. D. Boedeker and D. Sider, 148–63. Oxford: Oxford University Press.

Bommelaer, J. F. 1991. *Guide de Delphes: Le site.* Paris: De Boccard.

Bosworth, A. B. 1980. *A Historical Commentary on Arrian's History of Alexander: Commentary on Books I–III.* Oxford: Clarendon Press.

———. 1989. *Conquest and Empire: The Reign of Alexander the Great.* Cambridge: Cambridge University Press.

———. 1996. *Alexander and the East: The Tragedy of Triumph.* Oxford: Clarendon Press.

Bourguet, E. 1914. *Les ruines de Delphes.* Paris: Fontemoing et Cie.

———. 1929. *Fouilles de Delphes III 1: Inscriptions de l'entrée du sanctuaire au trésor des Athéniens.* Paris: De Boccard.

Bousquet, J. 1952. *Fouilles de Delphes II: Le trésor de Cyrène.* Paris: De Boccard.

———. 1963. "Inscriptions de Delphes." *BCH* 87: 188–208.

Bowie, E. 2014. "Rediscovering Sacadas." In *Patterns of the Past: Epitēdeumata in the Greek Tradition*, ed. A. Moreno and R. Thomas, 39–56. Oxford: Oxford University Press.

Braund, D. 2005. "Pericles, Cleon and the Pontus: The Black Sea in Athens, c. 440–421." In *Scythians and Greeks: Cultural Interactions in Scythia, Athens and the Early Roman Em-*

pire (Sixth Century BC–First Century AD), ed. D. Braund, 80–99. Exeter: University of Exeter Press.

Breglia, L. 2005. "The Amphictyony of Calaureia." *Ancient World* 36: 18–33.

Bruce, I. A. F. 1967. *An Historical Commentary on the Hellenica Oxyrhynchia*. Cambridge: Cambridge University Press.

Buck, R. J. 1985. "Boiotia and Political Theory in the Fifth and Fourth Centuries." In *La Béotie antique*, ed. P. Roesch and G. Argoud, 291–96. Paris: Éditions du Centre national de la recherche scientifique.

———. 1994. *Boiotia and the Boiotian League, 423–371 B.C.* Edmonton: University of Alberta Press.

Buckler, J. 1980. *The Theban Hegemony, 371–362 B.C.* Cambridge, Mass.: Harvard University Press.

———. 1982. "Alliance and Hegemony in Fourth-Century Greece: The Case of the Theban Hegemony." *Ancient World* 5: 84–86.

———. 1985. "Thebes, Delphoi and the Outbreak of the Third Sacred War." In *La Béotie antique*, ed. P. Roesch and G. Argoud, 237–46. Paris: Éditions du Centre national de la recherche scientifique.

———. 1989a. "Pammenes, die Perser und der Heilige Krieg." In *Boiotika*, ed. H. Beister and J. Buckler, 155–62. Munich: Maris=Buckler and Beck 2008: 224–32 (in English).

———. 1989b. *Philip II and the Sacred War*. Leiden: Brill.

———. 1998. "Epameinondas and the New Inscription from Knidos." *Mnemosyne* 51: 192–205.

———. 2000a. *Aegean Greece in the Fourth Century BC*. Leiden: Brill.

———. 2000b. "The Phantom *Synedrion* of the Boeotian Confederacy, 378–335 BC." In *Polis and Politics: Studies in Ancient Greek History Presented to Mogens Herman Hansen on His Sixtieth Birthday*, ed. P. Flensted-Jensen, T. H. Nielsen, and L. Rubinsetein, 431–46. Copenhagen: Museum Tusculanum Press.

———. 2003. *Aegean Greece in the Fourth Century BC*. Leiden: Brill.

Buckler, J., and H. Beck. 2008. *Central Greece and the Politics of Power in the Fourth Century BC*. Cambridge: Cambridge University Press.

Buraselis, K. 2014. "Contributions to Rebuilding Thebes: The Old and a New Fragment of *IG* VII 2419=*Sylloge* 3 337." *ZPE* 188: 159–70.

Bury, J. B., and R. Meiggs. 1975. *A History of Greece to the Death of Alexander the Great*. 4th ed. London: Macmillan.

Busolt, G. 1874. *Der zweite athenische Bund*. Leipzig: Teubner.

———. 1920–1926. *Griechische Staatskunde*. Ed. H. Swoboda. H.d.A. IV. 1. i. Munich: Beck.

Canevaro, M. 2010. "The Decree Awarding Citizenship to the Plataeans ([Dem.] 59.104)." *GRBS* 50: 337–69.

———. 2013. *The Documents in the Attic Orators: Laws and Decrees in the Public Speeches of the Demosthenic Corpus*. Oxford: Oxford University Press.

Cargill, J. 1981. *The Second Athenian League: Empire or Free Alliance?* Berkeley: University of California Press.

———. 1983. "*IG* II^2 and the Athenian Kleruchy on Samos." *GRBS* 24: 321–32.

Cartledge, P. 1987. *Agesilaos and the Crisis of Sparta*. London: Duckworth.

———. 2000. "Boiotian Swine F(or)ever? The Boiotian Superstate, 395 BC." In *Polis and Politics: Studies in Ancient Greek History*, ed. P. Flensted-Jenson, T. H. Nielsen, and L. Rubenstein, 397–418. Copenhagen: Museum Tusculanum Press.

Cawkwell, G. 1962. "Notes on the Social War." *Classica et Mediaevalia* 23: 34–49.

———. 1972. "Epaminondas and Thebes." *CQ* 22: 254–78.

———. 1976. "The Imperialism of Thrasybulus." *CQ* 26: 270–77.

———. 1981. "Notes on the Failure of the Second Athenian Confederacy." *JHS* 101: 40–55.

Chaniotis, A. 2002. "Ritual Dynamics: The Boiotian Festival of the Daidala." In *Kykeon: Studies in Honour of H. S. Versnel*, ed. H. F. J. Horstmanshoff, H. W. Singor, F. T. van Straten, and J. H. M. Strubbe, 23–48. Leiden: Brill.

———. 2004. "From Communal Spirit to Individuality: The Epigraphic Habit in Hellenistic and Roman Crete." In *Creta romana e protobizantina*, vol. 1, ed. Monica Livadiotti and Ilaria Simiakaki, 75–87. Padova: Bottega d'Erasmo.

Cloché, P. 1952. *Thèbes de Béotie: Des origines à la conquête romaine*. Louvain: Editions Nauwelaerts.

Constantakopoulou, C. 2007. *The Dance of the Islands: Insularity, Networks, the Athenian Empire, and the Aegean World*. Oxford: Oxford University Press.

Cooper, F. A. 2000. "The Fortifications of Epaminondas and the Rise of the Monumental Greek City." In *City Walls: The Urban Enceinte in Global Perspective*, ed. J. D. Tracey, 155–91. Cambridge: Cambridge University Press.

Corsten, T. 1999. *Vom Stamm zum Bund: Gründung und territoriale Organisation griechischer Bundesstaaten*. Munich: Oberhummer Gesellschaft.

Corvisier, J. 1985. *Santé et société en Grèce ancienne*. Paris: Economica.

Courby, M. F. 1927. *Fouilles de Delphes II 1: La terrasse du temple*. Paris: De Boccard.

D'Angour, Armand. 1999. "Archinus, Eucleides and the Reform of the Athenian Alphabet." *BICS* 43: 109–30.

Daux, G. 1936. *Pausanias à Delphes*. Paris: Picard.

Daux, G., and A. Salac. 1932. *Fouilles de Delphes III 3: Inscriptions depuis le trésor des Athéniens jusq'aux bases de Gélon*. Paris: De Boccard.

Defradas, J. 1954. *Les thèmes de la propagande delphique*. Paris: Librarie C. Klincksieck.

Deltenne, F. 2010. "La datation du débout de la troisième guerre sacrée: Retours sur l'interprétation des comptes de Delphes." *BCH* 134: 97–116.

Demand, N. H. 1990. *Urban Relocation in Archaic and Classical Greece: Flight and Consolidation*. Bristol: Bristol Classical Press.

Dow, S. 1961. "The Walls Inscribed with Nikomakhos' Law Code." *Hesperia* 30: 58–73.

———. 1983. "Catalogi Generis Incerti *IG* II^2 2364–2489: A Check-List." *Ancient World* 8: 95–106.

Dreher, M. 1995. *Hegemon und Symmachoi: Untersuchungen zum Zweiten athenischen Seebund*. Berlin: De Gruyter.

Ducat, J. 2008. "Sparta: Geography, Myth and History." *Revue Historique* 648: 924–26.

Ducrey, P., and C. Calame. 2006. "Notes de sculpture et d'épigraphie en Béotie, II: Une base de statue portant la signature de Lysippe de Sicyone à Thèbes." *BCH* 130: 63–81.

Edwards, A. T. 2004. *Hesiod's Ascra*. Berkeley: University of California Press.

Egger, E. 1878. "Note sur une inscription métrique." *BCH* 2: 22–27.

Elsner, J. 1992. "Pausanias: A Greek Pilgrim in the Roman World." *Past and Present* 135: 3–29.

———. 2001. "Structuring 'Greece': Pausanias' *Periegesis* as a Literary Construct." In *Pausanias: Travel and Memory in Roman Greece*, ed. S. E. Alcock, J. F. Cherry, and J. Elsner, 3–20. Oxford: Oxford University Press.

Faraguna, M. 2012. "Società, amministrazione, diritto: Lo statuto giuridico di tombe e periboloi nell' Atene classica." In *Symposion 2011: Études d'histoire du droit grec et hellénis-*

tique (Paris, 7–10 septembre 2011), ed. B. Legras and G. Thür, 165–85. Vienna: Verlag der Österreichischen Akademie der Wissenschaften.

Farinetti, E. 2008. "Fluctuating Landscapes: The Case of the Copais Basin in Ancient Boiotia." *Annuario della Scuola archeologica di Atene e delle Missioni italiane in Oriente* 86: 115–38.

———. 2011. *Boeotian Landscapes: A GIS-Based Study for the Reconstruction and Interpretation of the Archaeological Datasets of Ancient Boeotia*. Oxford: Archaeopress.

Federico, E. 2008. "Hektor sull'isola dei Beati: Memorie e realia tebani da Licofrone a Pausania." *Incidenza dell'antico: Dialoghi di storia greca* 6: 253–71.

Flament, Ch. 2010. *Contribution à l'étude des ateliers monétaires grecs*. Louvain-la-Neuve: Association de numismatique professeur M. Hoc.

Flower, M. A. 2000. "Alexander the Great and Panhellenism." In *Alexander the Great in Fact and Fiction*, ed. A. B. Bosworth and E. J. Baynham, 96–135. Oxford: Oxford University Press.

Forrest, W. G. 2000. "The Pre-polis Polis." In *Alternatives to Athens: Varieties of Political Organization and Community in Ancient Greece*, ed. R. Brock and S. Hodkinson, 280–92. Oxford: Oxford University Press.

Fossey, J. M. 1979. "Une base navale d'Épaminondas." In *Proceedings of the Second International Conference on Boiotian Antiquities*, ed. A. Schachter and J. M. Fossey, 9–13. Montreal: Tiresias.

———. 1988. *Topography and Population of Ancient Boiotia*. Vol. 1. Chicago: Ares.

———. 1991a. "Inscriptions from Orkhomenos 3 (='Επιγραφαὶ ἐξ 'Ορχομενοῦ 3)." In *Epigraphica Boeotica*, vol. 1, *Studies in Boiotian Inscriptions*, ed. J. M. Fossey, 65–87. Amsterdam: Brill.

———. 1991b. "Tanagran Tombstones." In *Epigraphica Boeotica*, vol. 1, *Studies in Boiotian Inscriptions*, ed. J. M. Fossey, 197–218. Amsterdam: Brill.

———. 2014. *Epigraphica Boeotica*. Vol. 2, *Further Studies on Boiotian Inscriptions*. Leiden and Boston: Brill.

Foucart, P.-F. 1879. "Inscriptions d'Orchomène: Dédicace des cavaliers ayant fait l'expédition d'Asie sous Alexandre; Pièces relatives à un prêt fait par une femme de Thespies à la ville d'Orchomène." *BCH* 3: 452–65.

Fraser, P. M., and T. Rönne. 1957. *Boeotian and West Greek Tombstones*. Lund: Gleerup.

Frazer, J. G. 1898. *Pausanias's Description of Greece*. 5 vols. London: Macmillan.

Frey, L. 1992. "Mathématiques anciennes et conception architecturale du trésor de Thèbes." In *Delphes: Centenaire de la "Grande fouille" réalisée par l'Ecole française d'Athènes (1892–1903)*, ed. J. F. Bommelaer, 233–49. Leiden: Brill.

Fröhlich, P. 2004. *Les cités grecques et le contrôle des magistrats (IVe–Ier siècle avant J.-C.)* Geneva: Droz.

Gabrielsen, V. 2007. "Trade and Tribute: Byzantion and the Black Sea Straits." In *The Black Sea in Antiquity: Regional and Interregional Economic Exchanges*, ed. V. Gabrielsen and J. Lund, 287–324. Aarhus: Aarhus University Press.

Gartland, S. D. 2013. "The Electrum Coinage of Thebes." *NChron* 173: 23–32 and plates 6–7.

Gehrke, H.-J. 1985. *Stasis: Untersuchungen zu den inneren Kriegen in den griechischen Staaten des 5. und 4. Jahrhunderts v. Chr.* Munich: C. H. Beck.

Georgiadou, A. 1997. *Plutarch's "Pelopidas": A Historical and Philological Commentary*. Stuttgart: Teubner.

Glotz, G. 1933. "Un Carthaginois à Thebes en 365 av. J.-C." In *Mélanges offerts à M. Nicolas Iorga*, 331–39. Paris: J. Gamber.

Gonzalez, J. P. 2010. "Un invierno 'clásico' en los lagos Beocios." In *Dialéctica histórica y compromiso social: Homenaje a Domingo Plácido*, ed. J. G. C. A. F. Vaquero and P. M. L. B. d. Quiroga, 1437–62. Zaragoza: Libros Pórtico.

Greenwalt, W. 1999. "Why Pella?" *Historia* 48 (2): 158–83.

Guarducci, M. 1930. "Per la cronologia degli arconti della Beozia (Richerche storico-epigrafiche)." *RFIC* 58: 311–38.

Gullath, B. 1982. *Untersuchungen zur Geschichte Boiotiens in der Zeit Alexanders und der Diadochen*. Frankfurt: P. Lang.

Habicht, C. 1985. *Pausanias' Guide to Ancient Greece*. Berkeley: University of California Press.

———. 2002. "Die Ehren der Proxenoi: Ein Vergleich." *MusHel* 59: 13–30.

Hall, J. 1997. *Ethnic Identity in Greek Antiquity*. Cambridge: Cambridge University Press.

Hammond, N. G. L. 1997. "What May Philip Have Learnt as a Hostage in Thebes? (Early Years of Philip II of Macedon)." *GRBS* 38 (4): 355–72.

Hanell, K. 1934. *Megarische Studien*. Lund: Lindstedt.

Hansen, M. H. 1995. "Boiotian Poleis: A Test Case." In *Sources for the Ancient Greek City-State*, ed. M. Hansen, Acts of the Copenhagen Polis Centre, vol. 2, 13–63. Copenhagen: Munksgaard.

———. 2006. *The Shotgun Method: The Demography of the Ancient Greek City-State Culture*. Columbia: University of Missouri Press.

———. 2008. "An Update on the Shotgun Method." *GRBS* 48: 259–86.

Hansen, M. H., and T. H. Nielsen. 2004. *An Inventory of Archaic and Classical Poleis: An Investigation Conducted by the Copenhagen Polis Centre for the Danish National Research Foundation*. Oxford: Oxford University Press.

Hansen, P. A., 1989. *Carmina epigraphica Graeca: Saeculi IV a. Chr. n. (CEG 2)*. Berlin: W. de Gruyter.

Hatzopoulos, M. B. 1996. *Macedonian Institutions under the Kings: A Historical and Epigraphic Study*. 2 vols. Athens: Kentron Hellenikes kai Romaikes Archaiotetos.

Head, B. V. 1881. *On the Chronological Sequence of the Coins of Boeotia*. London: Rollin and Fanardent.

———. 1897. *Catalogue of the Greek Coins of Caria*. London: Trustees of the British Museum.

———. 1911. *Historia Numorum*. 2nd ed. Oxford: Clarendon Press.

Hedrick, C. W., Jr. 1999. "Democracy and the Athenian Epigraphical Habit." *Hesperia* 68: 387–439.

———. 2000. "For Anyone Who Wishes to See." *Ancient World* 31: 127–35.

Hepworth, R. 1989. "Epaminondas' Coinage." In *Proceedings of the 10th International Numismatic Congress*, ed. I. A. Carradice, 35–40. London: International Association of Professional Numismatists in association with the UK Numismatic Trust.

———. 1998. "The 4th Century BC Magistrate Coinage of the Boiotian Confederacy." Νομισματικά Χρονικά 17: 61–96.

Heskel, J. 1997. *The North Aegean Wars, 371–360 B.C.* Stuttgart: F. Steiner.

Hobsbawm, E. 1994. *The Age of Extremes: The Short Twentieth Century, 1914–1991*. London: Michael Joseph.

Holleaux, M. 1895. "Sur une inscription des Thebes." *REG* 8: 7–48.

Homolle, T. 1891. "Nouvelles et Correspondances." *BCH* 15: 441–58.

Hoover, O., A. Meadows, and U. Wartenberg, eds. 2010. *Coin Hoards*. Vol. 10, *Greek Hoards*. New York: American Numismatic Society.

Hope Simpson, R., and D. K. Hagel. 2006. *Mycenean Fortifications, Highways, Dams and Canals*. Sävedalen: Paul Åströms Förlag.

Horden, P., and N. Purcell. 2000. *The Corrupting Sea: A Study of Mediterranean History*. Oxford: Blackwell.

Hornblower, S. 1982. *Mausolus*. Oxford: Oxford University Press.

———. 2011. *The Greek World, 479–323 BC*. 4th ed. London: Routledge.

Hubbard, T. K. 2004. "The Dissemination of Epinician Lyric: Pan-Hellenism, Reperformance, Written Texts." In *Oral Performance and Its Context*, ed. C. J. Mackie, *Mnemosyne* Suppl. 248, 71–93. Leiden: Brill.

Humphreys, S. C. 2004. *The Strangeness of Gods: Historical Perspectives on the Interpretation of Athenian Religion*. Oxford: Oxford University Press.

———. 2004–2009 [2010]. "Epheboi at Oropos." *Horos* 17–21: 83–90.

Hutton, W. 2005. *Describing Greece: Landscape and Literature in the "Periegesis" of Pausanias*. Cambridge: Cambridge University Press.

Imhoof-Blumer, F. 1877. "Zur Münzkunde Boeotiens und der peloponnesischen Argos." *NZeit* 9: 1–62.

Irigoin, J. 1952. *Histoire du texte de Pindare*. Paris: Klincksieck.

Isaac, B. 1986. *The Greek Settlements in Thrace until the Macedonian Conquest*. Leiden: Brill.

Isager, S., and J. E. Skydsgaard. 1992. *Ancient Greek Agriculture: An Introduction*. London: Routledge.

Iversen, P. A. 2007. "The Small and Great Daidala in Boiotian History." *Historia* 56 (4): 381–418.

———. 2010. "New Restorations and Date for a Fragment of Hestiatoria from Thespiai (IThesp, 39)." In *Studies in Greek Epigraphy and Hisory in Honor of Stephen V. Tracy*, ed. G. Reger, F. X. Ryan, and T. F. Winters, Études Ausonius Institute 26, 255–68. Bordeaux: Ausonius éditions.

Jacquemin, A. 1991. "Les chantiers de Pankratès, d'Agathôn et d'Euainétos au péribole du sanctuaire d'Apollon à Delphes." *BCH* 115: 243–58.

———. 1999. *Offrandes monumentales à Delphes*. Paris: De Boccard.

Jacquemin, A., and D. Laroche. 2010. "Constructions et reconstructions à Delphes au IVe s. av. JC." *Les Dossiers d'Archéologie* 342: 2–9.

———. 2012–2013. "Notes sur quatre édifices d'époque classique à Delphes." *BCH* 136–37: 82–122.

Jehne, M. 1994. *Koine Eirene: Untersuchungen zu den Befriedung- und Stabilisieurungsbemühungen in der Griechischen Poliswelt des 4. Jahrhunderts v. Chr.* Stuttgart: F. Steiner.

———. 1999. "Formen der thebanischen Hegemonial politik zwischen Leuktra und Chaironeia (371–339 v. Chr.)." *Klio* 81: 317–58.

Kaibel, G. 1878. *Epigrammata graeca ex lapidibus conlecta*. Berlin: G. Reimer.

Kalliontzis, Y. 2014. "Digging in Storerooms for Inscriptions: An Unpublished Casualty List from Plataia in the Museum of Thebes and the Memory of War in Boiotia." In *The Epigraphy and History of Boeotia: New Finds, New Prospects*, ed. N. Papazarkadas, 332–68. Leiden: Brill.

Keen, T. 1996. "Were the Boiotian Poleis Autonomoi?" In *More Studies in the Ancient Greek Polis*, ed. M. Hansen and K. Raaflaub, 113–25. Stuttgart: F. Steiner.

Keesling, C. 2006. "Heavenly Bodies: Monuments to Prostitutes in Greek Sanctuaries." In *Prostitutes and Courtesans in the Ancient World,* ed. C. Faraone and L. McClare, 59–76. Madison: University of Wisconsin Press.

Kisseoglu, L. 1955. Cited in "Proceedings of the Royal Numismatic Society." *NChron* 6 (15): xvi.

Knauss, J. 1987. *Wasserbau und Siedlungsbedingungen im Altertum. Die Melioration des Kopaisbeckens durch die Minyer im 2. Jt. v. Chr. (Kopais 2).* Munich: Technische Universität.

———. 1990. *Kopais 3: Wasserbau und Geschichte, Minysche Epoche—Bayerische Zeit (vier Jahrhunderte—ein Jahrzehnt).* Munich: Technische Universität.

———. 1992. "Purpose and Function of the Ancient Hydraulic Structures at Thisbe." In *Boeotia Antiqua,* vol. 2, ed. J. Fossey, 35–46. Amsterdam: J. C. Gieben.

———. 1993. "The Prehistoric Land Reclamation at the Valley of Thisvi in Southwest Boiotia, Middle Greece." *15th Congress on Irrigation and Drainage: Water Management in the Next Century* 1 (1): 133–43.

Knauss, J., B. Heinrich, and H. Kalcyk. 1984. *Die Wasserbauten der Minyer in der Kopais: Die älteste Flussregulierung Europas. Untersuchungsergebnisse (Kopais 1).* Munich: Technische Universität.

Knoepfler, D. 1978. "Proxénies béotiennes du IVe siècle." *BCH* 102: 375–93.

———. 1992. "Sept années de recherches sur l'épigraphie de la Béotie (1985–1991)." *Chiron* 22: 411–503.

———. 1993. "Adolf Wilhelm et la pentétèris des Amphiaraia d'Oropos: Réexamen de *A.P.* LIV 7 à la lumière du catalogue *IG* VII 414+*SEG* I 126." In *Aristote et Athènes: Fribourg (Suisse), 23–25 mai 1991,* ed. M. Piérart, 279–302. Paris: De Boccard.

———. 2000. "La loi de Daitondas, les femmes de Thèbes et le collège des Boétarques au IVe et au IIIe siècle avant J.-C." In *Presenza e funzione della città di Tebe nella cultura greca: Atti del Convegno Internazionale (Urbino 7–9 Luglio 1997),* ed. P. A. Bernadini, 345–66. Pisa: Istituti editoriali e poligrafici internazionali.

———. 2001a. *Eretria: Fouilles et recherches.* Vol. 11, *Décrets érétriens de proxénie et de citoyenneté.* Lausanne: Payot.

———. 2001b. "La fête des Daidala de Platées chez Pausanias: Une clef pour l'histoire de la Béotie hellénistique." In *Éditer, traduire, commenter Pausanias en l'an 2000,* ed. D. Knoepfler and M. Piérary, 343–74. Geneva: Librairie Droz.

———. 2001c. "La réintégration de Thèbes dans le *koinon* béotien après son relèvement par Cassandre, ou les surprises de la chronologie épigraphique." In *Recherches récentes sur le monde hellénistique: Actes du colloque international organisé à l'occasion du 60e anniversaire de Pierre Ducrey, Lausanne, Novembre 20–21, 1998,* ed. R. Frei-Stolba and K. Gex, 11–26. Bern: P. Lang.

———. 2004. "La découverte des *Histoires* de Polybe par Pausanias et la place du livre IX (Boiôtika) dans l'élaboration de la *Périégèse.*" *REG* 117: 468–503.

———. 2005. *Apports récents des inscriptions grecques à l'histoire de l'antiquité.* Paris: Collège de France.

———. 2008. "Épigraphie et histoire des cités grecques." *Annuaire du Collège de France, Résumés 2005–2006, 106e année,* 627–48. Paris: Collège de France.

———. 2009. "Bulletin épigraphique: Béotie-Eubée." *REG* 122: 443–79.

———. 2010 [2012]. "L'occupation d'Oropos par Athènes au IVe siècle avant J.-C.: Une clérouquie dissimulée?" In *Gli Ateniesi fuori dall'Attica: Modi d'intervento e di controllo del territorio (Torino, 8–9 aprile 2010), SAIA* 58: 439–54.

———. 2012. "Bulletin épigraphique: Béotie-Eubée." *REG* 125: 567–607.

Konecny, A., V. Aravantinos, and R. Marchese, 2013. *Plataiai: Archäologie und Geschichte einer boiotischen Polis*. Vienna: Österreichisches Archäologisches Institut.

Koumanoudes, S. A. 1877. "Ἄλλαι ἐπιγραφαί." *Athenaion* 6: 151–52.

Koumanoudes, S. N. 1966. "ΠΕΜΠΤΙΔΗΣ." In *Χαριστήριον εἰς Α. Κ. Ὀρλάνδον*, 2:1–21. Athens: Archaiologike Hetaireia.

Koutsoyiannis, D., and A. N. Angelakis. 2007. "Agricultural Hydraulic Works in Ancient Greece." In *Encyclopedia of Water Science*, ed. S. W. Trimble, 24–27. Boca Raton, Fla.: CRC Press.

Kraay, C. M. 1976. *Archaic and Classical Greek Coins*. London: Methuen.

Krasilnikoff, J. A. 2010. "Irrigation as Innovation in Ancient Greek Agriculture." *World Archaeology* 42 (1): 108–21.

Krentz, P. 1989. "Athena Itonia and the Battle of Koroneia." In *Boiotika: Vorträge von 5 Internationalen Böotien-Kolloquium (13–17 Juni 1986)*, ed. H. Beister and J. Buckler, 313–17. Munich: Editio Maris.

Kroll, J. H. 2011. "The Reminting of Athenian Silver Coinages, 353 B.C." *Hesperia* 80: 229–59.

Kuhr, A. 2006. *Als Kadmos nach Boiotien kam: Polis und Ethnos im Spiegel thebanischer Gründungsmythen*. Stuttgart: F. Steiner.

La Coste-Messelière, P. de. 1949. "Listes amphictioniques du IVe siècle." *BCH* 73: 201–47.

Lambert, S. D. 2002. "The Sacrificial Calendar of Athens." *BSA* 92: 353–99.

———. 2012. *Inscribed Athenian Laws and Decrees, 352/1–322/1 BC: Epigraphical Essays*. Brill Studies in Greek and Roman Epigraphy. Leiden: Brill.

Laroche, D., and M. Nenna. 1992. "Deux trésors archaïques en poros à Delphes." In *Delphes: Centenaire de la "Grande fouille" réalisée par l'Ecole française d'Athènes (1892–1903)*, ed. J. F. Bommelaer, 109–24. Leiden: Brill.

Larsen, J. A. O. 1955. "The Boeotian Confederacy and Fifth-Century Oligarchic Theory." *TAPA* 86: 41–50.

———. 1968. *Greek Federal States: Their Institutions and History*. Oxford: Clarendon Press.

Larson, S. 2007. *Tales of Epic Ancestry: Boeotian Collective Identity in the Late Archaic and Early Classical Periods*. Stuttgart: F. Steiner.

Leake, W. M. 1835. *Travels in Northern Greece*. Vol. 2. London: J. Rodwell.

Lewis, D. M. 1990. "The *Synedrion* of the Boeotian Alliance." *Teiresias* supp. 3: 71–73.

———. 1992. "The Thirty Years' Peace." In *The Cambridge Ancient History*, 2nd ed., vol. 5, ed. D. M. Lewis, J. Boardman, J. K. Davies, and M. Ostwald, 121–46. Cambridge: Cambridge University Press.

Liampi, K. 2008. "NIKA, ΛΕΙΑ: Graffiti on Sicyonian and Theban Staters in a New Hoard from Boeotia/Beginning of 2000." *AJN* 20: 209–26.

Liddel, P. 2007. *Civic Obligation and Individual Liberty in Ancient Athens*. Oxford: Oxford University Press.

Low, P. 2003. "Remembering War in Fifth-Century Greece: Ideologies, Societies, and Commemoration beyond Democratic Athens." *World Archaeology* 35: 104–9.

Lupu, E. 2003. "Sacrifice at the Amphiareion and a Fragmentary Sacred Law from Oropos." *Hesperia* 72: 326–31.

Luraghi, N. 2008. *The Ancient Messenians: Constructions of Ethnicity and Memory*. Cambridge: Cambridge University Press.

———. 2010. "The Local Scripts from Nature to Culture." *ClAnt* 29: 68–91.

Ma, J. 2008. "Chaironeia 338: Topographies of Commemoration." *JHS* 128: 72–91.

———. 2013. "Grandes et petites cités au miroir de l'épigraphie classique et hellénistique." *Topoi* 18: 67–86.

Mack, W. 2015. *Proxeny and Polis: Institutional Networks in the Ancient Greek World*. Oxford: Oxford University Press.

Mackil, E. 2004. "Wandering Cities: Alternatives to Catastrophe in the Greek Polis." *AJA* 108.4: 493–516.

———. 2008. "A Boiotian Proxeny Decree and Relief in the Museum of Fine Arts Boston and Boiotian-Lakonian Relations in the 360s." *Chiron* 38: 157–94.

———. 2013. *Creating a Common Polity: Religion, Economy, and Politics in the Making of the Greek Koinon*. Berkeley: University of California Press.

Mackil, E., and P. van Alfen. 2006. "Cooperative Coinage." In *Agoranomia: Studies in Money and Exchange Presented to John H. Kroll*, ed. P. van Alfen, 201–46. New York: American Numismatic Society.

MacMullen, Ramsay. 1982. "The Epigraphic Habit in the Roman Empire." *AJP* 103: 233–46.

Malkin, I., and N. Shmueli. 1988. "The 'City of the Blind' and the Founding of Byzantium." *Med. Hist. Rev.* 3: 21–36.

Manieri, Alessandra. 2009. *Agoni poetico-musicali nella Grecia antica*. Vol. 1. *Beozia*. Pisa: Istituti editoriali e poligrafici internazionali.

Markle, M. 1994. "Diodorus' Sources for the Sacred War in Book 16." In *Ventures into Greek History*, ed. I. Worthington, 43–69. Oxford: Clarendon Press.

Martin, T. R. 1985. *Sovereignty and Coinage in Classical Greece*. Princeton, N.J.: Princeton University Press.

Matthaiou, A. P. 2009. "Attic Public Inscriptions of the Fifth Century BC in Ionic Script." In *Greek History and Epigraphy: Essays in Honour of P. J. Rhodes*, ed. L. Mitchell and L. Rubinstein, 201–12. Swansea: Classical Press of Wales.

———. 2014. "Four Inscribed Bronze Tablets from Thebes: Preliminary Notes." In *The Epigraphy and History of Thebes: New Finds, New Prospects*, ed. Nikolaos Papazarkadas, 211–22. Leiden: Brill.

Mattingly, H. B. 1989. Review of I. Carradice and M. Price, *Coinage in the Greek World*. *NChron* 149: 228–32.

McKechnie, P. R. 1989. *Outsiders in Greek Cities in the Fourth Century BC*. London: Routledge.

Meadows, A., and U. Wartenberg, eds. 2002. *Coin Hoards*. Vol. 9, *Greek Hoards*. London: Royal Numismatic Society.

Meiggs, R., and D. Lewis. 1988. *A Selection of Greek Historical Inscriptions to the End of the Fifth Century B.C.* 2nd ed. Oxford: Clarendon Press.

Merkelbach, R. 1980. *Die Inschriften von Kalchedon*. Bonn: Habelt.

Merle, H. 1916. *Die Geschichte des Städte Byzantion und Kalchedon, von ihrer Gründung bis zum Eingriefen der Römer in die Verhältnisse des Ostens*. Kiel: H. Fiencke.

Michaud, J.-P. 1973. *Fouilles de Delphes II: Le trésor de Thèbes*. Paris: De Boccard.

Michell, H. 1940. *The Economics of Ancient Greece*. Cambridge: Cambridge University Press.

Migeotte, L. 1984. *L'emprunt public dans les cités grecques: Recueil des documents et analyse critique*. Quebec: Éditions du Sphinx; Paris: Les Belles Lettres.

Millender, E. G. 2001. "Spartan Literacy Revisited." *ClAnt* 20: 121–64.

Miller, M. C. J. 1996. "Kassandros, Thebes, Boiotia and Athens." In *Boeotia Antiqua*, vol. 6, ed. J. M. Fossey, 91–103. Amsterdam: Gieben.

Moggi, M. 1993. "Scrittura e riscrittura della storia in Pausania." *RFIC* 121: 396–418.

Morpurgo Davies, A. 1993. "Geography, History, and Dialect: The Case of Oropos." In *Dialectologia Graeca*, ed. E. Crespo, J. L. García Ramón, and A. Striano, 261–79. Madrid: Universidad Autónoma de Madrid.

Müller, C. 1996. "Les recherches françaises à Thespies et au Val des Muses." In *La Montagne des Muses*, ed. A. Hurst and A. Schachter, Recherches et Rencontres, 7, 171–83. Geneva: Librairie Droz.

Müller, H. 2005. "Ein Kultverein von Asklepiasten bei einem attalidischen Phrourion im Yüntdağ." *Chiron* 40: 427–57.

Munn, M. H. 1993. *The Defense of Attica*. Berkeley: University of California Press.

———. 1996. "The First Excavations at Panakton on the Attic-Boiotian Frontier." In *Boeotia Antiqua*, vol. 6, ed. J. M. Fossey, 47–58. Amsterdam: Gieben.

———. 1997. "Thebes and Central Greece." In *The Greek World in the Fourth Century*, ed. L. Tritle, 66–106. Oxford: Routledge.

Musti, M. 1988. "La struttura del libro di Pausania sulla Beozia." *Επετηρίς της εταιρείας Βοιωτικών μελετών* 1: 333–44.

Nauhaud, M. 1986. "Sur une allusion d'Eschine (*Ambassade*, 75) au stratège athénien Tolmidès." *REG* 99: 342–46.

Neer, R. T. 2004. "The Athenian Treasury at Delphi and the Material of Politics." *ClAnt* 23: 63–94.

Osborne, R. 2009. "The Politics of an Epigraphic Habit: The Case of Thasos." In *Greek History and Epigraphy: Essays in Honour of P. J. Rhodes*, ed. L. Mitchell and L. Rubinstein, 103–14. Swansea: Classical Press of Wales.

Osborne, R. Forthcoming. "Thespiai: The Epigraphic City Down to 171."

Page, D. L. 1981. *Further Greek Epigrams*. Cambridge: Cambridge University Press.

Papalexandrou, A. 2014. "Messenian Tripods: A Boiotian Contribution to the Symbolic Construction of the Messenian Past?" In *Attitudes towards the Past in Antiquity: Creating Identities; Proceedings of an International Conference Held at Stockholm University, 15–17 May 2009*, ed. B. Alroth and C. Scheffer, 127–37. Stockholm: Edita Bobergs AB.

Papazarkadas, N. 2009. "The Decree of Aigeis and Aiantis (Agora I 6793) Revisited." In *Ἀττικὰ Ἐπιγραφικά: Μελέτες πρὸς τιμὴν τοῦ Christian Habicht*, ed. A. A. Themos and N. Papazarkadas, 165–81. Athens: Hellēnikēs Epigraphikē Hetaireia.

———, ed. 2014a. *The Epigraphy and History of Boeotia: New Finds, New Prospects*. Leiden: Brill.

———. 2014b. "Two New Epigrams from Thebes." In *The Epigraphy and History of Boeotia: New Finds, New Prospects*, ed. N. Papazarkadas, 223–51. Leiden: Brill.

Pariente, A. 1992. "Le monument argien des 'Sept contre Thèbes.'" In *Polydipsion Argos: Argos de la fin des palais mycéniens à la constitution de l'état classique*, ed. M. Piérart, *BCH Supplement* 22, 195–229. Paris: De Boccard.

Parke, H. W., and D. E. Wormell. 1956. *The Delphic Oracle*. Vol. 1, *The History*. Oxford: Blackwell.

Parker, R. 1983. *Miasma: Pollution and Purification in Early Greek Religion*. Oxford: Clarendon Press.

Partida, E. 2000. *The Treasuries at Delphi: An Architectural Study*. Jonsered: Paul Aström Förlag.

Pausanias. 1918–1935. *Descprition of Greece*. 5 vols. Translated by W. H. S. Jones. Cambridge, Mass.: Harvard University Press.

Peake, S. 1997. "A Note on the Dating of the Social War." *G&R* 44: 161–64.

Perlman, S. 1968. "Athenian Democracy and the Revival of Imperialistic Expansion at the Beginning of the Fourth Century B.C." *CP* 63: 257–67.

Petrakos, B. C. 1967. "Τὸ Ἀμφιάρειον τοῦ Ὠρωποῦ: Τοπογραφικὰ καὶ ἐπιγραφικὰ θέματα." *AEph, Chronika*, 1–13.

———. 1968. *Ὁ Ὠρωπὸς καὶ τὸ ἱερὸν τοῦ Ἀμφιαράου*. Athens: Archaiologike Hetaireia.

———. 1997. *Οἱ ἐπιγραφὲς τοῦ Ὠρωποῦ*. Athens: Archaiologike Hetaireia.

Petropoulou, A. 1981. "The *Eparche* Documents and the Early Oracle at Oropus." *GRBS* 22: 39–63.

Picard, O., ed. 1991. *Guide de Delphes: Le musée*. Paris: De Boccard.

Pirenne-Delforge, V. 2008. *Retour à la source: Pausanias et la religion grecque*. Liège: Centre international d'étude de la religion grecque antique.

Pitt, R. 2014. "Just as It Has Been Written: Inscribing Building Contracts at Lebadeia." In *The Epigraphy and History of Boeotia: New Finds, New Prospects*, ed. N. Papazarkadas, 373–94. Leiden: Brill.

Plassart, A. 1926. "Fouilles de Thespies et de l'Hiéron des Muses de l'Hélikon: Les inscriptions (6e article)." *BCH* 50: 383–462.

Platon, N., and C. Feyel. 1938. "Inventaire sacré de Thespies trouvé à Chostia (Béotie)." *BCH* 62: 149–66.

Pleket, H. W. 2010. Review of Bintliff, Howard, and Snodgrass 2007. *Bulletin Antieke Beschaving* 85: 217–19.

Pouilloux, J. 1952. "Promanties collectives et protocole delphique." *BCH* 76: 484–513.

———. 1962. "La reconstruction du temple de Delphes au IVe siècle et les institutions delphiques." *REA* 64: 300–313.

Pretzler, M. 2007. *Pausanias: Travel Writing in Ancient Greece*. London: Duckworth.

Pritchett, W. K. 1985. *The Greek State at War*. Vol. 4. Berkeley: University of California Press.

———. 1999. *Pausanias Periegetes*. Vol. 2. Amsterdam: J. C. Gieben.

Psoma, S. 2001. *Olynthe et les Chalcidiens de Thrace: Études de numismatique et d'histoire*. Stuttgart: F. Steiner.

Rackham, O. 1983. "Observations on the Historical Ecology of Boeotia." *Annual of the British School at Athens* 78: 291–351.

Radicke, J. 1995. *Die Rede des Demosthenes für die Freiheit der Rhodier (or. 15)*. Stuttgart: Teubner.

Repapis, C. C. 1989. "A Quasi–Nine Year Oscillation of the Water Level in Lake Copais." *Climatic Change* 14 (1): 81–87.

Rhodes, P. J. 1994. *Thucydides: History III*. Warminster: Aris and Phillips.

———. 2005. *Euthynai (Accounting)*. Valedictory lecture. Durham: University of Durham.

———. 2010. *A History of the Classical Greek World, 478–323 B.C.* 2nd ed. Chichester: Wiley-Blackwell.

Rhodes, P. J., and R. Osborne. 2003. *Greek Historical Inscriptions, 404–323 BC*. Oxford: Oxford University Press.

Rigsby, K. J. 1996. *Asylia: Territorial Inviolability in the Hellenistic World*. Berkeley: University of California Press.

Robert, L. 1962. *Villes d'Asie Mineure: Études de géographie ancienne*. 2nd ed. Paris: De Boccard.

Robinson, E. W. 2011. *Democracy beyond Athens: Popular Government in the Greek Classical Age*. Cambridge: Cambridge University Press.

Roesch, P. 1965. *Thespies et la confederation Béotienne*. Paris: De Boccard.

———. 1978. *Teiresias: Epigraphica*.

———. 1979. "La citoyenneté fédérale en Béotie." In *Proceedings of the Second International Conference on Boiotian Antiquities*, ed. A. Schachter and J. M. Fossey, 27–31. Montreal: Tiresias.

———. 1982. *Études béotiennes*. Paris: De Boccard.
———. 1984a. "La base des Béotiens à Delphes." *CRAI*: 177–95.
———. 1984b. "Un décret inédit de la ligue thébaine." *REG* 97: 45–60.
———. 2007. *Les inscriptions de Thespies*. Electronic ed., ed. G. Argoud, A. Schachter, and G. Vottéro. Lyon: Maison de l'Orient et de la Mediterranée Jean Pouilloux.
Roller, D. W. 1987. "Tanagra Survey Project 1985: The Site of Grimadha." *Annual of the British School at Athens* 82: 213–32.
———. 1989. *Tanagran Studies*. Vol. 1, *Sources and Documents on Tanagra in Boiotia*. Amsterdam: Gieben.
Roux, G. 1976. *Delphes, son oracle et ses dieux*. Paris: Les Belles Lettres.
Roy, J. 2000. "The Arcadian League, 370–362 B.C." In *Alternatives to Athens*, ed. R. Brock and S. Hodkinson, 308–26. Oxford: Oxford University Press.
———. 2009. "Hegemonial Structures in Late Archaic and Early Classical Elis and Sparta." In *Sparta: Comparative Approaches*, ed. S. Hodkinson, 69–88. Swansea: Classical Press of Wales.
Rübel, A. 2001. "Hellespontophylakes—Zöllner am Bosporos? Überlegung zur Fiskalpolitik des attischen Seebundes (*IG* I[3] 61)." *Klio* 83: 39–51.
Ruggeri, C. 2004. *Gli stati intorno a Olimpia: Storia e costituzione dell'Elide e degli stati formati dai perieci elei (400–362 A.C.)*. Stuttgart: F. Steiner.
Rups, M. 1986. "Thesauros: A Study of the Treasury Building as Found in Greek Sanctuaries." PhD diss., Johns Hopkins University.
Russell, F. S. 1999. *Information Gathering in Classical Greece*. Ann Arbor: University of Michigan Press.
Ruzicka, S. 1998. "Epaminondas and the Genesis of the Social War." *CP* 93: 60–69.
Salviat, F. 1965. "L'offrande Argienne de l' 'hémicycle des rois' à Delphes et l'Héraclès Béotien." *BCH* 89: 307–14.
Schachter, A. 1979. "The Boiotian Herakles." In *Proceedings of the Second International Conference on Boiotian Antiquities*, ed. A. Schachter and J. M. Fossey, 37–44. Montreal: Tiresias.
———. 1981–1994. *Cults of Boiotia*. 4 vols. London: Institute of Classical Studies.
———. 1989. "Boiotia in the Sixth Century B.C." In *Boiotika: Vorträge von 5 internationalen Böotien-Kolloquium (13–17 Juni 1986)*, ed. H. Beister and J. Buckler, 73–86. Munich: Editio Maris.
———. 1996. "Reconstructing Thespiai." In *La Montagne des Muses*, ed. A. Hurst and A. Schachter, Recherches et Recontres, 7, 99–126. Geneva: Librairie Droz.
———. 2004. "Politics and Personalities in Classical Thebes." In *Daimonopylai*, ed. R. B. Egan and M. Joyal, 347–61. Winnipeg: University of Manitoba Centre for Hellenic Civilization.
———. 2014. "Tlepolemos in Boiotia." In *The Epigraphy and History of Boeotia: New Finds, New Prospects*, ed. N. Papazarkadas, 313–31. Leiden: Brill.
———. 2016. "From Hegemony to Disaster." In *Boiotia in Antiquity: Selected Papers*, ed. A. Schachter, 113–32. Cambridge: Cambridge University Press.
Schachter, A., and F. Marchand. 2013. "Fresh Light on the Institutions and Religious Life of Thespiai: Six New Inscriptions from the Thespiai Survey." In *Epigraphical Approaches to the Post-classical Polis: Fourth Century BC to Second Century AD*, ed. P. Martzavou and N. Papazarkadas, 277–99. Oxford: Oxford University Press.
Schild-Xenidou, W. 1972. *Boiotische Grab- und Weihreliefs archäischer und klassischer Zeit* (Inaugural-Dissertation des Doktorgrades). Munich: Ludwig-Maximilians-Universität.

Scott, M. C. 2007. “Putting Architectural Sculpture into Its Archaeological Context: The Case of the Siphnian Treasury at Delphi.” *BABesch* 82 (2): 321–31.

———. 2008. “Constructing Identities in Sacred Inter-state Space: The Case of the Arcadian Monument at Delphi.” In *SOMA 2005: Proceedings of the IX Symposium on Mediterranean Archaeology*, ed. O. Menozzi, M. Di Marzio, and D. Fossataro, 431–38. Oxford: British Archaeological Reports.

———. 2010. *Delphi and Olympia: The Spatial Politics of Panhellenism in the Archaic and Classical Periods*. Cambridge: Cambridge University Press.

———. 2014. *Delphi: A History of the Center of the Ancient World*. Princeton, N.J.: Princeton University Press.

Seager, R. 1967. “Thrasybulus, Conon and Athenian Imperialism, 386–86 B.C.” *JHS* 87: 95–115.

Sealey, R. 1993. *Demosthenes and His Time: A Study in Defeat*. Oxford: Oxford University Press.

Seymour, P. A. 1922. “Note on the Boeotian League.” *Classical Review* 36: 70.

Shiel, R. S. 2000. “Refuting the Land Degradation Myth for Boiotia.” In *Human Ecodynamics*, ed. G. Bailey, R. Charles, and N. Winder, 55–62. Oxford: Oxbow Books.

Shipley, G. 1987. *A History of Samos, 800–188 BC*. Oxford: Clarendon Press.

Shrimpton, G. S. 1971. “The Theban Supremacy in Fourth-Century Literature.” *Phoenix* 25: 310–18.

———. 1991. *Theopompus the Historian*. Montreal: McGill–Queen’s University Press.

Sickinger, J. P. 2009. “Nothing to Do with Democracy: ‘Formulae of Disclosure’ and the Athenian Epigraphic Habit.” In *Greek History and Epigraphy: Essays in Honour of P. J. Rhodes*, ed. L. Mitchell and L. Rubinstein, 87–102. Swansea: Classical Press of Wales.

Snodgrass, A. M. 1987. *An Archaeology of Greece: The Present State and Future Scope of a Discipline*. Berkeley: University of California Press.

Sordi, M. 1957. “La fondation du collège des naopes et le renouveau politique de l’Amphictionie au IVe siècle.” *BCH* 81: 38–75.

———. 1973. “La restaurazione della lega beotica nel <3>79–8 a.C.” *Athenaeum* 51: 79–91.

———. 1993. “La battaglia di Ceresso e la secessione di Tespie.” In *Boeotia Antiqua*, vol. 3, *Papers in Boiotian History, Institutions and Epigraphy in Memory of Paul Roesch*, ed. J. M. Fossey, 25–32. Amsterdam: J. C. Gieben.

Stamatakis, P. 1883. “Ekthesis peri tôn en Boiôtiai ergôn en etei 1882.” *Praktika tis en Athinais Arkhaiologikis Etaireias* 1883: 63–74.

Strasser, J.-Y. 2004. “La fête des Daidala de Platées et la ‘grande année’ d’Oinopidès.” *Hermes* 132: 338–51.

Stylianou, P. J. 1998. *A Historical Commentary on Diodorus Siculus, Book 15*. Oxford: Clarendon Press.

Svoronos, J. N. 1916. “Θησαυρὸς Νομισμάτων ἐκ τοῦ χωρίου Μύρου Καρδίτσας τῆς Θεσσαλίας.” *ADelt* 2: 273–335.

Swoboda, H. 1900. “Zur Geschichte des Epaminondas.” *Rh. Mus.* 55: 460–75.

Taillardat, J., and P. Roesch. 1966. “L’inventaire sacré de Thespies, l’alphabet attique en Béotie.” *RPh* 92: 70–87.

Taita, J. 2007. *Olimpia e il suo vicinato in epoca arcaica*. Milan: LED Edizioni.

Tejada, J. V. 2015. “Hegemony and Political Instability in the Black Sea and Hellespont after the Theban Expedition to Byzantium in 364 BC.” in *The Danubian Lands Between the Black, Aegean and Adriatic Seas (7th Century BC–10th Century AD): Proceedings of the Fifth International Congress on Black Sea Antiquities (Belgrade: 17–21 September 2013)*, ed. G. R. Tsetskhladze, A. Avram, and J. Hargrave, 53–58. Oxford: Archaeopress.

Thompson, M., O. Mørkholm, and C. M. Kraay. 1993. *An Inventory of Greek Coin Hoards*. New York: American Numismatic Society.

Threatte, L. 1980. *The Grammar of Attic Inscriptions*. Vol. 1. Berlin: W. de Gruyter.

Tod, M. N. 1948. *Greek Historical Inscriptions*. Vol. 2, *From 403 to 323 B.C.* Oxford: Clarendon Press.

Treves, P. 1940. "Les documents apocryphes du 'Pro Corona.'" *LEC* 9: 157–58.

Tuplin, C. J. 1984. "Pausanias and Plutarch's Epaminondas." *CQ* 34 (2): 346–58.

———. 1986. "The Fate of Thespiae during the Theban Hegemony." *Athenaeum* 64: 321–41.

———. 1987. "The Leuctra Campaign: Some Outstanding Problems." *Klio* 69: 72–107.

Turner, L. A. 1994. "*IG* VII 3073 and the Display of Inscribed Texts." In *Boeotia Antiqua*, vol. 4, ed. J. M. Fossey, 17–30. Amsterdam: Gieben.

Typaldou-Fakiris, C. 2004. *Villes fortifiées de Phocide et la IIIe guerre sacrée: 356–346 av. J.-C.* Aix-en-Provence: Presses de l'Université de Provence.

Ulrichs, H. N. 1863. *Reisen und Forschungen in Griechenland*. Vol. 2. Berlin: Weidmannsche Buchhandlung.

van Effenterre, H. 1997. "Aspects of Archaic Boeotia." In *Recent Developments in the History and Archaeology of Central Greece*, ed. J. Bintliff, 135–37. London: BAR.

van Straten, F. 2000. "Votives and Votaries in Greek Sanctuaries." In *Oxford Readings in Greek Religion*, ed. R. Buxton, 191–226. Oxford: Oxford University Press.

Vika, E. 2011. "Diachronic Dietary Reconstructions in Ancient Thebes, Greece: Results from Stable Isotope Analyses." *Journal of Archaeological Science* 38: 1157–63.

Vika, E., V. Aravantinos, and M. P. Richards. 2009. "Aristophanes and Stable Isotopes: A Taste for Freshwater Fish in Classical Thebes." *Antiquity* 83 (322): 1076–83.

Vincent, J.-C. 2010. "Pausanias en biographe: Réflexions sur la place des vies de Philopoimen et d'Epaminondas dans la vision historique du Périégète." *Dialogues d'histoire ancienne* 4 (1): 297–315.

Vlachogianni, E. V. 2004–2009. "Προξενικό ψήφισμα του Κοινού των Βοιωτών." *Horos* 17–21: 361–72.

Vottéro, G. 1996. "L'alphabet ionien-attique en Béotie." In *Le IVe siècle avant J.-C: Approches historiographiques*, ed. P. Carlier, Études anciennes, 15, 157–81. Nancy and Paris: ADRA and De Boccard.

———. 1998. *Le dialecte béotien (7e s.–2e s. av. J.-C.)*. Vol. 1, *L'écologie du dialecte*. Nancy and Paris: ADRA and De Boccard.

———. 2001. *Le dialecte béotien (7e s.–2e s. av. J.-C.)*. Vol. 2, *Répertoire raisonné des inscriptions dialectales*. Nancy and Paris: ADRA and De Boccard.

Walbank, F. W. 1957–1979. *A Historical Commentary on Polybius*. 3 vols. Oxford: Clarendon Press.

Wallace, P. W. 1979. *Strabo's Description of Boiotia: A Commentary*. Heidelberg: Winter.

Wallace, W. P. 1956. *The Euboian League and Its Coinage*. Numismatic Notes and Monographs 134. New York: American Numismatic Society.

Wankel, H. 1976. *Demosthenes: Rede für Ktesiphon über den Kranz*. Vol. 1. Heidelberg: Carl Winter.

Warner, R. 1979. *Xenophon: A History of My Times*. Revised with introduction and notes by G. L. Cawkwell. Harmondsworth: Penguin.

Warren, J. A. W. 2000. "The Silver Coins of Sikyon in Leiden: Analysis and Some Comments on the Coinage." In *Pour Denyse: Divertissements numismatiques*, ed. S. M. Hurter and C. Arnold-Biucchi, 201–13. Bern: Schuler AG.

Wartenberg, U. 1997. "The Alexander-Eagle Hoard: Thessaly, 1992." *NChron* 157: 179–88.

Wickersham, J. M. 2007. "Spartan Garrisons in Boeotia, 382–379/8 BC." *Historia—Zeitschrift fur alte Geschichte* 56 (2): 243–46.

Wilhelm, A. 1909. *Beiträge zur griechischen Inschriftenkunde, mit einem Anhange über die öffentliche Aufzeichnung von Urkunden*. Österreichisches archäologisches Institut, Vienna, Sonderschriften, vol. 7. Vienna: Alfred Hölder.

Wilson, P. 2007. "Pronomis and Potamon: Two Pipers and Two Epigrams." *JHS* 127: 141–49.

Winter, F. E. 1971. *Greek Fortifications*. London: Routledge and Kegan Paul.

Wolters, P. 1940. *Das Kabirenheiligtum bei Theben*. Vol. 1. Berlin: W. de Gruyter.

Worthington, I. 1990. "Alexander the Great and the Date of the Mytilene Decree." *ZPE* 83: 194–214.

Zahrnt, M. 1971. *Olynth und die Chalkidier: Untersuchungen zur Staatenbildung auf der Chalkidikischen Halbinsel im 5. und 4. Jahrhundert v. Chr.* Munich: C. H. Beck.

CONTRIBUTORS

Samuel D. Gartland is departmental lecturer in ancient history at the University of Oxford.

John Ma is professor of ancient history at the University of Oxford and professor of classics at Columbia University.

Robin Osborne is professor of ancient history at the University of Cambridge.

Nikolaos Papazarkadas is associate professor at the University of California–Berkeley.

P. J. Rhodes is emeritus professor of ancient history at the University of Durham.

Thom Russell has recently completed a DPhil at St. Hilda's College, Oxford.

Albert Schachter is Emeritus Hiram Mills Professor of Classics at McGill University.

Michael Scott is associate professor of classics and ancient history at the University of Warwick.

Anthony Snodgrass is Emeritus Laurence Professor of Classical Archaeology at the University of Cambridge.

GENERAL INDEX

INDEX OF SOURCES

ACKNOWLEDGMENTS

To paraphrase Winston Churchill's withering comment on Clement Attlee, Boiotia is often thought of as "a modest region with much to be modest about," but this volume seeks to move away from any timidity about claiming the centrality, in every sense, of Boiotia to Greek history. This collection is designed to improve our understanding of an important part of the ancient world, and it is hoped that it will be only part of a wider reimagining of both the region and the period.

The catalyst for this volume was a colloquium on Boiotia held at Corpus Christi College, Oxford, where the appetite for more discussion of Boiotia in print became apparent. But the ultimate origin of the collection lies much earlier, when a fiery young lecturer took his undergraduate audience on a journey to Chaironeia in 338 BC to discuss not glory but suffering, the violence and loss of conflict, and the lasting effect on Boiotia and the Boiotians. An extended meditation on the damage done to the skulls of fallen Thebans by the butts of the Macedonian sarissa might not have been quite so compelling and memorable had the lecture not concluded with a haiku encapsulating the day of defeat from a Theban perspective. To the inimitable John Ma I owe many debts, and this book is perhaps a small repayment for telling me, in no uncertain terms, to go off and "do Boiotia."

During the period of preparation I have been indebted to the hospitality of the Faculty of Classics at the University of Oxford, Corpus Christi College, and the Department of Classics at the University of Leeds. In both Leeds and Oxford I have relied on the sagacity of many, but particular thanks for advice about the necessity and form of such a volume must go to Roger Brock, Albert Schachter, and Peter Thonemann. I must also gratefully recognize the generosity of Emily Mackil in providing the invaluable, beautifully clear general map of Boiotia.

The production of the volume was rendered painless by the unstinting work and assistance of the editor for the University of Pennsylvania Press, Deborah

Blake, whose patience, experience, and knowledge have been invaluable in guiding the book to completion. This gratitude must be extended to Penn Press more widely for its enthusiasm and support, particularly Hannah Blake, who has helped organize and prepare the manuscript. I am also grateful for the comments, criticism, and sage advice from the anonymous reader of the book for the press, which helped improve the final form of the volume. More broadly, I called in too many favors and ran up too many debts to mention everyone involved, but I am particularly grateful to the large body of reviewers, drawn from three continents, for the individual chapters.

The warmest thanks must of course be reserved for the authors of the chapters, who have been unfailingly diligent, generous, and tolerant of the questions and queries leveled at them. It has been a great pleasure to work with all of them, and I have learned a great deal from the experience.

My final thoughts are of home. In fourth-century Boiotia the landscape is regrettably almost devoid of women whose lives can be reconstructed at any level of detail, but throughout the course of putting this book together I have been lucky to be surrounded by three unique and powerful female voices. To Korinna, Nemea, and Nicola I dedicate my own small contribution to this book.